Suicidal Youth

John M. Davis
Jonathan Sandoval

Suicidal Youth

School-Based
Intervention and Prevention

Jossey-Bass Publishers

San Francisco • Oxford • 1991

SUICIDAL YOUTH
School-Based Intervention and Prevention
by John M. Davis and Jonathan Sandoval

Copyright © 1991 by: Jossey-Bass Inc., Publishers
350 Sansome Street
San Francisco, California 94104

&

Jossey-Bass Limited
Headington Hill Hall
Oxford OX3 0BW

Library of Congress Cataloging-in-Publication Data

Davis, John M. (John Martin), date.
  Suicidal youth : school-based intervention and prevention / John
M. Davis, Jonathan Sandoval.
      p.   cm.—(The Jossey-Bass social and behavioral science
series) (The Jossey-Bass education series)
  Includes bibliographical references (p.) and index.
  ISBN 1-55542-329-9
  1. Teenagers—United States—Suicidal behavior. 2. Students—
United States—Suicidal behavior. 3. Suicide—United States—
Prevention—Handbooks, manuals, etc. 4. Personnel services in
education—United States—Handbooks, manual, etc. I. Sandoval,
Jonathan. II. Title. III. Series. IV. Series: The Jossey-Bass
education series.
  HV6546.D38   1991
  373.17'13—dc20   90-25453
                                                              CIP

Manufactured in the United States of America

The paper in this book meets the guidelines for
permanence and durability of the Committee on
Production Guidelines for Book Longevity of the
Council on Library Resources.

JACKET DESIGN BY WILLI BAUM

FIRST EDITION

Code 9129

A joint publication in
The Jossey-Bass
Social and Behavioral Science Series
and
The Jossey-Bass
Education Series

Consulting Editors
Psychoeducational Interventions:
Guidebooks for School Practitioners

Charles A. Maher
Rutgers University

Joseph E. Zins
University of Cincinnati

For Jeffrey and Marian

Contents

10. Making Institutions Sensitive to Suicide   153

11. Legal and Ethical Issues   173

12. Conclusion: Toward a Better Understanding of
     Adolescent Suicide   193

     Resource A: Films, Filmstrips, and Videotapes
     on Suicide   201

     Resource B: Resources for Prevention Programs   215

     Resource C: Readings on Suicide for Children and
     Young Adults   218

     References   225

     Name Index   253

     Subject Index   261

Preface

Suicide is the second leading cause of death among U.S. adolescents. That fact makes suicide a public health problem. School districts and professionals are being sued by claimants who believe that an adolescent suicide could have been prevented. That fact makes suicide a legal problem. First and foremost, however, suicide is a *human* problem.

Why We Wrote This Book

Much writing and research about adolescent suicide have been done by people from a number of disciplines. These works have appeared in a variety of journals and books, most with necessarily restrictive perspectives. The purpose of *Suicidal Youth* is to bring this information together and formulate it to present theoretically and clinically sound approaches that can be readily translated into immediate intervention and prevention strategies for potentially suicidal adolescents.

Intended Audience

This book is designed to provide school-based personnel, especially those working in academic training programs, school psychology, school social work, counseling, and administration—and clinicians who work with suicidally at-risk adolescents who want to collaborate more effectively with school personnel—with material that will help them become more sensitized to, aware of, and competent in identifying and screening youth in need of suicide evaluation or treatment. *Suicidal Youth* is designed to serve each group by offering knowledge at a variety of levels, from current theory and research to practical procedures and advice. This multilevel approach is one of the major contributions of the book. It is also meant to provide information and resources that will enable a school site or district to set up programs for suicide screening, evaluation, prevention, and postevent intervention ("postvention").

Another major contribution of *Suicidal Youth* is that it bridges the gap between what is of interest to mental health professionals and what is of interest to educators in a language that should be clear to both. Both clinicians and educators need to be able to cope with suicidal adolescents, and they need to be able to collaborate to prevent an at-risk adolescent from falling through the cracks. This book provides a variety of frameworks applicable to these problems.

Overview of the Contents

Part One provides an introduction to the book's purposes and premises. Chapter One focuses on epidemiological issues, presenting the most recent statistics available on incidence rates of completed suicides, attempted suicides, and ideation from both clinical and survey populations. It also discusses demographic variation in the epidemiological data. Chapter Two explores the variety of models available to classify, explain, or predict suicidality. It examines the risk and precipitating factors that have been isolated in the research literature and discusses the different ways in which suicide is understood. This chapter introduces many of the variables that must be taken into consideration when prevention and intervention strategies are planned.

Part Two presents action strategies for school practitioners— what school-based professionals must know and do. Chapter Three describes models of suicide evaluation and explains how context and referral source influence the choice of a model. Since there are a number of ways in which school personnel may learn that a student is suicidal, this chapter presents alternative strategies that are context specific. It also provides three intervention models that are particularly sensitive to adolescent issues. Chapter Four focuses on how to determine whether an adolescent is in imminent danger or should be referred for a complete psychiatric evaluation for suicidal potential. Although, even in the best of situations, school-based personnel should not be the final arbiters of whether an adolescent is suicidal, they do need to know enough to be able to determine whether the potential for suicide is serious enough that a student should be referred for a complete evaluation. The chapter also addresses what should be done if an adolescent exhibits a low or moderate level of suicidality, presents alternative referral processes and techniques, and provides a brief overview of treatment models. This overview is intended not to prepare school-based personnel to engage in therapy but rather to provide them with an understanding of what types of treatment are available and to acquaint them with the relevant terminology so that they may act as liaisons between the mental health and educational systems. Since suicides do occur among the student population in spite of our best efforts, Chapter Five focuses on postventive efforts and possible responses to suicide attempts and completions in the schools.

Part Three is devoted to a discussion of suicide prevention programs in the public schools. Chapter Six describes methods for screening for suicidality, providing alternative strategies that could be implemented by a school site or district to identify children who may be at risk. Even if a school district is unwilling or unable to screen its entire population, school-based mental health practitioners are still responsible for identifying students at risk. Chapter Seven discusses findings identifying populations that seem to be at particularly high risk for suicide—students suffering from substance-abuse problems, runaways, gay and lesbian youth, students who have suffered physical or sexual abuse, special education students, and students transferred to a continuation or alternative high school campus—and discusses ways to intervene with these young people. Chapter Eight presents a variety of educational programs and processes available for schools interested in these types of preventive approaches, focusing on a program developed by the state of California, which is one of the most comprehensive programs currently being implemented in the public schools. Finally, Chapter Nine discusses the use of peers in prevention programs. It explores ways to implement peer helping models, such as peer counseling, and to provide school-site opportunities, such as clubs and work-experience programs, pointing out the risks that may be associated with some peer programs.

In Part Four, *Suicidal Youth* turns to broader programmatic and societal issues. Chapter Ten addresses systemic issues, exploring ways to design preparedness policies for the district, community, and societal levels, reviewing ways of implementing suicide prevention programs, and pointing out the accommodations that systems will have to make to allow for and support changes. Chapter Eleven discusses the legal and ethical issues in school prevention and intervention programs and their implications for the educational system. It also addresses current efforts to research and evaluate these programs and the controversies surrounding some of these efforts. In Chapter Twelve, we summarize the major conclusions of the book, underscoring program elements that have the best potential to reduce many of the problems in schools that contribute to the risk of suicide among students. The three resources at the end of the book discuss media presentations and readings on suicide and suggest resources for prevention programs.

Acknowledgments

We would like to thank a number of people who have helped us to complete this work. First, we are grateful to our wives, Holly and Susan, for their encouragement and tolerance of our frequent disappearances into the library or our offices. Next, we wish to thank the word-processing staff at the Division of Education, University of California, Davis, who stuck with the project through disc failure and poor handwriting. We especially appreciate the efforts of Donna Coulston, Judy Gullicksen, and Brenda Travis. We were pleased to have the opportunity to work with series editor Joseph Zins and Jossey-Bass editors Gracia Alkema, who prodded and nurtured this effort, and Lesley Iura, who saw the manuscript through production. Finally, we must acknowledge the assistance and support over the years of California's premier school psychologist, Milton Wilson, of the California Department of Education.

Davis, California   John M. Davis
February 1991   Jonathan Sandoval

The Authors

John M. Davis is lecturer in education at the University of California, Davis. He received his B.S. degree (1972) in humanities and social sciences from Drexel University and his M.A. (1975) and Ph.D. (1979) degrees in education (school psychology) from the University of California, Berkeley.

Davis's main research interests are in family systems theory, school-based consultation, and adolescent suicide. He worked for four years as a school psychologist and for four years in the Department of Psychiatry at Kaiser Hospital in San Rafael, California. He has published a number of articles on suicide, consultation, and other topics of interest to school psychologists. He has been active in the National Association of School Psychologists' special interest group in family systems and does collaborative research involving a number of school districts in Northern California.

Jonathan Sandoval is professor of education and director of the school psychology program at the University of California, Davis. He earned his B.A. degree (1964) in psychology at the University of California, Santa Barbara, and both his M.A. degree (1966) in education (counseling psychology) and his Ph.D. degree (1969) in education (school psychology) at the University of California, Berkeley. Before joining the faculty at Davis, he was a district school psychologist for three years.

Sandoval's main research activities have focused on the prevention of school failure and the promotion of mental health and learning in schools. He has published articles on nonpromotion, psychological testing, suicide prevention, and crisis management. He has coauthored a number of articles on consultation and suicide with Davis. Sandoval is editor of *Crisis Counseling, Intervention, and Prevention in the Schools* (1988).

Sandoval has served as president of the Trainers of School Psychologists and is currently president-elect of the Division of School Psychology of the American Psychological Association. Sandoval works with a number of organizations, including local school district staffs, state commissions and associations, and national associations and test publishers.

Suicidal Youth

Part One:
Understanding Suicide

The Prevalence
of the Problem

"The suicide rate for teenagers has increased 300 percent since 1950." "Youth suicide is an epidemic sweeping the United States." "In absolute numbers, 5,000 youths took their life last year." We regularly encounter sobering statements such as these in the popular press. How serious is the youth suicide "epidemic," and is there cause for alarm because of a new ill brought by modern life?

Sui, Latin for "of oneself," and *cide,* meaning "a killing," together give us *suicide:* the killing of oneself. This phenomenon has been with us for millennia. Evans and Farberow (1988) tell us that the first known writing about suicide appeared in Egypt somewhere between 2280 and 2000 B.C. A central theme of the anonymously written treatise, entitled *A Dispute over Suicide,* is ambivalence about the choice of life over death. Although it was most probably not written by an adolescent, its motif is familiar to those of us who work with adolescents. We must listen to and cope with such ambivalence all too often. A succinct example is found in *Vivienne: The Life and Suicide of an Adolescent Girl:* "Why live? Why die? One is equal choice to the other. What do I do?" (Mack and Hickler, 1981, p. 63).

This chapter focuses on the prevalence of adolescent suicide. After a brief review of definitions, we explore the issues of the accuracy of incidence statistics, offer historical and current perspectives on the incidence of suicide, present some of the relevant demographics, and review available statistics on suicide attempts and suicidal ideation among adolescents.

Epidemiology of Adolescent Suicide

Definitions

Before reviewing the data on the incidence of adolescent suicide, we must define a few important terms. First is *completed suicide*. A completed suicide was once referred to as a "successful" suicide, but the term was changed to avoid unwanted value implications of *successful*. In this chapter and the rest of the book, a completed suicide is defined as a death caused by the initiation of a deliberate set of actions leading to loss of life. A second important term is *attempted suicide*. This phrase refers to behavior directed against oneself that leads to self-harm or is considered by the adolescent (or evaluator) to have had a strong potential for self-harm. A third important concept is *suicidal ideation*. A person has suicidal ideation who has seriously considered suicide as an option at some point in his or her life. Although there is a logical progression from ideation to completed suicide, this sequence may not be exactly how the process functions, as we will discuss later. Also, since the seriousness of suicidal ideation exists on a continuum—no suicidal thoughts to many suicidal thoughts during a given period—this concept is more difficult to quantify than the other terms.

Accuracy of Incidence Statistics

Some suicidologists believe that the quality of official suicide statistics is so poor that they should not be used for research (Douglas, 1967) or descriptive purposes (Linden and Breed, 1976). However, most researchers collect the data, check the validity of the information, and then make estimates regarding "true" rates.

A number of studies on the accuracy of suicide statistics appear in the literature. All agree that suicide is an underreported statistic. Examples of estimated "true" suicide rates range from 1.2 (Holding and Barraclough, 1975) through 1.4–1.8 (Warshauer and Monk, 1978) to 3.8 (McCarthy and Walsh, 1975) times the officially reported rate. A variety of explanations have been offered to account for underestimates: misreporting of suicides as accidents (Adelstein and Mardon, 1975), false reporting to protect the feelings of the survivors (Hawton, 1986), inadequate information, certifier bias, and lack of a death certificate (Evans and Farberow, 1988). For a comprehensive review of validity and reliability of suicide mortality data, see O'Carroll (1989).

Current Incidence Data on Suicide Completion

As United Press International (1988) announced, "The suicide rate of young people continues to rise, the only category in one of the nation's lists of health objectives for 1990 not responding to control efforts, federal health officials reported yesterday." Suicide was the fifth leading cause of death among fifteen- to twenty-four-year-olds in 1960, and the rate has increased steadily since then. Figure 1 provides a striking illustration of the increase in the suicide rate for this age group relative to other age groups between 1970 and 1980.

Between 1979 and 1983, there was a slight decrease in incidence for this population, but in 1984, there was an upturn, and suicide became the second leading cause of death for fifteen- to twenty-four-year-olds. The 1984 rate for this group was 12.5 per 100,000. A breakdown of the total group revealed that the rate for fifteen- to nineteen-year-olds was 9.0 and that for twenty- to twenty-four-year-olds was 15.6 (Saltzman, Levenson, and Smith, 1988). The National Center for Health Statistics (1988) reported rates among fifteen- to twenty-four-year-olds of 12.7 in 1986 and 12.8 in 1987 (the 1987 data are provisional and based on a 10 percent sample of deaths).

Disaggregating the data to look for trends among the two age subgroups, we find that for the twenty- to twenty-four-year-olds, the rate seems to have peaked in 1979, when it was 18.2 per 100,000, whereas the rate for fifteen- to nineteen-year-olds is still increasing (see Table 1). In general, the rate for fifteen- to twenty-four-year-olds has hovered between 12.0 and 13.0 for the past ten years.

Our focus in this book is on adolescence, since there is a very low rate of incidence of completed suicide among younger children. Shaffer and Fisher (1981) reported that in 1977 only 2 children under the age of ten in the United States completed suicide, and only 1 in 102,000, or .98 per 100,000, of ten- to fourteen-year-olds completed

Figure 1. Percentage Change in Suicide Rates by Age Group and Sex,
United States, 1970 and 1980.

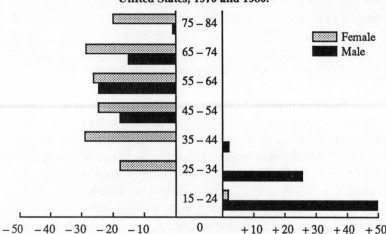

Percentage Change

Source: From THE ENCYCLOPEDIA OF SUICIDE, by Glen
Evans and Norman L. Farberow, Ph.D. Copyright © 1988 by Glen Evans.
Reprinted with the permission of Facts on File, Inc., New York.

suicide, with the majority being over the age of twelve. The 1987
estimate for the group fourteen years old and younger is 0.4 per
100,000 (National Center for Health Statistics, 1988). Disaggregating the 1982–1985 data for this group gives a 1.3 ratio for the ten-
to fourteen-year-olds and no figures for those under age ten (U.S.
Department of Health and Human Services, 1989).

Demographic Differences in Suicide Rates

Table 1 provides a consistent report of incidence data for
sixteen years for five-year age spans covering those ages of most
interest to us: ten to fourteen years, fifteen to nineteen years, and
twenty to twenty-four years. It also allows us to look at the issues
of sex and race in adolescent suicide.

Age

It is clear from Table 1 that rates of completed suicide vary
by age, sex, and race. Although the suicide rate for ten- to fourteen-

Table 1. Death Rates from Suicide Among Adolescents and Young Adults in the United States, by Sex and Race, Selected Years, 1970–1986.

	1970	1974	1978	1982	1986
Ages 10–14					
All races	0.6	0.9	0.8	1.1	1.5
Male	0.9	1.4	1.2	1.7	2.3
Female	0.3	0.4	0.4	0.4	0.7
White	0.7	1.0	0.9	1.1	1.6
Male	1.1	1.5	1.4	1.7	2.4
Female	0.3	0.4	0.4	0.5	0.7
All other	0.4	0.6	0.5	0.9	1.2
Male	0.3	0.7	0.6	1.6	1.8
Female	0.4	0.4	0.5	0.2	0.5
Black	N/A	N/A	N/A	0.8	1.0
Male	N/A	N/A	N/A	1.5	1.5
Female	N/A	N/A	N/A	0.2	0.4
Ages 15–19					
All races	5.9	7.2	8.0	8.7	10.2
Male	8.8	11.0	12.8	14.1	16.4
Female	2.9	3.2	3.1	3.2	3.8
White	6.2	7.6	8.7	9.6	11.3
Male	9.4	11.9	13.8	15.5	18.2
Female	2.9	3.3	3.4	3.4	4.1
All other	4.2	4.5	4.5	4.6	5.3
Male	5.4	6.2	7.5	7.2	8.0
Female	2.9	2.8	1.6	1.9	2.5
Black	N/A	N/A	N/A	3.9	4.6
Male	N/A	N/A	N/A	6.2	7.1
Female	N/A	N/A	N/A	1.5	2.1
Ages 20–24					
All races	12.2	15.1	16.9	15.1	15.8
Male	19.3	24.1	27.4	25.1	26.6
Female	5.7	6.2	6.4	5.1	4.9
White	12.3	15.5	17.5	16.0	17.0
Male	19.3	24.5	26.1	26.4	28.4
Female	5.7	6.4	6.7	5.4	5.3
All other	12.0	12.8	13.8	10.6	10.1
Male	19.4	21.3	23.3	17.5	17.5
Female	5.5	5.0	5.0	3.9	2.9
Black	N/A	N/A	N/A	9.3	9.0
Male	N/A	N/A	N/A	16.0	16.0
Female	N/A	N/A	N/A	2.9	2.4

Note: During the years 1970, 1974, and 1978, the statistics for blacks were included in the "all other" category.

Source: National Center for Health Statistics, 1988.

year-olds has doubled over the sixteen years represented by the data, it is clearly still an extremely rare event. The increases among fifteen- to nineteen-year-olds and twenty- to twenty-four-year-olds, however, are certainly a cause for major concern, especially since it appears that the rate for the fifteen- to nineteen-year-old group is still increasing.

Gender

Gender is also a highly significant variable, with males completing suicide at five times the rate of females. At the extreme, the black male-to-female ratio for the twenty- to twenty-four-year-old group in 1986 was 6.6:1. Some of these ratios are reversed for attempted suicide (discussed later).

Ethnicity

With respect to race, suicide has been viewed predominantly as a white male problem. Although Table 1 supports this view, some caveats are in order. First, Native American and black (male) suicide rates are the only ones that peak during the young adult years. Also, as suggested by the black male-to-female ratio cited above, almost all of the increase in the overall black suicide rate has been due to the increase among black males age twenty to twenty-four (Gibbs, 1988).

Geography also seems to play a more powerful role in black suicides than in white suicides. Although not conclusive, there are data to support the notion that young urban blacks complete suicide more frequently than their rural counterparts and perhaps as frequently as their white urban peers (Hendin, 1969; Linden and Breed, 1976; Shaffer and Fisher, 1981).

Native Americans have the most alarming suicide rates. Frederick (1984) reported that the death rate from suicide among fifteen- to twenty-four-year-old Native Americans in the United States during the years 1977–1979 was an astounding 44.7 per 100,000, the highest rate of completed suicide for the Native American population. However, intertribe variability is high. Berlin (1987) reports a rate for Navajo adolescents of 11.8 to 12.0, a rate for Apache adolescents of about 43.3, and a rate for adopted Native American adolescents of about 70 per 100,000. Even with high variability among the Native American nations, the *lowest* rate is about equal to the national average.

Methods

Some researchers (for example, Lester and Beck, 1980) argue that choice of method is significant in terms of how seriously suicidal a person is. Smith, Conroy, and Ehler (1984) have employed this notion to develop a lethality-of-suicide-attempt rating scale to help evaluators to determine how serious an attempt has been made. Peck (1984), on the other hand, argues that this theory does not hold for completers and suggests that perseverance with a method is more significant than the method itself. He also suggests that we may be confusing issues by not considering completers and attempters as two separate but overlapping populations. However, all would agree that method used or fantasy of method to be used must be part of any clinical evaluation, so knowledge of prevalence is helpful.

Table 2 lists the methods and percentages of completions per method for 1979. It is clear that firearms and explosives play a major role in the killing of our young. The second most chosen method is gender related; males most often choose some mode of asphyxiation, and females favor poisons or medication. These preferences have changed over time, as illustrated by Table 3. In general, there has been an increase in the use of firearms; the most recent data on female use of firearms indicate that it has declined somewhat, but the rate is still higher than in 1970.

Nationality

Not surprisingly, different nations have different suicide rates and different method patterns. Table 4 compares rates of suicide among fifteen- to nineteen-year-olds in nine different nations. Among males, those in the United States rank third highest, after Canadian and Australian males; U.S. females also rank third, but after Sweden and Germany. Many speculations could be made

Table 2. Completed Suicides by Method, United States, 1979
(in Percentage).

Method	White			Black		
	Total	Male	Female	Total	Male	Female
Ages 15–19						
Firearms and explosives	64.6	67.7	50.8	53.0	54.0	50.0
Hanging/strangulation/ suffocation	15.5	16.2	12.1	23.5	29.0	6.2
Solid and liquid substances (poisons, medication, and so on)	7.3	3.8	22.6	9.1	3.0	28.1
Gases and vapors (for example, carbon monoxide)	6.5	6.8	5.4	1.5	2.0	0.0
Jumping	2.6	2.2	4.0	3.8	5.5	6.2
Cutting and piercing	0.6	0.6	0.3	0.8	0.0	3.1
All other	2.1	2.0	2.3	3.8	4.0	3.1
Ages 20–24						
Firearms and explosives	60.9	63.1	51.6	56.2	55.7	58.6
Hanging/strangulation/ suffocation	14.1	15.6	8.0	19.0	21.8	7.7
Solid and liquid substances (poisons, medication, and so on)	9.5	6.3	23.0	7.3	4.8	18.5
Gases and vapors (for example, carbon monoxide)	7.5	7.2	7.8	1.1	1.4	0.0
Jumping	3.3	2.8	5.0	6.8	6.9	6.2
Cutting and piercing	1.0	1.1	0.7	0.6	0.7	0.0
All other	2.1	2.1	1.9	4.5	4.5	4.6

Source: National Center for Health Statistics, 1988.

Table 3. Completed Suicides by Method, Ages Fifteen Through Nineteen,
1970, 1980, and 1986 (in Percentage).

Method	1970			1980			1986		
	Total	Male	Female	Total	Male	Female	Total	Male	Female
Firearms and explosives	47.9	52.3	34.2	63.3	64.9	55.7	61.0	64.2	45.0
Hanging/strangulation/suffocation	18.3	21.4	8.5	20.0	21.8	11.1	19.4	20.8	12.7
Solid and liquid substances (poisons, medication, and so on)	17.6	10.0	41.5	6.2	3.9	17.2	6.5	3.5	20.6
Gases and vapors (for example, carbon monoxide)	8.9	9.4	7.4	5.3	4.9	7.3	9.8	8.4	16.0
All other	7.3	6.9	8.5	5.2	4.5	8.6	3.6	3.1	6.1

Source: National Center for Health Statistics, 1988.

Table 4. Suicide Rates Among Fifteen- to Nineteen-Year-Olds in
Nine Industrialized Countries (per 100,000 Population).

Country	Male	Female
United States	16.0	3.7
Germany	13.3	4.1
France	9.1	2.6
The Netherlands	5.7	1.3
England and Wales	4.3	1.1
Sweden	9.0	5.3
Canada	18.4	3.6
Japan	6.8	3.3
Australia	16.6	3.6

Source: U.S. Department of Health and Human Services, 1989.

about the differences. The purpose of presenting these data here is
only to create a perspective.

Another interesting set of data on method chosen in different
countries, provided by Hawton (1986), encourages even more speculation. Table 5 is drawn from his work. The most glaring difference is the much lower rate of firearm suicides by the English and
Welsh adolescents, although there are smaller but corresponding
increases in asphyxiation, poisoning, and "other" categories.

Geography

We previously mentioned that geography plays a role in
black adolescent suicides. Geography seems to have some effect in
other groups as well. Perhaps because of weather, increased mobil-
ity, or somewhat higher divorce rates, the western United States has
had a consistently higher suicide rate than the rest of the nation. As
Figure 2 shows, suicide rates were higher in the West than in other
areas during the years 1970 to 1980, although there has been a trend
for the rates in other geographical regions to approach that of the
West.

Seasons

We are beginning to see research reported on "seasonal affective disorders" (American Psychiatric Association, 1987, p. 224) and

Table 5. Suicide Methods Used by Fifteen- to Nineteen-Year-Olds in
the United States (1981) and England and Wales (1983).

	United States (Percentages)	England and Wales (Percentages)
Firearms	66.0	5.9
Hanging/strangling/suffocation	18.0	29.4
Poisoning by liquids and solids	2.2	23.5
Poisoning by gas	7.8	5.9
Other	5.9	35.3a

a Jumping from high places was common among the "other" methods in England and Wales.

Source: Hawton, K., Suicidal Behavior in Children and Adolescents, p. 31, copyright © 1986 by Sage Publications, Inc. Reprinted by permission of Sage Publications, Inc.

have always had anecdotal evidence of how depressing holidays are and how stressful the end of summer vacation can be. In fact, seasons and weather patterns do seem to affect suicide rates. Coleman (1987) reports that spring is traditionally the most suicidal season for adults, with a peak in May, although he has also found that suicide clusters, a more commonly adolescent phenomenon, occur most often in February. Some contradictory data have been collected by Bollern (as reported in Evans and Farberow, 1988), who found November to be a peak month in his sample of fifteen- to twenty-nine-year-olds. Golombek and Garfinkel's (1983) study also found autumn and winter to be times of mildly increased suicide rates among young people in Ontario, Canada. Although these data on seasons and suicide are intriguing, the correlation between suicide and time of year is not strong.

Special Education

The final population whose prevalence of completed suicide we discuss is children participating in special education and other school programs. This group of children is one of great interest to school-based personnel. Ironically, considering the fairly alarming statistics, not much research has been done with this population. Warning papers have been written about suicide among the gifted

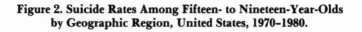

Figure 2. Suicide Rates Among Fifteen- to Nineteen-Year-Olds
by Geographic Region, United States, 1970–1980.

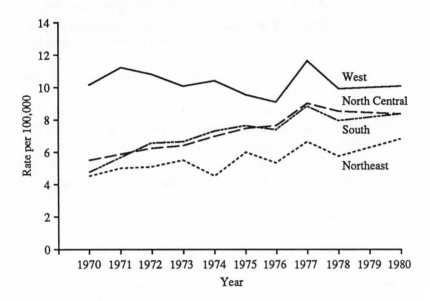

Source: From THE ENCYCLOPEDIA OF SUICIDE, by Glen
Evans and Norman L. Farberow, Ph.D. Copyright © 1988 by Glen Evans.
Reprinted with the permission of Facts on File, Inc., New York.

(Delisle, 1986; Leroux, 1986), the mentally retarded (Carter and
Jancer, 1983; Kaminer, Feinstein, and Barrett, 1987), and the learning disabled (Bryan and Herjanc, 1980; Hayes and Sloat, 1988), but
little in the way of epidemiological or intervention data has
followed.

The pioneering work of Jan-Tausch (1964) and Shaffer
(1974) first revealed problems in this group. The young adolescents
from their samples of completed suicides tended to be bright, but
of Jan-Tausch's forty-one children who completed suicide, seventeen, or 41.5 percent, were described as reading retarded. Peck (1985),
using data from Los Angeles County, found that of fourteen suicide
completers under age fifteen, seven, or 50 percent, had been diagnosed as learning disabled. Larger bodies of work with a greater age
span are needed.

Incidence of Suicide Attempts and Suicidal Ideation

National data on attempted suicide are not available for the United States or most other countries, and so suicidologists conduct studies using a variety of data sources to estimate the rates. Their consensus is that the rate of attempted suicide has easily paralleled if not exceeded the rise in completed suicide rates for adolescents (see, for example, Diekstra and Moritz, 1987). The data used for these estimates are collected primarily from two sources: survey data from "normal" populations (junior and senior high schools, colleges) and data from clinical populations in both outpatient (mental health and psychiatric clinics and hospital emergency rooms) and inpatient (usually psychiatric) settings.

Data from "Normal" Populations

Attempts. In many ways, information from normal adolescents is of most interest to us, since it is derived directly from school-based sources. Unfortunately, there are differences among the results of these studies, depending on such factors as where the study was done, how the research questions were phrased (for example, whether the suicide attempt was made in the past month, six months, year, and so on), and perhaps even the season during which the study was conducted. Even though these differences exist, the studies report findings that are fairly comparable, if alarming. Survey reports of prior suicide attempts range from a low of 8.4 percent of 313 midwestern high school students (Smith and Crawford, 1986) through 9 percent of 380 high school students from New York (Harkavy-Friedman, Asnis, Boeck, and DiFiore, 1987) and 13 percent of 120 San Mateo, California, high school students (Ross, 1985) to a high of 20 percent of students in a small northeastern community (Rubenstein and others, 1989). A major difference between Rubenstein and others' questionnaire and those of the other researchers was that it contained the statement "I tried to hurt myself," while the others did not, and the students who chose this statement were included in the "attempters" category. Rubenstein and others contend that putting respondents choosing this statement into the "attempters" category is closer to the spirit of the definition of a suicide attempt and that because other researchers omitted this statement, their estimates are probably lower than is realistic. Theirs is an interesting, albeit arguable, position.

Rubenstein and others' study differed from the other studies in another significant way: They found that suicidal behavior was as common among males as among females. They suggest that the reason for this difference may be that "attempt" samples are often drawn from studies of hospital or emergency room populations, and these facilities may be used more often by females than by males. In fact, however, two studies that drew from "normal" populations—those of Harkavy-Friedman, Asnis, Boeck, and DiFiore, (1987) and Smith and Crawford (1986)—found female-to-female ratios of 3:1 and 5.6:1, respectively. Perhaps the different finding of Rubenstein and others was attributable to their added question; that is, "hurting self" perhaps was less threatening than "attempting to kill oneself" and therefore allowed more frequent than usual male responses. This possibility cannot be clarified from the data as they are reported.

These studies did reveal some troubling problems. Smith and Crawford (1986) found that only 12.1 percent of the attempters received medical treatment following their attempts, and Harkavy-Friedman, Asnis, Boeck, and DiFiore (1987) found that only about one-third of the attempters told anyone before their attempts, and fewer than two-thirds of the attempters told anyone after their attempts. How to reach these adolescents is a significant issue, which we address in later chapters. If there is a "silver lining" to any of these data, it is that studies have found the majority (usually 75 to 90 percent) of attempts to be of low lethality, predominantly mild overdoses and superficial wrist slashing.

Ideation. In a search for studies on suicidal ideation, we were able to find only one study of incidence in a junior high sample. In this study of sixty-three seventh- and eight-graders from suburban Philadelphia, 35 percent acknowledged current suicidal ideation (Albert and Beck, 1975). Studies with high school samples report a wider range of results on ideation than on attempts. The major reason for the differences among results regarding ideation is probably different wording of questionnaire items. Wright (1985) reported that only 10.6 percent of a central Texas high school population had seriously considered a suicide attempt in the last six months, while Teri's (1982) data on a Vermont high school sample revealed a 37.2 percent incidence of suicidal ideation. Other studies have found the incidence to be much higher, in the 50 to 65 percent range (Harkavy-Friedman, Asnis, Boeck, and DiFiore, 1987; Ross, 1985; Rubenstein and others, 1989; Smith and Crawford, 1986).

Summary. These statistics can be made concrete through the following example. If you were working in a high school with 2,000 students, given the data we have presented, you would be likely to lose one student or former student to suicide about every five years, have somewhere between 168 and 400 attempt to kill or hurt themselves per year, and have 660 to 1,300 of your students at some time during that year walking about your campus considering suicide. Of course, the actual number of these that school-based personnel will hear about will be far fewer.

Data from Clinical Populations

Garfinkel, Froese, and Hood (1982) found that 0.25 percent, or 1 in every 400, of admissions to the emergency room at a large children's hospital was precipitated by a suicide attempt. Pfeffer (1986) reported that from 1 to 12.8 percent of psychiatric outpatients had made a suicide attempt; for inpatients, the figures rose to between 27 and 34 percent. Cohen-Sandler, Berman, and King (1982) also found that 28 percent of their inpatient population had made some kind of suicide attempt.

Another statistic of particular import to us is the finding that 24.6 percent of inpatient children and adolescents who had attempted suicide were also learning disabled (Myers, Burke, and McCauley, 1985). These kinds of data are also being found by researchers in the field of learning disabilities. There is a suggestion that a particular subtype of learning disabilities, a form of nonverbal learning disabilities, may predispose adolescents to greater risks of depression and suicide (Kenny and others, 1979; Rourke, Young, and Lenaars, 1989). This disability seems to interfere with the learning of social skills such as social perception, social judgment, social interaction, and so on in ways that can lead to withdrawal and isolation, common characteristics of depressed and suicidal adolescents.

Method. What methods do attempters use? Studies indicate that self-poisoning is the most common suicide attempt. A range from 71 percent (Gispert, Wheeler, Marsh, and Davis, 1985) to 87.9 percent (Garfinkel, Froese, and Hood, 1982) of all suicide attempts have been found to be self-poisonings. This method is somewhat preferred by females; it accounted for 84.6 percent of attempts by females and 78.3 percent attempts by males (Withers and Kaplan, 1987). The second most common attempt method is some form of cutting behavior, usually accounting for about 10 percent of adolescent attempts (Garfinkel, Froese, and Hood, 1982; Withers and Kaplan, 1987). The ranking of other methods varies among studies; the third most common may be jumping, hanging, alcohol overdose, or firearms. It is very clear that attempter methods are different from and tend to be less lethal than completer methods.

Suicide Attempts and Referral to Clinics. One last disturbing statistic should be mentioned in this section. Cohen-Sandler, Berman, and King (1982) found that whereas 23 percent of their nonsuicidal inpatient sample were referred by school personnel, *none* of their suicidal subjects was. Whether this may be due to lack of sensitivity, lack of school attendance, or some other variable unfortunately was not addressed. The referral process is discussed more fully in Chapter Four.

Conclusion

In spite of the differing definitions, methodologies, interpretations of data, and other problems inherent in epidemiological research, the data do clarify the severity and importance of the problem and justify our and others' position that this is an area that school-based personnel need to know about.

In order to better focus our interventions, we need to know more about our populations. The information on child and adolescent suicide is much less complete than that on adult populations,

but such knowledge is essential for more refined prevention and
intervention efforts. And, as we will discuss, there is a great need for
more evaluation and research on these prevention and intervention
efforts. To some extent, we must ultimately gauge our efforts
against epidemiological data.

Much of what the professionals in this area need to know
about is the subject of the remainder of this book. To create some
"advanced organizers" for this material, the next chapter presents
models available to begin to help us understand this sad and per-
plexing problem of adolescent suicide.

2

Explaining
and Predicting Suicide

Mary Ann, age sixteen, has just been grounded for the week. She has a long history of conflict with her parents even though she does well in school, has friends, and is liked by her high school teachers. Enraged at her parents, she goes into the bathroom, takes ten aspirin tablets, and runs out of the bathroom sobbing loudly.

Bobby is seventeen. He has not done well in school. He has no close friends, few acquaintances, and a somewhat distant relationship with his teachers and parents. On Thursday morning, "God" speaks directly to him, telling him that if he simply jumps off the top of his high school building, the secrets of heaven will be opened to him. Telling no one, ignoring all but the voice, he heads for the stairs at his high school.

Is every suicide the same? Clearly, the answer is no. Each suicide has elements in common with others, but each is different from all others. The intent of this chapter is to explore some of the variety of ways theorists and researchers have tried to understand, classify, and explain suicide. We find it useful to distinguish three basic approaches to viewing suicide. The first approach is to be purely descriptive, the second is to develop typologies or models that explain through classification or categorization, and the third is to develop a model that attempts not only to explain but also to isolate specific variables that can be used for prediction, prevention, intervention, and postvention.

A Descriptive Model

The model presented in Figure 3 uses the variables *intent to die* and *outcome of action* to conceptualize four possible suicidal

Figure 3. Descriptive Model of Suicide Phenomena.

Intent to Die

	High	Low
Death	Completed Suicide	Accidental Death
Life	Attempted Suicide	Parasuicide

Outcome of Action

Source: California Suicide Intervention Training Program, 1988.

phenomena. When a high level of intent to die in fact leads to death, the phenomenon is termed a *completed suicide*. It is termed an *attempted suicide* when there is a high level of intent to die but the suicide is thwarted through some unplanned event; for example, the unexpected arrival of a friend before a self-poisoning becomes lethal. The validity of such a classification is supported by cases such as that of the suicide attempter who awakens both angry at still being alive and determined to complete the self-destructive act. The term *accidental,* or *undetermined, death* is applied when there is low or no intent to die but death results from an act. This category is examplified by an action that is truly accidental; for example, a single-vehicle accident misclassified as a suicide. Finally, when there is a low level of intent to die and no resulting death, the act is referred to as a *parasuicide*. This classification consists of behaviors such as certain autoerotic practices, borderline personality disorder "cutting" behavior, manipulative gestures, and so on. Although this term was originally introduced by Kreitman, Philip, Greer, and Bagley (1969) to replace the term *attempted suicide* (to avoid arguments about such issues as intention), its meaning here has been modified.

These descriptions are useful not only clinically but also for legal and statistical record keeping. The issues related to descriptive approaches and their complications are further addressed by Peck (1984, 1987). The strength of this model, its phenomenological approach, is also its major shortcoming: The absence of an attempt to explain or understand suicidal dynamics makes it difficult to generate interventions from such a model.

Explanatory Models

The first typological explanatory model was sociological in origin. It was proposed in 1897 by Émile Durkheim (1951), who, after analyzing data about suicides in France, proposed four types of suicides based on the individual's ties to society: (1) altruistic—sacrificing oneself for the community; (2) egoistic—resulting from few ties with or isolation from the community; (3) anomic—resulting from failure to adjust to social change (crises); and (4) fatalistic—resulting rom excessive regulation or overcontrol. Althoughthis typology is not particularly clinically useful, one can see potential applications of it to current prevention and intervention strategies.

Later, a somewhat more dynamically oriented typology was formulated by Menninger (1938). Whereas Durkheim stressed connections with people and society as a causative factor in suicide, Menninger stressed anger with self and others. For Menninger, suicide consisted of the wish to kill, the wish to be killed, and the wish to die. These thoughts connecting suicide and anger are more currently represented in the writings of Everstine and Everstine (1983), who place suicide in an interactional context. They suggest that (1) suicide is an event intended to send a message from one person to another; (2) there is one specific person who is expected to receive the message of suicide and for whom, above all, the suicidal act is performed; and (3) the primary content of the message being conveyed is anger (p. 207).

Another dynamic model of historical interest is Shneidman's (1968). He proposes a classification of committed suicides as dyadic, egotic, or ageneratic. The dyadic suicide is similar to Everstine and Everstine's (1983) "interactional" suicide, because the focus is on the expression of rage and frustration directed at another. The egotic suicide, according to Shneidman, results primarily from an intrapsychic rather than an interpersonal struggle, such as the hallucinating Bobby described at the beginning of this chapter. The ageneratic suicide is one caused by the withdrawal of the individual from "the transgenerational flow of human life" (Beck and Greenberg, 1971, p. 14), as epitomized by the isolated elderly who become depressed and no longer feel useful or productive.

A more current model focused specifically on young suicide attempters (self-poisoners) is offered by Hawton (Hawton, Cole, O'Grady, and Osborn, 1982; Hawton, 1986). He proposes three categories defined by the duration of the adolescent's problems and the level of his or her behavioral disturbance. The *acute* group consists of suicide attempters who have problems persisting less than one month and no overt behavior problems. The *chronic* group consists of attempters who have psychological problems persisting for longer than one month and no behavior problems. Finally, a group labeled *chronic with behavior disturbance* have problems lasting longer than one month and a history of recent behavioral disturbances, such as stealing, fighting, or abusing drugs.

More sophisticated statistical analyses—cluster and factor analyses—have brought about newer models. For instance, two British studies using cluster analytical techniques on groups of suicide attempters each derived three fairly similar groups of attempters (Henderson and others, 1977; Paykel and Rassaby, 1978). One group evidences high levels of *alienation, self-destructive* motivation, and *life endangerment.* The second group is overtly *hostile* and *angry.* The attempters in the third group were more difficult to characterize but were probably somewhat *less psychiatrically disturbed,* and their reasons for the attempt were less clear. The primary factors emerging as correlates of suicide from these studies seem to be levels of anger, depression, and psychopathology.

All of these models spring from the approach of grouping people and behaviors in ways that reveal similar characteristics, enabling us to better understand the suicidal phenomena. The characteristics identified can further be used to help us understand and generate the more explanatory-predictive models next considered. They go beyond the "descriptive" models but still struggle more with explaining or understanding the phenomenon of suicide than pushing into the realm of prediction.

Explanatory-Predictive Models

When we develop a model for suicide prediction, we must first know what it is that we are trying to predict and what our focus is. Are we trying to predict completed suicide, attempted suicide, or parasuicide? Are we trying to predict acute-imminent suicides (those likely to be attempted within the next twenty-four hours), with a focus on immediate intervention, or "chronic" suicides (those likely to be carried out sometime in the future), with a focus on prevention, or both? We also must know the context with which we are most concerned. As Litman, Wold, Farberow, and Brown (1974) point out, different cues or signs may be more relevant in some settings or contexts than in others. Even though, theoretically, all adolescents go through the school system, there are data to indicate that as many as 45 percent of suicide attempters are usually truant or not attending school at all (Gispert, Wheeler, Marsh, and Davis, 1985). However, other data indicate that adolescents making more lethal attempts tend to be more successful in school than their less lethal counterparts (Golombek and Garfinkel, 1983).

In Chapter Four, we address the assessment of imminent danger, and in Chapter Six we discuss screening. In the remainder of this chapter, we focus on the signs and symptoms most helpful to us in predicting and understanding nonacute suicide crises in adolescents. A useful model for organizing this section has been provided by Blumenthal and Kupfer (1988). This "threshold model," presented in Figure 4, considers four types of factors for the assessment of suicidal behavior. We review predisposing risk factors, risk factors, and precipitating factors here; protective factors are addressed in Chapters Eight and Nine.

Predisposing Risk Factors

These factors may be grouped in three primary clusters: genetics, biological factors, and personality traits or temperament.

Figure 4. Threshold Model for Suicidal Behavior Assessment.

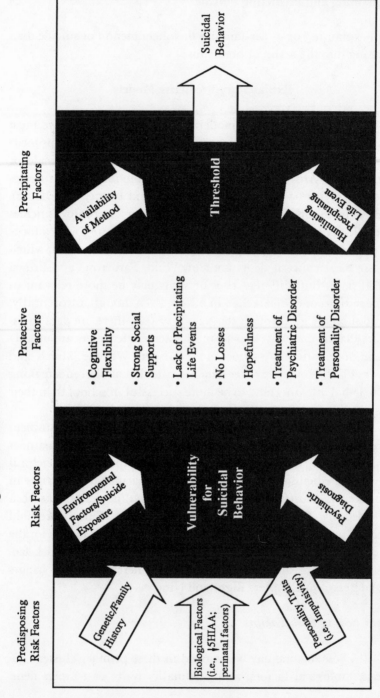

Source: From Blumenthal, S. J., and Kupfer, D. J. "Overview of Early Detection and Treatment Strategies for Suicidal Behavior in Young People," in JOURNAL OF YOUTH AND ADOLESCENCE, 17, 1–23 (1988), Plenum Publishing Corporation. Reprinted with permission.

Although we discuss these as if they were separate factors, in all likelihood they are highly related.

Genetics. Findings related to genetics tend to be conceptualized in one of two ways: (1) a higher incidence of suicide in families of attempters and completers or (2) a higher incidence of psychopathologies (most often affective disorders or schizophrenia) in the families of attempters and completers.

In a study of completed suicides, Shafti, Carrigan, Whittinghill, and Derrick (1985) found that six out of twenty suicide victims had parents or adult relatives who had completed or attempted suicide or were considered seriously suicidal, compared to two out of seventeen controls. Although this was not a statistically significant difference, when they added siblings or friends who attempted suicide to both groups, the completers' rate rose from six to twelve out of twenty, while that of the controls did not change. Unfortunately, it was not clear how many of the "siblings and friends" were actual biological siblings.

In studies of inpatient attempters, Roy (1983, 1986a) found that 50 percent came from families with a history of attempted suicide, and Garfinkel, Froese, and Hood (1982) found that significantly more of their attempters came from families with a history of suicide. In a study comparing the incidence of suicide among the biological and adoptive relations of adopted completers, there was a six times greater incidence of suicide among the biological relatives of adoptee completers than among those of the adoptee controls (Schulsinger, Ketz, Rosenthal, and Wender, 1979).

Biological Factors. In terms of a possible biological predisposition to psychopathology being highly correlated with suicide, the two primary candidates are the affective disorders and the schizophrenias (Roy, 1982, 1986b; Tsuang, 1977, 1983). Although no studies prove causality, the possibility of predisposition cannot be ignored.

A major finding in this area is that completers and violent attempters often have a deficit in the functioning of the neurotransmitter serotonin (Asberg, Traskman, and Thoran, 1986; Stanley and Stanley, 1989). This reduced central serotongenic activity is correlated more highly with suicidal behavior than with any particular psychiatric diagnosis (Brown and Goodwin, 1986). Furthermore, it has been suggested that violent suicide attempters with decreased serotonin activity may have a risk of completed suicide as much as ten times that of attempters with normal serotonin levels (Asberg, Traskman, and Thoran, 1986). Even though physiological correlates are always striking, it is important to remember that "normals" may also have this deficit without suicidal behaviors. Whatever the mediating or triggering variable might be has yet to be uncovered.

Personality Traits and Temperament. The term *temperament* refers to how a child behaves and the levels or extremes of that behavior, but not necessarily why the child behaves that way (Thomas and Chess, 1977). However, there is an underlying assumption that temperaments are phenotypical behavioral differences (Berger, 1985).

There are no current data to support a theory that an adolescent possessing any particular temperament or cluster of temperamental characteristics is any more likely to become suicidal than another. In the Chess and Thomas (1984) New York Longitudinal Study, adolescents with a depressive neurosis or an adjustment disorder with depressed mood showed an extreme tendency on one of the study traits or a cluster of traits during early childhood, but the particular traits were different from child to child. Chess and Thomas speculated that these "neurosis" cases were probably due more to poor "fit between parental expectations and demands and the child's capacities and characteristics" (p. 192) than to genetics. But they caution that they did not find evidence for their "fit" model for the two cases of major depression among their subjects, which they feel were likely to have been more directly influenced by genetics.

For the purposes of assessing predisposition, temperament can help us better understand how some of the increased stress in families with suicidal adolescents may have been generated. In this way, this conceptual framework may be very helpful for intervention.

Risk Factors

The risk factors in Blumenthal and Kupfer's model are those intrapsychic, cognitive, and environmental elements that have been found to be significantly correlated with suicidality. In this section, we examine the elements of hopelessness, depression, psychopathology, stress, the family system, and coping or problem-solving abilities.

Hopelessness. Social isolation (Durkheim, 1951) and depression (Freud, [1915] 1957) have long been considered the interpersonal and intrapsychic hallmarks of suicide. Clinical theory and practice were generally built around these concepts until the pioneering research in the measurement of suicidal potential (for example, Cohen, Motto, and Seiden, 1966; Beck, Schuyler, and Herman, 1974; Zung, 1974). Evidence for another, perhaps more powerful predictor of suicide, hopelessness, has emerged from the work of Beck and his colleagues (Beck, 1986; Beck, Kovacs, and Weissman, 1975; Beck, Steer, Kovacs, and Garrison, 1985). An extremely important aspect of this conceptualization is that "hopelessness is a core characteristic of depression and serves as the link between depression and suicide. Furthermore, hopelessness associated with other psychiatric disorders also predisposes the patient to suicide" (Beck, Steer, Kovacs, and Garrison, 1985, p. 559). This finding has been supported by other researchers, such as Dyer and Kreitman (1984), Goldney (1979), and Pallis and others (1982).

Although hopelessness was defined initially in adult populations, its high correlation with adolescent suicidality is also well supported in the literature on child and adolescent suicide (Asarnow, Carlson, and Guthrie, 1987; Brent and others, 1986; Friedman and others, 1984; Garfinkel, Froese, and Hood, 1982; Kazdin and others, 1983; Kazdin, Rodgers, and Colbus, 1986). Orbach (1986) provides us with a clinical example of the impact of hopelessness, which he relates to his concept of the "insolvable problem." According to Orbach, an insolvable problem is a situation confronting a child or adolescent that he or she cannot solve because of developmental, familial, or life constraints. Failure to discover a way out of a predicament leads to a variety of feelings, especially hopelessness. In Orbach's example, "A 13-year-old boy who tried to electrocute himself was subject to this confusing experience by his parents and it was demonstrated time and again during the family sessions. The parents used to maneuver themselves into a bitter confrontation and the mother would turn to the boy for help, pressuring him to support her against the father. As soon as the boy complied she hastily quieted him down, accusing him of disrespectful behavior toward his father. The same maneuver was repeated by his father, leaving the boy confused, overwhelmed, and helpless" (Orbach, 1986, p. 515). We postulate that this young adolescent would most probably develop feelings of hopelessness as well as confusion.

There are, however, some exceptions noted in the literature. In particular, Rotheram-Borus and Trautman (1988) found that black and Hispanic, chiefly Puerto Rican and Dominican, adolescent female suicide attempters were not more hopeless than a matched group of psychiatrically disturbed nonattempters. Hopelessness, as measured by the Beck Hopelessness Inventory, was higher for both clinical groups than for a group of nondisturbed controls.

A means of understanding this difference is offered by Brent and others (1986), who state that "this discrepancy might be explained by the existence of two different populations of suicide attempters: a dysphoric, hopeless group, whose attempts are planned and of high intent, and an impulsive, externalizing group whose attempts are of variable intent" (p. 666). Again, this explanation is compatible with the model illustrated by Figure 3. We should note, however, that the evidence available on adolescents' planning of their suicide attempts indicates that forethought is seldom extensive. Hawton, Cole, O'Grady, and Osborn (1982) found that more than 50 percent of their self-poisoning survivors reported thinking seriously about the suicide act for less than fifteen minutes, 16 percent thought about it for fifteen to sixty minutes, and only 8 percent thought about it for more than one day. Taylor and Stansfield (1984) found that three-quarters of their group of adolescent self-poisoners spent less than two hours thinking about it. Of course, one could still argue that since poison is lower on lethality scales than firearms or hanging, Brent's dichotomy could still be valid. Self-poisoners as a group may be impulsive.

The research on hopelessness has also moved us away from the simplistic Freudian model of melancholia leading to suicide. The current view is that a variety of psychopathologies potentially lead to suicide when mediated by hopelessness. Thus, other variables, such as stress and family dynamics, become important.

Psychopathology. There is convincing evidence that adults who complete differ from those who attempt but do not complete suicide (Segal and Humphrey, 1970; Shneidman and Farberow, 1965). This difference also seems to be true for adolescents. In a group of children and adolescents who completed suicide, Shaffer (1974) found that twenty-two of thirty had antisocial or conduct disorder symptoms, twenty-one had affective symptoms, primarily depression, and seventeen had a combination of both. He comments that "a model viewing suicide as the consequence of the distortion of perception or judgment which characterizes individuals who are psychiatrically ill is the most useful and valid framework for conceptualizing its causes" (Fisher and Shaffer, 1984, p. 139). The most common diagnosis for completers is affective disorder, with conduct and personality disorders and substance abuse following. The co-occurrence of affective disorders with other psychiatric disorders increases the risk of suicide (Blumenthal, 1988; Garfinkel, Froese, and Hood, 1982).

The data on psychopathology among suicide attempters are more varied. Percentages of attempters with diagnosable psychiatric illness start from a high of almost 100 percent in an inpatient setting (Clarkin and others, 1984), drop to 68.3 percent in a hospital emergency room setting (Garfinkel, Froese, and Hood, 1982), drop further to 42 percent in an outpatient psychiatric setting (Carlson and Cantwell, 1982), and fall to a low of about 20 percent in a general British hospital setting (Hawton, Cole, O'Grady, and Osborn, 1982). Thus, depending on diagnostic criteria and setting, estimates differ. Hawton (1986) further suggests that the majority of adolescent suicide attempts are most appropriately categorized as an adjustment reaction or situational crisis. It seems likely that attempters who suffer from a psychiatric illness would be more apt to be placed in the "suicide attempt" cell of our model and that the adjustment reaction and situational attempters are more appropriately placed in our "parasuicide" cell.

There is also evidence supporting the theory that suicidality is not dichotomous but rather exists on a continuum of behaviors from ideation through completed suicide. In a very interesting study of hospitalized suicidal youngsters and nonhospitalized, school-based adolescents who had anonymously admitted to "hurting themselves" or attempting suicide within the past year, it was found that the hospital and school groups were psychologically similar with respect to stress, depression, and hopelessness (Rubenstein and others, 1989). Suicidal adolescents in a high school setting, then, were not significantly different from suicidal adolescents in an in-patient psychiatric unit. Although only one study, it has very important implications for school-based practitioners, especially when coupled with the earlier Cohen-Sandler, Berman, and King (1982) study documenting how few suicidal students we refer for inpatient services (none in that particular study).

Stress. Life stress contributes to suicidality in children and adolescents. "Unlike depressed and psychiatric control children, suicidal children experienced an increasing amount of stress as they matured. Moreover, from the pre-school years through the year prior to admission [to an inpatient psychiatric faculty], the amount of stress children experienced increasingly differentiated the suicidal group, reaching statistical significance by later childhood" (Cohen-Sandler, Berman, and King, 1982). During the year prior to the suicide attempt, stress scores have been reported to be 33 percent higher than those of nonsuicidal adolescents (Rubenstein and others, 1989).

Rubenstein and others found the types of stress that increase the probability of suicide clustered into four groups: sexuality, achievement pressure, family suicide (suicide within the extended family network), and personal loss (death of friends or family members due to causes other than suicide). They state, "92 percent of the teenagers who score very high on all four risk factors are expected to be suicidal" (p. 65), whereas only 3 percent of those who score low are expected to be suicidal. The questions regarding sexuality did not ask about abuse or homosexuality, which might have made this an even more powerful variable. Rather, they asked more developmentally oriented questions about feeling stress about sex, sexual activity, parents' upset about sexual activity, and so on. Achievement pressure was also more developmentally focused, and

64 percent of the population reported difficulties with parental and societal pressure about academics or athletics. (The sample for this study was from the middle class. These two clusters in particular may be different for a population of lower socioeconomic status.)

Family Systems. When a suicide has been attempted by an adolescent, it is clinically sound to assume that the family is involved. How the family is involved is a more complex question. Some clinicians have written about the family's causative role. Sabbath (1982) talks about the "expendable child," and Rosenbaum and Richman (1970) discuss family hostilities and death wishes toward the child pressuring the child toward suicide. Other, somewhat more benign views are that the families of these adolescents failed to provide security and opportunities for developing resources for coping with stress (Rosenberg and Latimer, 1966) or fostered the use of suicide as a coping strategy (Cohen-Sandler, Berman, and King, 1982).

The best-documented family characteristics contributing to adolescent suicidality are the higher rates of suicide (Blumenthal and Kupfer, 1988; Garfinkel, Froese, and Hood, 1982), higher rates of medical and psychiatric illness (Friedman and others, 1984; Garfinkel, Froese, and Hood, 1982), often increased economic stress (Garfinkel, Froese, and Hood, 1982), and the adolescent's perception of the family as high in conflict and low in support or cohesion (Asarnow, Carlson, and Guthrie, 1987; Cohen-Sandler, Berman, and King, 1982; Garfinkel, Froese, and Hood, 1982; Kosky, 1983; Rubenstein and others, 1989; Withers and Kaplan, 1987; Wright, 1985). An important footnote to these data is offered by Rubenstein and others (1989), who found that "sexuality, loss, and pressure to achieve involve the adolescent directly, and were found to be more salient for suicidal behavior than were family problems such as family emotional disorder or family conflict-issues over which the adolescent has less control and less responsibility" (p. 68), although it is clear that the adolescent's family must be involved in some way in the ongoing processes around sexuality, loss, and achievement pressure. A clinical caveat is offered by Garfinkel, Froese, and Hood (1982), who caution against attributing blame to the family but prefer to look at inabilities to reach out, support, and/or problem solve on the part of all family members.

Problem-Solving Ability. Earlier, we reviewed data supporting the notion that suicidal adolescents experience more stress in their lives than nonsuicidal adolescents. The data in this section underline the importance of this difference. Suicidal children and adolescents do not seem to be as good at problem solving as their nonsuicidal counterparts, and we find that this manifests itself in a variety of ways.

One of the earliest studies of this nature was by Levenson and Neuringer (1971). Using both nonsuicidal psychiatric and normal control groups, they found that adolescent suicide attempters performed significantly less well on the Wechsler Adult Intelligence Scale (WAIS) Arithmetic subtest and the Rokeach Map Test Problems. They concluded that suicidal adolescents had a diminished problem-solving capacity. This result clearly ties in with the information in Chapter One on learning disabilities and suicide.

The research by George Clum and his associates (Luscomb, Clum, and Patsiokas, 1980; Patsiokas, Clum, and Luscomb, 1979: Schotte and Clum, 1982, 1987) has also supported the link with cognitive or "impersonal" problem-solving deficits over a variety of cognitive measures. Their research has taken this thought a step further in that they have also found that suicidal people are less proficient *inter*personal problem solvers, as measured by the Means-End Problem-Solving Procedure (Platt, Spivack, and Bloom, 1971). Linehan's research (Linehan and Nielsen, 1983; Linehan and others, 1987) also supports the existence of deficits in interpersonal problem solving. She states that "those [psychiatric inpatients] admitted following a parasuicide scored lower in active interpersonal problem solving than did those admitted for current suicide ideation without parasuicide" (Linehan and others, 1987, p. 9). (In our nomenclature, Linehan's parasuicide could be either a suicide attempt or a parasuicide.)

A similar line of research has looked at coping behaviors. Here again, differences in interpersonal coping abilities and styles have been found. Using a coping strategies test, Asarnow, Carlson, and Guthrie (1987) found that "suicide ideators, when compared with nonsuicidal children, were significantly less likely to generate active cognitive coping strategies" (p. 364); however, there were no differences between ideators and attempters. They found that some of the suicidal children even generated suicide as a coping strategy.

An attempt to better delineate the variety of coping strategies available has been made by Spirito (Spirito, Overholser, and Stark, 1989; Spirito, Stark, and Williams, 1988). Using a checklist that he has devised that he calls "Kidcope," he reports that suicide attempters more often use social withdrawal as a coping mechanism and less often use emotional regulation than do controls.

The last study we found relating to coping also attempted to be more specific about the mechanisms used. Khan (1989) sums up his findings as follows: "the main difference between the suicidal and non suicidal adolescents appeared to be in two areas: (1) ability to cope with angry and sad feelings and (2) cognitive capacity to think through the consequences of their action" (p. 681). Related to lack of coping skills is proclivity for substance abuse. Substance abuse may be seen as a substitute for coping and a form of escapism. (We discuss the important relationship between substance abuse and suicide in Chapter Seven.)

Thus, it is becoming clear that suicidal adolescents tend to be raised in families that are higher in stress and conflict and lower in support and cohesiveness, experience higher levels of stress, and are not as able to cope with what must be experienced as a disharmonious world about them than the families of nonsuicidal adolescents. What is needed for suicide is something to set it off.

Precipitating Factors

Precipitating factors are perhaps one of the most important issues for school-based personnel, because they are often how we make things worse for adolescents. Shaffer (1974) found that more than one-third of the completed suicides were precipitated by a "disciplinary crisis" and that for half of those (or roughly one-sixth of the completed suicides), "the disciplinary crisis consisted of the child's having been told by a school official that their parents would be informed by letter of truanting or some other antisocial behavior about which the parents had not previously been aware" (Shaffer and Fisher, 1981).

A powerful example of how school personnel can precipitate a crisis is found in the film *Up the Down Staircase,* in which an English teacher returned a love note, corrected and graded, to an infatuated student, which led to a completed suicide. Support for the potential negative impact of insensitive school discipline has also been documented by Spirito, Overholser, and Stark (1989), who found that 10 percent of their suicide attempters reported that school problems had precipitated their suicide attempts. If we use the statistics cited in Chapter One that estimate attempts by 8.4 to 20 percent of the school population, given a school population of 2,000, school personnel could be precipitating as many as 16 to 40 attempts per year. We do not impute causality to these events, but we do suggest that unempathic or ill-informed interventions can make things worse and, in fact, can at times become the precipitating factor in a suicide or suicide attempt.

Of course, other precipitating factors do exist. Spirito, Overholser, and Stark (1989) grouped three other categories of precipitating events: 53 percent of their sample talked about problems with parents, 27 percent talked about problems with a boyfriend or girlfriend, and 10 percent reported problems with friends. These findings are supported by those of Shaffer (1974), whose subjects had similar experiences.

Hawton, Cole, O'Grady, and Osborn (1982), trying to elucidate the motivation behind the attempts they studied, found that their attempters were most likely to say that they wanted to get relief from distress, to escape for a while from an impossible situation, or to make people understand how desperate they were feeling. Interestingly, when asked to suggest the reasons behind the attempt, the evaluators of these attempters were most likely to see the attempt as a way of influencing or manipulating a person, a way to get others to change their mind about something, or a way to get people's sympathy or to frighten or get back at them for some perceived injustice.

Conclusion

In this chapter, we have presented many ways of trying to classify, understand, and predict suicide. The descriptive models have a heavily epidemiological emphasis, the explanatory models are more sociologically oriented, and the explanatory-predictive models have a clinical focus. Obviously, the explanatory-predictive models offer practitioners the most useful information for prevention and intervention. However, the most important point made in this chapter is that suicide is a multicausal, multifaceted, complex process. It is not useful to see a suicidal adolescent as "crazy," nor is it useful to see the adolescent as normally reacting to developmental stress. What is most likely is that the adolescent is in emotional turmoil and is being bombarded by more than just developmental stress. Also, it should be clear from the chapter that there is no one suicidal type of adolescent. Rather, suicide or a suicide attempt is the end result of a variety of complex patterns and sequences. But it is equally obvious that we do not have at this point and probably will not have at any point in the near future a complete understanding of the suicidal process.

However, we do have enough knowledge to begin to take action—action with a strong likelihood of a positive impact on the lives of our students. *Understanding* of the potential complexity of the suicidal adolescent's life and *empathy* with the concomitant feelings provide the necessary leverage for action.

Part Two:
Strategies for
School Practitioners

3

Evaluating
Suicide Potential

A survey of the personnel from five public high schools in the southwestern United States indicated that 79 percent of the classroom teachers and 47 percent of the special education staff would turn to the school psychologist first if worried about a student they believed to be depressed (Maag, Rutherford, and Parks, 1988). In a study of twelve Boston area public high schools, almost 50 percent of the school professionals wanted to have well-trained professionals from within the school system available to them and to their students, including those at risk for suicide (Grob, Klein, and Eisen, 1983). School-based support personnel (psychologists, counselors, social workers, nurses), whether or not they see it as their job, are going to be approached for their advice and expertise regarding students with problems and crises, including suicidal crises. Each of them needs to be clear about what they need to know to be able to intervene helpfully in the lives of their students and to provide helpful consultation to their parents and to school colleagues. One set of skills they need concerns how to make an assessment of suicidal risk and what to do with the data and the adolescent after they have finished the assessment. This chapter focuses on these skills.

The following example of a failure to intervene and the resulting dire consequences poignantly illustrates how costly not knowing what to do can be: Scott was a relatively new kid in the sixth grade. One Monday, he turned in to his teacher an essay entitled "Suicide Mistake." Later, the investigating police chief described the essay: "It starts with One—Introduction. Two—The New Boy. Three—Making Friends. Four—Committing Suicide.

Under item one, he changed his name from Scott to Dan. He put down that his story is based on a true story and taken from [Scott's life]. On the second page, he talks about moving to [a small town in Illinois]. He wrote that in the school he left everybody liked him. On the third page, he becomes upset that it is difficult to make friends and trying to be liked. On the last page, well, we're trying to suppress the information about the actual suicide" ("A Stubborn Suicide Rate," 1986, p. A4).

On Monday evening, Scott's teacher read the essay, including the part on the last page that described "Dan" having trouble making friends at the new school and killing himself by suffocation with a plastic bag. The teacher immediately called the principal, and they agreed to help Scott get counseling in the morning. Scott's mother found his body at 9:24 P.M. This example illustrates the two primary concerns addressed in this chapter: How school-based mental health professionals get access to potentially suicidal students and what they do with or for them once they learn about their thoughts or plans.

Referral Sources

School-based mental health professionals have four basic ways to come into contact with their clients: screening, self-referral, psychological and/or educational evaluations and interviews, and informal referrals. This chapter focuses on the latter three; screening is discussed in detail in Chapter Six.

Self-Referral

Relatively few troubled students approach helping professionals on their own to ask for specific help in controlling suicidal impulses. However, when suicide does come up in a student interview, it is vitally important to keep in mind the fact that because the student is aware of and talks about suicide does not mean that he or she will not do it. In fact, in his study of male adolescent suicide completers, Motto (1984) found that they often sought help and that their suicidal intent was very clear. Although having a client initiate the topic provides the interviewer with a straightforward approach to a suicide assessment, a thorough assessment is still very much needed. Recently, a counselor told us of a near disaster. A bright, sixteen-year-old male student came into her office and directly stated that he had not done well on his report card and was feeling suicidal and scared. The counselor, being rushed as they often are, commended him on knowing himself well and seeking help and, as she was putting her things together to leave, asked him whether he felt that they could begin working on this first thing the next morning. He silently nodded his acquiescence, but as they were about to leave, he broke into tears. This outburst stopped them both; she did a more thorough assessment and helped to arrange for what turned out to be a brief psychiatric hospitalization. We must make time whenever the topic of suicide comes up in counseling.

Evaluations

School-based professionals are often called on to do psychoeducational, educational, vocational, and other types of evaluations of students. In this role, they need to be cognizant of the fact that they are coming into contact with clients possibly at risk for suicidal behavior and need either to be sensitive to possible indirect messages or directly inquire about suicidal ideation and behavior. The latter approach is espoused by Cynthia Pfeffer, who found that 33 percent of a serially selected group of thirty-nine six- to twelve-year-old children coming to an outpatient clinic for an evaluation displayed suicidal ideas, threats, and/or attempts (Pfeffer, Conte, Plutchik, and Jerrett, 1980). She recommends that all children and, by implication, all adolescents who are being psychiatrically evaluated should be assessed for suicidal potential. Her position, which is shared by many others (for example, Hawton, 1986; Orbach, 1988; Weiner, 1982), is that children and adolescents are most interested in talking openly about suicidal thoughts and feelings with adults who can talk about it openly with them.

One of our own assessment experiences provides an example of how an indirect message during a psychoeducational reevaluation led to a suicide assessment. Susan was sixteen and a junior in high school. She was in a learning disability pull-out program for help in reading and was due for a three-year reevaluation for continued placement. Reevaluations are seldom high among a school psychologists' priorities, and these evaluations are sometimes approached with less sensitivity than we would care to find in ourselves. Susan was very cooperative, and the reevaluation was proceeding smoothly until she began the comprehension subtest of the WISC-R. When she was asked what she would do if she lost an object belonging to a friend, her affect shifted and her motivation began to fade, but she reluctantly answered the question. Although the psychologist wanted to continue the assessment, he was also curious about the shift in demeanor. He finally went back and commented on the shift and discovered that one of her best friends had recently died, so that she had lost a friend. With relatively little empathic listening, Susan revealed that she was very depressed and that this had become exacerbated by some relatively mild suicidal ideation, which was very frightening to her.

Informal Referrals

Informal referrals to school-based personnel usually come from teachers, administrators, secretaries or other school personnel, parents, or students' peers who report information about a student's despair or statements about suicidality. This situation is very difficult because it requires acting on data gathered and organized through another's framework. Depending on who makes the referral and the nature of the information given, the professional may (1) begin intervening with the suicidal student on the basis of the other's data, (2) consult with the referrer about how he or she can further engage and assess the student, (3) decide to collect more data directly through individual or joint interviews with the student, or (4) if the student is unwilling to talk to anyone, inform the parent or guardian and suggest referral when there are concerns about serious suicidal intent.

First-category decisions are often the easiest to make, because these cases are usually extreme. For example, if a teacher presents with a student who seems high on drugs, is abusive, and is verbally threatening suicide, it is clear that the parents and/or police must be called and the student helped to regain control.

The choices around the second and third categories are often more difficult, but these cases are usually resolved by further assessments of the suicidal student's level of intention. Factors that will influence the choice of who will make the further assessment include the student's fears of mental health personnel or fears of being stigmatized by seeing a mental health professional and the referring person's level of comfort with and skill to conduct further evaluation. If the student's fears of being stigmatized are high and the referral source is able and willing, working initially through the referral source may be more profitable.

The fourth category presents difficulties because the student's unwillingness to talk makes it impossible to make an assessment. Although mistakingly referring a student without suicidal intent may cause some psychological trauma, we believe that it is better to err on the side of caution, since the outcome of erring in the other direction is usually more tragic. Following are two examples.

Craig, an excellent high school student in his junior year, from a first-generation Asian family in San Francisco, was scheduled to take the Scholastic Aptitude Test within the next month. His teacher reported that Craig was very nervous about the test, because his family expected him to be accepted into a prestigious university, and he did not know what he would do if he performed poorly. The teacher suggested to Craig that he talk to the counselor about his fears in order to learn some relaxation techniques to help with his anxiety. Craig declined, because he believed that talking to a counselor would be viewed as an admission of "craziness" and make his parents ashamed of him. Because of the lack of clues suggesting imminent suicide and the fears associated with seeking out a counselor, the counselor consulted with the teacher rather than directly intervening. The teacher was able to get Craig to agree to a parent conference to discuss some of his anxieties and to get parental permission and support to work with the counselor to decrease his anxieties. The parents also agreed to meet with the counselor to talk about Craig's and their aspirations and expectations for his college career.

A clear example of when to use a direct intervention was provided by an Oakland school psychologist. While she was working in one of her schools, a principal from another of her schools called in a panic, stating that Tyrone, a sixth-grader in his school, was standing in his office angry, upset, and threatening suicide. She immediately went over to the school, interviewed Tyrone, and called his mother, asking that she come to the school for a crisis conference. The school psychologist knew the principal and knew that she normally would not call her except in an emergency.

One exception to these guidelines of urgency, competence of referral source, and the suicidal child's willingness to talk to a counselor is the case when the referring person is another student. If a student has struggled within him- or herself to come to a counselor out of fear for and loyalty to a friend, the counselor would not want to increase the burden on that adolescent by suggesting that he or she go back to collect more data or intervene. We feel that the increased level of responsibility and guilt that would result should the victim complete suicide is an unacceptable risk (see also Ruof, Harris, and Robbie, 1987). However, some students may offer no other choice. If students come to talk to us about "a friend," and the counselor is certain that this is not a metaphor for themselves, yet they absolutely refuse to reveal who their friend is, the counselor may be forced to use them as an intermediary while educating them on the risks that they are taking.

Up to this point, we have discussed assessment as if there were only one way to go about it. Actually, there are a variety of approaches. In the next section, we explore a number of models and issues regarding suicide assessment in the interview.

Models of Suicide Assessment

As we have stated earlier, the goal of this book is not to make anyone a suicidologist or an expert in the interventions and treatment of suicidal adolescents but to help school-based practitioners become suicide sensitive and knowledgeable. In this section, we present guidelines for evaluating an adolescent for suicidal risk. We do believe that the evaluator should possess the skills, knowledge, and attitudes suggested by Pfeffer (1986, p. 178):

1.   The clinician should be knowledgeable about diagnosis, treatment, and outcome of suicidal children.

2. The clinician must be aware of his or her conscious feelings about death and suicide.

3. The clinician must be able to evaluate his or her unconscious feelings about death and suicide.

4. All suicidal ideas and actions are serious and warrant extensive evaluation.

5. The degree of acute suicidal risk should be evaluated.

6. A commitment should be obtained from the child to work with the therapist and not attempt to harm him- or herself.

7. The family should be involved in the initial interviews.

8. A verbal mode should be the predominant format for evaluations.

We think that most school-based personnel do not have the time or the training to treat seriously suicidal clients; therefore, our focus is on assessment, referral, and collaboration (although Chapter Four includes some suggestions for working with adolescents who have some suicidal ideation but who are assessed to be at minimal risk).

Assessment Approaches

While Patrick and Overall (1969) report the successful development of a brief psychiatric rating scale able to discriminate between suicidal and nonsuicidal patients, they admit that the scale does not provide results as accurate as would be obtained by simply asking the patient about suicidal concerns. Standard psychological tests, such as the Rorschach, the Minnesota Multiphasic Personality Inventory (MMPI), and the Thematic Apperception Test (TAT), have also been found lacking as predictors of suicidal risk (Brown and Sheran, 1972; Clopton and Jones, 1975; Lester, 1974; Neuringer, 1974). We follow in the tradition of Gordon Allport and George Kelly, who believed that it is usually best to ask people directly about those issues that concern them. For these reasons, the three basic approaches advocated here, although they vary somewhat, all take a direct questioning approach. Developed by Corder, Reynolds, and Rotheram, these strategies were chosen because they are the most relevant to an adolescent school-based population. Many other models are useful but are oriented either toward young and older adults (Beck, Kovacs, and Weisman, 1975; Lettieri, 1974; Zung, 1974) or toward preadolescents (Kazdin and others, 1983; Pfeffer, 1986).

Before proceeding to the models, let us review what may be obvious. What questions are asked as part of an assessment depends on what seems to be important for understanding the problem. For instance, depression has long been thought to be a contributor to suicide (Carlson and Cantwell, 1982; Freud, [1915] 1957; Toolan, 1962, 1988; Ross and Lee, n.d.). Over the years, however, the work of Beck and others has brought into question the relative importance of depression in suicide among adults and older adolescents (Beck, Schuyler, and Herman, 1974; Beck, Weisman, Lester, and Trexler, 1974), and Kazdin's work with inpatient children and young adolescents also supports the notion of a smaller role for depression (Kazdin and others, 1983). Both research teams concluded that suicidal intent was more consistently correlated with and better explained by hopelessness than depression. Or, as another study found, "Although 65 percent of our suicidal children also were diagnosed as depressed, only 38 percent of depressed children engaged in suicidal behavior. This discrimination is essential in understanding that despite the overlap or association between suicide and depression, it is possible to differentiate the two groups. Depressed children are not necessarily suicidal; conversely, not all suicidal children meet the criteria for depression" (Cohen-Sandler, Berman, and King, 1982).

Therefore, we deemphasize the diagnosis of depression as part of the suicide assessment. However, since suicidal adolescents can manifest a variety of psychopathologies and diagnoses, we feel that it is important to do a brief mental status examination to look for evidence of psychosis, depression, psychosomatic concerns, organicity, disorientation due to use of drugs or alcohol, and so on. The use of a mental status examination ties in with our belief that we should have some beginning measures of potential psychopathology as well as suicidality. It is also important because it has been found that almost all psychiatric symptoms increase with the severity of suicidal ideation and make a suicide attempt more likely (Brent and others, 1986). The following list, adapted from Tishler,

McKenry, and Morgan (1981, p. 89), is an example of a mental status examination to be used for adolescents. This is best conducted with the adolescents alone in a private setting, as is the suicide interview, after a rapport has been established.

After this general psychiatric interview to rule out or establish a level of signs of pathology, the questions need to be shifted to the more direct and thorough assessment of suicidal thoughts and feelings.

Orientation	1.	What is your name?
	2.	Where are you?
	3.	What day is it?
Memory	4.	Do you have problems thinking or remembering things?
	5.	Do you have problems concentrating in school?
Sleep	6.	What time do you go to bed at night?
	7.	What time do you fall asleep at night?
	8.	How many times per week do you have trouble falling asleep at night?
	9.	Do you ever wake up in the early morning (2 A.M.–5 A.M.)?
Weight	10.	Have you lost or gained weight over the past two to three months?
Somatic complaints	11.	Have you had aches, pains, headaches, or problems with your body lately?
Hallucinations	12.	Have you heard or seen anything recently that you were not sure was really there?

Problems	13. Do you have any family problems or problems of any kind (such as with boy- or girlfriends) that you would like to talk about?
Affect	14. How often do you cry or feel like crying?
	15. Do you ever feel like crying but you can't?
	16. Do you ever feel sad but don't know why?
School history	17. Have you been attending school regularly? If not, why not?
	18. Are there people that you are close to, friends or relatives, that you talk to about your thoughts and feelings?
Sexual history	19. Are you currently dating or finding yourself especially attracted to someone?
	20. Are you sexually involved with anyone? Has a pregnancy occurred [if heterosexual]?
Drug and alcohol history	21. Have you been using any kinds of drugs or alcohol over the last two weeks? How much and how frequently?
Abuse history	22. Has there been any sexual or physical abuse in your family?
	23. Have you been the recipient of abuse?

Corder's Strategy of Suicidal Evaluation

Corder has taken a very pragmatic, clinical approach to the evaluation of suicidal children and their families (Corder and Haizlip, 1982; Corder, Page, and Corder, 1974; Corder, Shorr, and Corder, 1974). Although she has worked primarily in a medical setting and her objective is assisting nonpsychiatric medical doctors, particularly pediatricians, to identify suicidal adolescents, her interview questions are also an excellent working model for a school-based professional's assessment of suicidal risk. We have modified her questions (Corder and Haizlip, 1982) for use by school-based personnel as follows:

For Child

- It seems things haven't been going so well for you lately. Your parents and/or teachers have said _____ . Most adolescents would find that upsetting.
- Have you felt upset, maybe some sad or angry feelings you've had trouble talking about? Maybe I could help you talk about these feelings and thoughts?
- Do you feel like things can get better, or are you worried (afraid, concerned) things will just stay the same or get worse?
- Other teenagers I've talked to have said that when they feel that sad and/or angry, they thought for a while that things would be better if they were dead. Have you ever thought that? What were your thoughts?
- What do you think it would feel like to be dead?
- How do you think your father and mother would feel? What do you think would happen with them if you were dead?
- Has anyone that you know of killed or attempted to kill themselves? Do you know why?
- Have you thought about how you might make yourself die? How often have you had these thoughts? How long do they stay with you? Do you have a plan?
- Is there anyone or anything that would stop you?
- Do you have (the means) at home (available)?
- Have you ever tried to kill yourself before?

- On a scale of 1 to 10, how likely is it that you will kill yourself? When are you planning to or when do you think you will do this?
- What has made you feel so awful?

For Parents

- Has any serious change occurred in your child's or your family's life recently (within the last year)?
- How did your child respond?
- Has your child had any accidents or illnesses without a recognizable physical basis?
- Has your child experienced a loss recently?
- Has your child experienced difficulty in any areas of his or her life?
- Has your child been very self-critical, or have you or his or her teachers been very critical lately?
- Has your child made any unusual statements to you or others about death or dying? Any unusual questions or jokes about death or dying?
- Have there been any changes you've noticed in your child's mood or behavior over the last few months?
- Has your child ever threatened or attempted suicide before?
- Have any of your child's friends or family, including yourselves, ever threatened or attempted suicide?
- How have these last few months been for you? How have you reacted to your child (anger, despair, empathy, and so on)?

For Teachers

- Have you noticed any major changes in your student's schoolwork since school started (or from last year)?
- Have you noticed any behavioral, emotional, or attitudinal changes? (same time frame)
- Has the adolescent experienced any trouble in school for abusive language or behavior to peers and/or adults?
- Does the adolescent appear depressed and/or hostile and angry to you? What clues does he or she give?
- Has the student either verbally, behaviorally, or symbolically (in

an essay or story) threatened suicide or expressed statements associated with self-destruction or death?

For Family Members

- Would family members describe themselves as being closer to each other within their immediate family than they perceive the average family as being? Are doing things together and being close a high priority?
- Has the family experienced any major changes due to work, death, moving, separation, and so on?
- Has the adolescent in question been special or significant for any particular reasons in his or her family?
- Has the adolescent disappointed the family over the last year as a result of behavioral, attitudinal, or any other changes?
- Does the family think that they have been more critical of this adolescent recently than during the last year?
- Has anyone in the family or close to the family or adolescent attempted or completed suicide?

As can be seen, these questions recognize the importance of the demographic data discussed in the previous chapter and the relevant clinical data and the necessity of gathering data about the child or adolescent from the family, from the school, and directly from the child or adolescent. Although the point is not discussed in Corder's articles, we believe that the parents and teachers should be questioned in private, and the child should be questioned alone and in private. For the family questions, as many as practically possible of the family members should be present and respond. If there is a discrepancy between the parents' and the adolescent's reports, the more serious report should receive the greatest weight (Brent and others, 1986).

The value of the Corder model is that it can be used very flexibly and it pays explicit attention to all available resource groups within a school that can be used for gathering data on the student or aid in the intervention. As in many instances in life, some of the strengths of this approach could also be seen as its weaknesses. A clinical model also entails having some clinical expertise. Therefore, school-based personnel who have not had enough training or do not feel comfortable with their clinical skills may be intimidated by its openness.

Reynolds's Strategy of Suicidal Evaluation

Reynolds and his associates (Klosterman-Fields, 1985; Reynolds and Graves, 1987; Reynolds, 1987a, 1988) have developed the Suicidal Ideation Questionnaire (SIQ), with a thirty-item high school form and a fifteen-item junior high school form. Reynolds (1988) suggests that it can be used for either screening or clinical evaluations. In this section, we discuss its usefulness in guiding an assessment interview for school-based professionals who desire a more structured, psychometric approach.

Reynolds's questionnaire is very much in the tradition of cognitive orientations such as Beck's Scale for Suicide Ideation (Beck, Kovacs, and Weissman, 1975). Each item on the SIQ begins with an "I thought . . . ," "I wondered . . . ," or "I wished . . . ," and the respondent is asked to choose along a seven-point continuum. The following excerpt presents the directions and the first item from the SIQ high school form (Reynolds, 1987a):

Directions

Listed below are a number of sentences about thoughts that people sometimes have. Please indicate which of these thoughts you have had in the past month. Fill in the circle under the answer that best describes your own thoughts. [In the original there are circles associated with each of the seven possible responses.] Be sure to fill in a circle for each sentence. Remember, there are no right or wrong answers.

1. I thought it would be better if I was not alive . . . This thought was in my mind:
    - Almost every day.
    - Couple of times a week.
    - About once a week.
    - Couple of times a month.
    - About once a month.

- I had this thought before but not in the past
  month.
- I never had this thought.

It can be seen that the instrument focuses on getting at specific
suicidal thoughts and the frequency of those specific thoughts over
a one-month period. The form is structured so that it can be filled
out by the client or the clinician can use it to ask the client questions. It is then scored by the clinician.

The scores can be used in four basic forms: total score, cutoff
scores, critical items, or individual items. Reynolds (1987b, 1988)
provides norms (raw scores and conversions to percentile ranks),
based on a normative sampling of 890 students for the high school
form and 1,280 students for the junior high form. He also provides
cutoff scores for his two instruments on the basis of his norming
and clinical research data: "Although not a diagnostic or predictive
measure, the S.I.Q. provides valuable clinical information on suicidal thoughts of adolescents. A cut-off score on the S.I.Q. may be
used to judge the severity of suicidal thoughts reported by adolescents" (Reynolds, 1987b, p. 22).

Reynolds reports eight critical items on the high school form
and six on the junior high form. He considers them critical because
they tap into actual thoughts and plans for suicide. He suggests that
if these items are answered "a couple of times a week" or "every
day," there is evidence of a critical level of danger. He suggests a
further clinical rule of thumb: If three or more of the eight critical
items on the thirty-item scale or two or more of the six critical items
on the fifteen-item scale are chosen, the respondent should be considered at serious risk, regardless of the total or cutoff scores.

Finally, a glance at the individual items can reveal patterns
or conflicts that may be useful for a specific client. In addition, a
client may personalize the instrument by adding or changing an
item. Reynolds (1987b) gives an example of a fifteen-year-old girl
who changed an item on the instrument to specifically shift the
focus from "parents" to her mother, thereby revealing a highly
conflicted relationship.

The strength of this inventory approach is that it is highly
structured and normed specifically for a school-based population,

so that it has high utility for school-based personnel involved in assessing potentially suicidal adolescents. Among its problematic aspects is that in questioning adolescents only, it leaves out family or school personnel as respondents. Perhaps more importantly, the questionnaire does not yield a measure of "imminent danger." Reynolds has addressed the "imminent danger" aspect in a semistructured clinical interview, which he calls the Suicide Potential Interview, that serves as a follow-up evaluation with adolescents who score high on the SIQ (personal communication, 1987). This instrument addresses the where's, when's, how's, and so on that would be necessary for a complete suicide evaluation. Unfortunately, this is not yet commercially available. Added to the screening or interview format, it would make Reynolds's approach the most structured model available for direct assessment of the adolescent. The last model presented here is the one that perhaps best addresses the assessment of "imminent danger."

Rotheram and Bradley's Strategy of Suicide Evaluation

Out of their work with runaway adolescents within the Division of Child Psychiatry at Columbia University–New York State Psychiatric Institute, Rotheram-Borus and Bradley (Bradley and Rotheram-Borus, 1989; Rotheram, 1987) have devised an evaluation procedure that they refer to as the Evaluation of Imminent Danger for Suicide. It is based on the assessment of the adolescent's current psychological state and coping mechanisms along with associated statistically based risk factors. They have conceptualized the evaluation as a three-step process. The first part takes about ten to fifteen minutes and is composed of five areas of inquiry. Sections focus on (1) current suicidal ideation, recent (during the past two weeks) attempts, and any current plan; (2) past suicidal behavior; (3) focus on level of depression during the most recent two weeks; (4) exploration of the adolescent's behavior problems; and (5) exploration of family and/or peer suicide attempts.

The second part, the Screening Checklist, requires the interviewer to pay attention to the statistically based risk factors affecting the client. It also includes a "decision rule" providing clinical cutoff scores as a way of utilizing the data gathered. The authors suggest that a high score, which means that the adolescent either has spoken of current suicidal ideation or exhibits five or more of the risk factors, necessitates moving on to part three, the Imminent Danger Assessment (IDA). A medium score, from three to five risk factors, necessitates referral to a treatment or support group. A low score, fewer than three risk factors, requires no clinical intervention at that time. They stress that the focus of the assessment is on imminent danger, which they define as covering a three-day period, not on any longer-range suicide prediction.

The IDA is a very innovative addition to suicide assessment. The authors explain that "This assessment does not involve information gathering or statistically-based risk related factors, but rather a clinical interaction with the adolescent which determines if she/he is in current danger of suicidal behavior. The worker attempts to elicit five nonsuicidal behaviors which a youth in imminent danger of a suicide attempt should not be likely to accomplish. The evaluation utilizes a strategy which views teenagers' suicidal feelings as related to their perceptions of the world, and themselves and to a lack of problem-solving skills which would enable them to cope in difficult stressful situations" (Bradley and Rotheram, n.d., p. 37). They state that the IDA should be administered as a continuing part of the first assessment interview and that it takes about twenty minutes to complete. The five interviewer activities that constitute this part of the evaluation are designed to encourage the adolescent to (1) make complimentary or positive statements about him- or herself, (2) identify suicide-provoking situations, (3) engage in problem solving for ways to avoid the identified suicide-provoking situations, (4) identify supports, and (5) make a "no-suicide" contract (Drye, Goulding, and Goulding, 1973).

Self-Statements. The goal of evoking complimentary or positive self-statements is to make a small move away from the hopeless and negative self-statements characteristic of suicidal people, often referred to as the "cognitive triad" of negative views of the self, the world, and the future (Beck, Rush, Shaw, and Emery, 1979; Bedrosian and Epstein, 1984), and toward positive coping skills. Any positive self-statements are encouraged.

The interviewer can begin with questions such as "What are the things about yourself you like best?" and "What things about you, or going on with you, do you like best?" Or the interviewer can use a modeling-questioning approach focusing on any relevant topics; for example, "I like that you had the (courage, honesty) to be able to talk with me today. What things do you like about yourself?" "I really appreciate the way you've dressed today; you must like the way you look. What other ways do you take care of yourself, or what do you like to do with yourself?" The interviewer is encouraging and gives feedback to see whether the adolescent can make any independent positive self-statements. Then the interviewer makes some summary statement and moves on to the potentially suicide-provoking situations.

Identifying Suicide-Provoking Situations. Can the adolescent identify distressing suicide-provoking contexts by being aware of his or her feelings? One of our clients, Nancy, a suicidal nineteen-year-old, had made two suicide attempts (ingestion of pills) after what she described as horrible fights with her live-in boyfriend. She was unable to monitor her feelings, so interactions seemed to move from loving to disaster to suicide without any recognition of the gradation. Bradley and Rotheram (n.d.) suggest what they call the "feeling thermometer" technique. It uses a six-point continuum of feeling statements (feeling good, feeling okay, beginning to be upset, upset, most upset, out of control and suicidal) to teach awareness to interviewees (any other Likert-like technique or metaphor could also be used). In this case, Nancy had to recognize when she began to get angry, awareness being the key issue. With a recognition of anger comes the ability to leave the field. This recognition of feeling is important, because adolescent attempters often express an inability to assess their feelings and describe their act as impulsive (Bradley and Rotheram, n.d.; Orbach, 1988). During this phase, the adolescents are also reminded of the transience of the suicidal impulse or hopeless feelings and encouraged about their ability to monitor and cope with their feelings. The old adage "Suicide is a permanent solution to a temporary problem" is appropriate to point out.

Problem Solving for Avoidance. If the adolescent can be aware of these suicide-provoking situations, the next step is to investigate whether the adolescent can *avoid* them. The adolescent is assisted in developing "clear, simple, concrete plans for avoiding situations in which an attempt might be provoked . . . [and] the alternatives considered should be realistic, accessible, and as safe and supportive as possible" (Bradley and Rotheram, n.d., p. 44). The intent is not to cure the problem. Because we are dealing with imminent danger, there must be action. Can the adolescent avoid the situation long enough to stay alive to work on the situation? The underlying goal here is to avoid hospitalization if possible *and* appropriate.

Nancy was able to recognize that when her boyfriend began to talk loudly, she began to get upset in a way that she felt unable to prevent from escalating. Therefore, a strategy was negotiated with her. Regardless of the time or circumstance, she was to leave and go to one of two specific friends' apartments or to her parents' home, for which she had the key, to remove herself from the suicide-provoking situation.

Identifying Supports. As can be seen, the strategy for Nancy also encompassed the ability to identify emergency supports. Although her parents were not her best supports, they agreed to at least be tolerant. Her friends were considered very supportive. This strategy of identifying supports also ties in with Beebe's (1975) concept of a "lifeline." He suggests that if there is not at least one person in the suicidal person's life to whom he or she feels able to turn, it is a *very* high-risk situation. Bradley and Rotheram (n.d.) suggest that at least three people should be available. In a highly unstable situation, a counselor, therapist, pastor, and so on can be identified as a support person if that person is easily accessible. Along with Fairchild (1988), we recommend that school-based personnel do not get involved with high-risk suicidal students unless the district has a program for this purpose or the school-based professional feels that he or she has the knowledge and expertise to do the work and is willing to be accessible in person and by phone to the client. It is often a very anxiety-provoking and emotionally draining experience, yet obviously it is also very rewarding when properly handled.

Contracts Setting. The last element of the IDA is taken from the work of Drye, Goulding, and Goulding (1973) and is referred to as the "no-suicide contract." Before the end of the evaluation, the adolescent is asked whether he or she will sign a statement that reads "No matter what happens, I will at no time do anything self-destructive, by accident or on purpose." Bradley and Rotheram (n.d.) add to this that with adolescents, it is important to have a "clear, realistic, short-term commitment" (p. 46) as part of the contract. The term of the contract can be as short as a day, with recontracting as necessary. At the beginning of the intervention, the contract term is usually the period between contacts with the helping person. Bradley and Rotheram add that "identified provoking situations" and "strategies to cope with these situations" that have been discussed prior to contracting should also be included in the contract. We have found it useful to have the client read the contract aloud before signing it to enhance its impact and to allow us to listen to the emotional content in the client's voice. As simple as this technique seems, Drye, Goulding, and Goulding (1973) stated that no client among the 600 (mostly adults) with whom they had worked over a five-year period committed suicide while under this type of contract. Exhibit 1 is the treatment contract form used with Nancy. This contract is presented only as an illustration; it may need to be modified to fit a particular client or situation.

As a working model, the Bradley and Rotheram evaluation procedure is an excellent overall methodology for an imminent danger assessment. As with Corder's model, its strengths lie in its clinical flexibility, but its power is somewhat enhanced by decision rules and cutoff scores. Among its weaknesses, as with Corder's model, are that it does not provide norms as Reynolds's model does, and its structure is not as clear and well delineated as is that of Reynolds's model. However, its shares with Reynolds's model the weakness that it does not tap into all the information potentially available to school-based personnel, as Corder's model does. Depending on one's comfort with and style of clinical interviewing, some integration of models might be most appropriate. However,

Exhibit 1. Sample No-Suicide Contract.

1. No matter what happens, I will at *NO* time, during the time for which we contract, do anything self-destructive, by accident or on purpose.
2. Furthermore, should I find myself in any of the following situations:

   a. at the beginning stages of a fight with my boyfriend

   I will:

   a. regardless of the time or the circumstances, leave the scene and go to Linda's apartment, Fran's apartment, or my parents' home.
3. If other situations arise with which I am having a problem and I begin to feel suicidal or think seriously about suicide, I will:

   a. call my friends Fran, Linda, or Mary, or
   b. call the Suicide Hotline or
   c. call you [counselor-therapist].

I promise to keep this contract from [current date] to [next meeting date].

_____

signature of patient/client

_____

signature of counselor/therapist

---

the Rotheram-Borus model (Rotheram, 1987; Bradley and Rotheram-Borus, 1989) does seem to us to be the most clinically powerful. The next section describes two other evaluation approaches that hold promise for clinicians and may be incorporated into any of the above or other assessment models.

Other Evaluation Approaches

The Reasons for Living Inventory (RFL) developed by Marsha Linehan (Linehan, Goodstein, Nielsen, and Chiles, 1983) consists of forty-eight items designed to assess a range of beliefs about life and suicide that have been disguised to differentiate suicidal from nonsuicidal individuals. It is most appropriate for adults but could also be useful with older adolescents. It is composed of six short subscales (suicidal and coping belief, fear of suicide, responsibility to family, child-related concerns, fear of social disapproval, moral objections) that can be very useful in guiding interventions. In fact, it is this information-providing aspect, even more that its ability to differentiate groups, that would make it an interesting addition to a suicide evaluation, especially if the evaluator were to continue as treatment person.

Also potentially useful in intervention are the findings of Orbach (1983, 1988) that suicidal children and adolescents have a different level of attraction to death than do normal children and adolescents. The more suicidal the adolescents become, the more attractive death becomes. Orbach claims that even though their desire to live remains strong (in fact, it is no different from that of nonsuicidal adolescents), their attraction to death, which he considers a defense serving their self-destructive tendencies, increases. He believes that suicidal adolescents tend to have very optimistic views of death as some kind of improved condition. They describe it as a place of "peace and calm," a place where "no one can hurt me anymore," and so on. The more positive the view of death, the higher the risk of suicide. Although Orbach provides no norms or specific guidelines, his findings seem another useful addition to one's clinical armamentarium.

Conclusion

The interventions that we have reviewed are very useful in guiding practitioners toward the data necessary to make decisions regarding the level of risk for suicide. However, practitioners must be careful not to place themselves under undue pressure to prevent suicidal ideation or to think that they can stop all suicide attempts. Adolescent suicide attempts are more impulsive than we would like and thus are less possible to prevent than we would like.

Two recent British studies support this concept of impulsivity. One found that three-quarters of a sample of adolescent self-poisoners contemplated their self-poisoning for less than two hours (Taylor and Stansfield, 1984), while another reported that more than half the adolescents in a self-poisoning study thought about the act for fewer than fifteen minutes, 16 percent for somewhere between fifteen and sixty minutes, and only 8 percent for more than one day (Hawton, Cole, O'Grady, and Osborn, 1982). These results are presented not as a note of pessimism but as an example of realism. While practitioners must strive for sensitivity and quick action when needed, they need to be aware of their limitations.

This chapter has illustrated the different ways in which potentially suicidal students can come to the attention of school-based personnel and presented some available models and techniques for assessing suicide potential. We do not propose that these are the only models available; rather, they are the most appropriate for adolescents, and we and others have found them to be extremely useful.

We do want very strongly to recommend that a model be used. Especially in the schools, where one does not routinely perform suicide evaluations, professionals quickly get out of practice and need a structure to help support and guide them. Also, models help them to develop and organize their clinical sensitivities to their client populations. Suicide is a crisis, and during a crisis, anxiety increases, yet it is extremely important that all the relevant questions be asked and the appropriate interventions taken. These methods can be used to facilitate the appropriate management of a serious adolescent problem.

4

Intervention: Determining the Best Course of Action

In this chapter and the next, we cover the two major issues of suicide intervention and postvention from our school-based perspective. By *intervention*, we mean any number of a range of professional behaviors used after it has been decided that an adolescent needs help in coping with thoughts and feelings engendering suicidal ideation or behavior. After an assessment, the question for the professional becomes, given this information regarding this adolescent, what help is needed, and how do I increase the likelihood that he or she gets it?

Postvention, a relatively new term, has been defined by Shneidman (1973) as a series of planned interventions made with people thought to be put at increased risk by a completed suicide. Although postvention efforts are directed at friends or family, an affected survivor could be anyone connected to or identified with the suicide victim and thereby placed at risk for suicide or other psychological problems. The whole issue of the construct of "contagion" and adolescent suicide makes these efforts particularly important (see Chapters Ten and Eleven for a full discussion of contagion). Postvention, then, is a form of prevention for the survivors.

Choosing an Intervention

In order to choose an appropriate intervention, the practitioner must answer two basic questions. First, is the adolescent in imminent danger? Second, given the answer to the first question, what interventions would be most beneficial for this youth? Figure 5 lists answers to the first question and possible interventions given each answer. The remainder of this section focuses on these possible interventions.

Imminent Danger—Yes

Given the framework developed by Bradley and Rotheram-Borus and discussed in Chapter Three, any youth considered to be

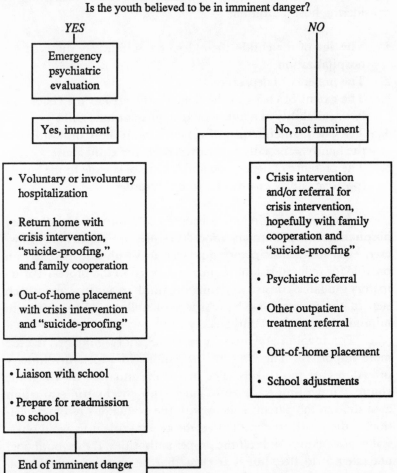

Figure 5. School-Based Personnel Intervention Flow Chart.

Is the youth believed to be in imminent danger?

in imminent danger must receive a thorough emergency evaluation. The school-based professional's job is to provide that service if trained and competent to do so or to collaborate as needed with other competent professionals, such as hospital emergency room staff or community mental health workers, in the evaluation process. The emergency evaluator will then have three primary options: to hospitalize, to return to the family, or to place in a different home or shelter.

Choosing to Hospitalize. Adams and Fras (1988, p. 547) list the following as some of the information necessary when one is considering hospitalization:

1. The age of the child—the older, the more likely the need for hospitalization
2. The presence of depression
3. The extent of chaos in the family—the greater the chaos, the less availability of adults who can safeguard the child
4. The extent and intensity of violence, aggression, or hostility in the family, especially as it carries over into child abuse
5. The presence of depression and history of suicide in the family (positive family history of affective disorders)

An obvious distinction is between voluntary and involuntary hospitalizations. Voluntary procedures are straightforward; however, even here, anticipatory guidance to youth and parents can provide for reduced risk of trauma connected to the process. Anticipatory guidance consists of telling the youth in advance about each step in the process that he or she will undergo. The idea is to minimize surprise and thus anxiety.

For involuntary procedures, anticipatory guidance is even more important. There are two situations in which involuntary procedures are most likely. The first is the situation in which the youth is unwilling to agree to emergency psychiatric evaluation even though the parents concur with the evaluator's recommendation. If the youth attempts to flee, the general rule is to avoid physical confrontation and call the proper authorities. If the youth does not attempt to flee, but it is clear that he or she would be too difficult or dangerous for the parents to transport for further evaluation, the police or crisis intervention team must be called. Should others be brought in to assist, it is very important that the parents be informed about what will happen—that is, that their child may well be handcuffed and taken away in a police vehicle.

A clinical colleague described an incident where anticipatory guidance was not provided, and the family, after agreeing to the necessity of an involuntary psychiatric evaluation, became very upset when two burly police officers started to put handcuffs on their crying, struggling, petite fourteen-year-old daughter. The parents attempted to "help" their daughter, enabling her to escape and run out of the building and in front of a moving automobile. Luckily, she survived, receiving only bruises and a mild concussion. All involved were terrified, however, and this incident increased the complexity of the case enormously.

A second instance when involuntary procedures are probably necessary is the case in which neither the parents nor their child concur with the recommendation of an emergency psychiatric evaluation or placement. Assuming that the professional believes that an emergency psychiatric evaluation is necessary to protect the adolescent's life, and assuming that the professional has exhausted all apparent approaches to developing a realistic working relationship with the family, the school-based helper should inform the family that child protective services and/or the police will be called if they fail to cooperate. If no convincing change of attitude occurs, the necessary calls should be made.

Returning the Child to the Family. If the family is willing and able to help control the child's self-destructive behavior, and some empathic bond or caring still exists, the first step is for them to "suicide-proof" their home. Before the adolescent returns home, all guns, poisons, and other suicidal means must be removed. With a safe environment ensured, the person doing the emergency evaluation may choose to send the adolescent and family home after initiating crisis intervention procedures.

Turning the Child over to Other Nonprofessionals. It is also possible, although much less likely, that the suicidal youth may be returned to the family of a relative or friend. However, the level of responsibility and monitoring that the youth needs usually prohibits this alternative. In some localities, a foster home system may be in place to manage suicidal youth.

Imminent Danger—No

The judgment of no imminent danger opens up a whole range of potential interventions. The first decision, however, must focus on the role of the school-based evaluator. There are basically three choices: (1) take on the case as counselor–therapist–crisis interventionist, (2) refer the student and/or family to another agency or practitioner and maintain a consulting, supporting, or monitoring role, or (3) refer the case to a community-based helper with no further contact. We believe the third option to be inadvisable, so we discuss only the first two.

Fine (1982) reviews several considerations affecting the choice of whether to treat or refer, including the professional's level of competence and comfort with the client's problem, the school's attitude or policy about working with "potentially" suicidal clients, and the availability of other competent personnel to receive a referral. We would like to add to these the consideration of the school as a system.

It is clear that if the evaluator is not competent or the school forbids personal counseling or intervening with students at suicidal risk, referral will be the intervention of choice. If no reasonably appropriate referral sources are available, a very real ethical dilemma arises (Davis and Sandoval, 1982). Assuming that the evaluator is competent to work with low-risk suicidal clients and wants to work with the student and family and that school policy allows it, one needs to remember that working with a suicidal client is a large commitment, very often with ups, downs, and emergencies. And schools as systems are not structured to be able to respond quickly to crises: for example, they lack twenty-four-hour availability.

All things considered, if one does decide to function as a direct intervener, the diagnostic model outlined in Chapter Two can be helpful. Although opinions about the level of psychopathology of suicidal adolescents differ (for contrasting opinions, see Hawton, 1986, and Shaffer and Fisher, 1981) it is fairly certain that if an adolescent is actively thinking about suicide or has made an attempt, he or she is very likely to be somewhere on the continuum from at least some psychological pain to a great deal of pain and psychopathology. We and others (for example, Fairchild, 1988) recommend that, if at all possible, anyone who has made an attempt within the last two years be treated in a system that has the backup necessary to cope with all the potential complications. If, however, (1) no attempts have been made, (2) after a thorough evaluation, the professional believes that the attempts have been parasuicidal and of low level of lethality, or (3) evaluation indicates that a youth who has made no suicide attempt has a low level of intent to die and a low level of pathology (adjustment reaction, mild neurosis), it may be appropriate to intervene directly, especially if there are no other appropriate referral possibilities or if the client(s) cannot be persuaded to accept a referral.

The Referral Process

As Figure 5 indicates, there are a variety of potential interventions and modalities. We briefly review each of the possibilities in the following section; here we review the referral process itself, since it underlies many of the options.

For as integral a part of the profession as the referral process is, there is relatively little empirical research in the school psychology literature. However, what is available is valuable and informative (Conti, 1971, 1973, 1975; Zins and Hopkins, 1981). Also, given that suicide is potentially life-threatening, the stakes involved in whether a referral is completed are substantial. Perhaps even more importantly, it seems likely that it is the referrer and the referral process rather than patient characteristics that contribute most to referral failures (Knesper, 1982; Paykel and others, 1974; Rogawski and Edmundson, 1971).

In the only study dealing with adolescents being referred because of suicidal ideation or attempts that we discovered, Litt, Cuskey, and Rudd (1983) found that only 33 percent of adolescents seen in an emergency room (nine of twenty-seven patients) kept follow-up appointments offered to them. This rate is lower than the success rates of 50 to 80 percent reported for referrals to psychological counseling in general (Zins and Hopkins, 1981). Thus, it is possible that those who may be in most need are least likely to comply. For this reason, school-based personnel are obligated to do their best when referring suicidal students. Following are some general rules for enhancing the referral process:

- Know where and to whom to refer.
- Build rapport with the client and/or family prior to the referral.
- Refer with the conviction that the referral agency or person can be helpful.
- If at all possible, when referring to an agency, refer to a specific person in that agency.
- Be interested and active.
- Ask about and help the client work through reactions to being referred.
- If at all possible, have the client call at the end of the referral session. If needed, make the initial contact while the client is in the office.
- If it is not possible to call at the end of the session, call the referral person to alert them that the client should be calling. Arrange for a follow-up call to the client to support the call for appointment and provide follow-up.
- If the client will not call but you believe the client to be imminently suicidal, call police, a crisis intervention team, and/or child protective services as needed.
- Document all that has transpired.

First and foremost, evaluators need to know where and to whom to refer. Next, they must transmit to the client their belief that the designated person or agency can in fact be helpful (Zins and Hopkins, 1981). The evaluator should maintain reasonable control of the interview process and needs to be interested and active so that the client does not feel that the referral is generic. Also, the thoughts and feelings stirred by the referral need to be explored until they are worked through (Knesper, 1982; Rogawski and Edmundson, 1971).

Although first appointments are usually better attended

when the client makes the call for the appointment (Slaikeu, Tulkin, and Speer, 1975), success rates can be increased by 25 to 45 percent when the appointment is made at the end of the evaluation and problem-solving process (Rogawski and Edmundson, 1971; Kogan, 1957). In addition, follow-up, outreach, and client support not only increase the rate of attendance at first appointments but also decrease the rate of dropping out of treatment (Welu, 1977; Zins and Hopkins, 1981). Although following these guidelines can never guarantee success, it does increase the odds of getting potentially suicidal clients into treatment.

Available Treatment Methods

The next logical question is what type of treatments and interventions are most successful for these clients. As one might expect, there is considerable disagreement. Here we present a discussion of various treatment approaches that may help professionals decide in what areas they need more education or training if they are to counsel suicidal students and improve their understanding of available community resources and what they might offer to suicidal youth.

Before treatment is initiated, two questions need to be addressed: Is treatment always necessary? And, if it is necessary, what are we trying to treat? Since school-based professionals are working within a system that deals primarily with "normal" adolescents, and since mild forms of suicidal ideation are the norm for high school students, it is very likely that they may at least sometimes be presented with a student about whom others are worried but who may not be in need of treatment. In fact, Hawton (1986) suggests that some adolescents who have even made a suicide attempt (probably what we refer to as a parasuicide) may need no more intervention than informing the youth's physician so that he or she may monitor the situation. He states that about one-third of his adolescent self-poisoners "often appear to have problems that largely resolve as a result of the attempt. The attempt itself may appear to have been an out-of-character response to an acute stress in an otherwise normally adjusted young person. Following a thorough assessment, referral back to the care of the family doctor may be all that is necessary" (pp. 110–111). Pfeffer (1984a, p. 175) states that "suicidal behavior in children requires, at the very least, exploratory psychiatric intervention." The consensus would seem to be that at least a thorough assessment or evaluation by a competent assessor is an absolute necessity and that, depending on the results of the evaluation, it may be followed by some kind of monitoring or "watch and consult" system that is school-based, family-physician-based, or, preferably, both.

The answer to the second question—what it is that we are trying to treat—is that we are attempting to treat a number of thoughts, feelings, and behaviors. One of the few things that most of the experts agree on is that suicide is not a diagnosis (Hawton, 1986; Motto, 1985; Trautman and Shaffer, 1984). Rather, suicide is the result of a constellation of biopsychosocial factors that most often require a multimodel approach (Pfeffer, 1984b). Even though the following treatments are presented as distinct options, they are not mutually exclusive. And, as Paul Trautman (1989, p. 253) says, "there are no specific treatment modalities for adolescent suicide attempters. That is, there are no treatment studies—psychothera-peutic, behavioral, or psychopharmologic—which show that a clearly defined treatment approach is superior to no treatment or to some other treatment."

Brief, Crisis-Oriented Treatment

There are a variety of books available on crisis intervention (for example, Sandoval, 1988; Slaikeu, 1984). Trautman (1989) recommends brief, crisis-oriented treatment as the treatment of choice for most adolescent attempters. Hawton and Catalan (1987) agree. They have developed a brief problem-focused form of crisis intervention based on their work with self-poisoning suicide attempters. Their model has five closely interrelated stages: assessment, problem solving, preventive measures, termination, and follow-up. We believe that this model could be useful to school-based personnel if they have the option and training to employ it. The following example illustrates the procedure.

Lisa presented herself in the counselor's office, referred by her English teacher. Lisa was a fourteen-year-old from a family of four. Her father had a heart condition, and her relationship with her mother had been deteriorating over the last year. Her twenty-year-old brother, with whom she had only a distant relationship, had moved out during the past year, and her academic work was deteriorating. Her teacher had referred her because she had become very upset during a conference and revealed suicidal ideation.

During her assessment phase, the counselor had to first and foremost evaluate her suicidal potential. The counselor assessed Lisa's level of suicidality as low to moderate and found her to be open to problem solving and parental involvement and willing to make a no-suicide contract. Lisa stated that the problems of most concern to her were her father's health, her relationship with her parents, and her school fears. Lisa and the counselor decided to meet alone again the next day to rehearse a third meeting, which would include her parents. They called Lisa's parents, who agreed to meet within three days (prior to the weekend).

In the individual session, Lisa and the counselor focused first on her concern about schoolwork. After Lisa's input and the counselor's review of her school records, they decided to request her parent's permission for further psychoeducational evaluation. They also decided that Lisa would share with her family her concerns about her father's health and the problems with family communication. Role playing was used to practice expressing her feelings.

The family meeting seemed very productive. All three family members expressed satisfaction that they had finally been able to share fears and worries about the father's illness. They decided that the further evaluation should be conducted, that the family would continue their dialogue about communication at home once a week to evaluate and monitor their progress, and that they would have another meeting in three weeks. During those three weeks, Lisa and the counselor would touch base at least twice a week at specified times for ten to fifteen minutes each time. If any crises or questions arose in the family, they would call the counselor, who also provided Lisa with her home telephone number. This practice conforms to Pfeffer's (1984b, p. 366) advice that "the therapist must be available to his suicidal patient willingly, without delay, and at all hours."

As one might guess, it is difficult enough to be on call; the inherent personal costs and problems presented to school-based personnel by their school system forces them to decide how realistic it is to work with suicidal youth. But in this instance, further contact with Lisa went well. Although she remained somewhat depressed, her suicidal ideation had stopped. The school psychologist joined in the beginning of the next session with the family to discuss the testing results. The remainder of the session focused on interventions based on assessment data—one period a day spent in the resource program for additional work in English—and, after the school psychologist left, a discussion of how family communications were going. In an effort to deal with preventive measures, the family members were advised to think about how each of them could contribute to a renewal of problems—a strategic technique to reinforce responsibility and awareness of behaviors (Watzlawick, Weakland, and Fisch, 1974). Another family session would be held later; during that time, Lisa would meet with the counselor for fifteen to twenty minutes at least once a week.

The next family meeting focused on termination and how things were progessing, what the family members had decided they could do to bring the problems back, and new ways to cope with the thoughts or feelings that might reintroduce the problems. The counselor and Lisa agreed to monthly meetings lasting about twenty to thirty minutes each, and a follow-up family meeting was scheduled for the end of the year.

Although the case of Lisa is an example of a fairly successful use of crisis intervention, it does not work this well in every case. While Hawton and Catalan (1987) feel that crisis intervention is the treatment of choice for everyone, others disagree. For example, Peck (1985), reviewing a study conducted at the Los Angeles Suicide Prevention Center, suggests that "fewer than one-third of the subjects in the L.A.S.P.C. sample satisfied the criteria for crisis. Not only were the majority not in crisis, but traditional crisis intervention approaches were deemed not suitable for most persons in the sample" (p. 114). Most of the center's population of young suicide attempters had diagnosable chronic maladjustment, rather than adjustment reactions or context-specific crises. Again, we have evidence that in working with suicidal youth, evaluation and diagnosis are very important parts of the process.

Psychodynamic Psychotherapy

Toolan (1962, 1984, 1988) has probably been the most consistent and strongest proponent of long-term psychodynamic work with suicidal youth. He has always stated that long-term individual rather than crisis intervention treatment is needed to adequately deal with all the complex psychodynamics underlying the suicidal act. Nor is he alone in this belief. Pfeffer (1984b, pp. 368–369) has very explicitly stated that "First, psychiatric treatment [of suicidal youth] is a long-term process lasting more than one year. Second, an intense patient-therapist relationship is needed to resolve the child's conflicts that produced the suicidal behavior. Third, expression of aggression is a central problem for suicidal children. Finally, suicidal behavior is a symptom with multiple conscious and unconscious meanings."

It is highly unlikely that school-based personnel will engage in long-term psychodynamic psychotherapy. However, given the range and depth of psychopathology that can be found among suicidal youth, this intervention may be the treatment of choice for some of the students that they encounter in the schools. Here again, knowing and having relationships with community resources can be invaluable. When school-based personnel know what people in the community work within this framework, they can call on those people as consultants to aid them in making a good referral, as well as referring students to them directly.

Cognitive Behavioral Therapy

From the research presented in Chapter Two, it is clear that cognitive factors are associated with suicide. Beck and his colleagues have probably been the most active in tying research in this area to therapy for depression and suicide (Beck, Rush, Shaw, and Emery, 1979; Bedrosian and Epstein, 1984; Hollon and Beck, 1979). Beck's model is built on the interrelated concepts of the cognitive triad, cognitive schemes, and cognitive errors. This model is applicable to suicide. However, we must remember that Shaffer's latest estimate is that only about 25 percent of adolescents who complete suicide could have been diagnosed as depressed (Shaffer and Bacon, 1989).

The Cognitive Triad. Beck's cognitive triad model suggests that most depressed people and many suicidal people have (1) a negative view of themselves, (2) a negative view of the world as a cold, unrewarding place, and (3) a negative view of the future or a sense of hopelessness. Echoing Orbach (1986), Beck, Rush, Shaw, and Emery (1979) postulate that "suicidal wishes can be understood as an extreme expression of the desire to escape from what appears to be insolvable problems or an unbearable situation" (p. 12).

Cognitive Schema. Developmentalists such as Piaget (1973) have conceptualized "cognitive schema" as mental structures used to differentiate, code, and retain stimuli. The cognitive schema that have developed in depressed individuals predispose them toward attending to and organizing data in ways that support their negative views. Beck hypothesizes that these schema develop and are reinforced through cognitive errors or faulty information processing.

Cognitive Errors. In general, the cognitive processes of depressed and suicidal individuals are similar to developmentally primitive thinking, which is absolutistic, invariant, irreversible, and so on, rather than more developmentally mature information processing, which is relativistic, reversible, variable, and so on. The focus of the theraputic work with such individuals is thus working with cognitive processes in ways that affect cognitive schema and the cognitive triad. Treatment is a kind of "collaborative empiricism" whereby empirical methodologies are used to challenge faulty beliefs.

An example from a typical cognitive therapy session is provided by Bedrosian and Epstein (1984, p. 358). The dialogue is between a therapist and a patient, a seventeen-year-old female with a long-standing history of suicidal ideation and two previous attempts:

Patient: I've got big problems. Bruce's parents say he can't see me any more. I'm gonna lose him.

Therapist: How do you know that?

Patient: He's the kind of guy who does what his parents want.

Therapist: Have you spoken to him?

Patient: No, but I will tonight or tomorrow.

Therapist: So you don't know for sure yet if you're even going to lose him. Let's say you do, what's going to happen to you?

Patient: I'm gonna have a rough time. He means a lot to me.

Therapist: Do you think you'll make it?

Patient: I don't know.

Therapist: Will you try to kill yourself?

Patient: I don't think so. But I know I'll be real depressed.

Therapist: Do you remember what you told me when you broke up with Carl?

Patient: That no one else would ever want me again.

Therapist: Then what happened?

Patient: I met Bruce. I didn't think I'd meet anyone again.

Therapist: You're not even sure you're going to lose Bruce, yet. If you do, I'm sure it will be a big disappointment. But, I want you to remember that when you lost Carl you told yourself that things were hopeless and it turned out they weren't.

The focus of this example is on the patient's cognition, soft confrontations with "reality" to deal with her distortions (primarily of global and irreversible thinking), and direct questioning about her suicidality. These features make this interview highly representative. Beck, Rush, Shaw, and Emery (1979) have found that treatment usually lasts for about twenty sessions interspersed over twelve weeks, but Bedrosian and Epstein (1984) suggest that therapy with adolescents may require a few more sessions to allow time for building and maintaining rapport.

Family Therapy

Whether we view the family as causative, reactive, or caught in a mutually harmful situation, there is no one who would not recommend some kind of consulting, counseling, or training for the family of a suicidal adolescent. Probably the most vociferous advocate of family therapy for suicidal people is Joseph Richman (1979, 1984, 1986), although he is by no means alone in this position (for example, Brown, 1985; Pfeffer, 1986, 1988). Richman (1984) suggests that there are four basic dynamics associated with most families that have a sucidial member: (1) a strong link between separation and death, often based on early traumatic experience, especially at a time of crisis; (2) a double bind that isolates the suicidal person within the family yet condemns outside support; (3) conflicts about family rules governing the expression of aggression; and (4) covert and/or overt messages to the adolescent that suicide is an acceptable act (see also Sabbath, 1982).

There are many models of family treatment available, and it is not our goal to review them all here. However, in a situation involving a suicidal adolescent, almost all approaches would agree that getting the parents to understand the seriousness of a sucidial threat or attempt, getting them to work together appropriately to help their child, and getting them to keep their conflicts defined and remediated between themselves would be primary tasks. Pfeffer (1986, p. 262) lists further goals for family therapy:

1. Establish empathic relationships between family members
2. Open avenues for communication between parent and child
3. Plan alternative ways of dealing with disagreements between parent and child
4. Develop awareness of feelings, ideas, and needs of others
5. Achieve a tolerance for change while maintaining a consistently stable family atmosphere
6. Promote individual autonomous functioning
7. Decrease tendencies for impulsive and severely aggressive behaviors in both parents and child
8. Diminish fears of separation between parents and child

Although working with families can be exciting and rewarding, a somber note is provided in a study by Shapiro and Budman (1973), who found a significantly higher rate of dropouts from family therapy than from individual therapy. Again, knowing who in the community might best be able to engage a family is critical. Shapiro and Budman also found that the father's expressed motivation to participate in family therapy was a key clinical indicator for continuing in family treatment.

Group Treatment

As with the other forms of intervention discussed here, there are no empirical data to substantiate the effectiveness of group work with suicidal adolescents. However, there is some evidence that groups may be a more powerful vehicle for adolescents than for adults. In contrast to the findings in most studies of the importance of one or two intimate friends to lessen suicidal risk among adults (for example, Beebe's, 1975, notion of a "lifeline"), Rubenstein and others (1989) found that being integrated into a *group of friends*, especially when those friends were accepted by parents, was a more powerful deterrent to attempting suicide for adolescents than was having one or two intimate friends. This sense of connectedness to a group also has many implications for prevention (discussed in Part Three).

Ross and Motto (1984) describe their experience with the "Peer Befriender Group," a group counseling project focused on adolescents at risk for suicide. The two cotherapists began the first group session by outlining the group rules (punctuality, prior notification of absence, prohibition on smoking, drugs, and alcohol while attending group, confidentiality), presenting them in an interpersonal context of caring and consideration. They gave each member a card with their home telephone numbers, and then had everyone introduce themselves. The group format began as dynamically oriented, closed, and time-limited, with group content chosen by members. Although the dynamic orientation was maintained, the group extended its time limit and opened up to new members. It is important to recognize that the group was not the only intervention for these youth. Each had an individual "therapist of rec-

ord" for at least one assessment session, and all were encouraged to
continue with individual treatment (although not all did). Further,
all at-risk adolescents were provided "befrienders"—other young
adults and adults who functioned as "big brothers" or "big sisters."
Ross and Motto rated the group as basically successful. There were
no completed suicides over its span of two years, a fact that the
authors attribute to the increased support provided by this peer
network.

Another group experience documented in the literature
(Comstock and McDermott, 1975), although targeted on adults, may
be useful to anyone interested in brief group treatment with low-
risk suicidal adolescents. In this group strategy, concurrent individual therapy was not required, but a thorough assessment was. The
goals of these brief groups (usually six weeks) were (1) confrontation of suicidal preoccupation and exploration of situational difficulties and current problems, (2) fostering of psychological-
mindedness, with emphasis on self-observation and self-
responsibility, and (3) helping group members to recognize their
tendency toward impulsivity, which often leads to suicidal behaviors, and emphasizing that better alternatives existed. It is unclear
whether a brief, somewhat confrontative approach would work
with adolescents, but the goals seem clinically useful.

One of our experiences with similar groups made clear to us
the significant emotional toll a group such as this takes on its
leaders and also the absolute necessity for contingency planning
and backup. But with adolescents who are mildly ideational and
have a low level of psychopathology, a supportive group focusing
on enhancement of peer networks may be effective.

Psychopharmacological Therapy

The research on the treatment of children and adolescents
with medication shows mixed results. Almost all of the studies have
consisted of interventions with depressed populations, even though,
as previously mentioned, Shaffer and Bacon (1989) contend that
only 25 percent of adolescents who complete suicides can be diagnosed as depressed.

The class of drugs most commonly researched is the tricyclic antidepressants, primarily imipramine and amitriptyline. The literature generally suggests that patients with a major affective disorder, rather than dysthymia, and with endogenous or melancholic symptoms, such as diurnal mood variation and weight loss, have the best responses to these medications (Anderson, 1982). The *Diagnostic and Statistical Manual* lists the following criteria for a major depressive episode:

A. At least five of the following symptoms have been present during the same two-week period and present a change from previous functioning; at least one of the systems is either (1) depressed mood, or (2) loss of interest or pleasure. (Do not include symptoms that are clearly due to a physical condition, mood-incongruent delusions or hallucinations, incoherence, or marked loosening of associations.)

   (1) depressed mood (or can be irritable mood in children and adolescents) most of the day, nearly every day, as indicated either by subjective account or observation by others

   (2) markedly diminished interest or pleasure in all, or almost all, activities most of the day, nearly every day (as indicated either by subjective account or observation by others of apathy most of the time)

   (3) significant weight loss or weight gain when not dieting (e.g., more than 5 percent of body weight in a month), or decrease or increase in appetite nearly every day (in children, consider to make expected weight gains)

   (4) insomnia or hypersomnia nearly every day

   (5) psychomotor agitation or retardation nearly every day (observable by others, not merely subjective feelings or restlessness or being slowed down)

   (6) fatigue or loss of energy nearly every day

(7)   feelings of worthlessness or excessive or
       inappropriate guilt (which may be delu-
       sional) nearly every day (not merely self-
       reproach or guilt about being sick)

(8)   diminished ability to think or concentrate,
       or indecisiveness, nearly every day (either by
       subjective account or as observed by others)

(9)   recurrent thoughts of death (not just fear of
       dying), recurrent suicidal ideation without
       a specific plan, or a suicide attempt or a
       specific plan for committing suicide

B. (1) It cannot be established that an organic fac-
         tor initiated and maintained the disturbance

    (2) The distrubance is not a normal reaction to
         the death of a loved one (Uncomplicated
         Bereavement)
         Note: Morbid preoccupation with worth-
         lessness, suicidal ideation, marked func-
         tional impairment or psychomotor retarda-
         tion, or prolonged duration suggest
         bereavement complicated by Major
         Depression.

C. At no time during the disturbance have there
    been delusions or hallucinations for as long as
    two weeks in the absence of prominent mood
    symptoms (i.e., before the mood symptoms devel-
    oped or after they have remitted).

D. Not superimposed on Schizophrenia, Schizo-
    phreniform Disorder, Delusional Disorder, Psy-
    chotic Disorder NOS. [Reprinted with permission
    from the *Diagnostic and Statistical Manual of
    Mental Disorders, Third Edition, Revised,* Copy-
    right 1987 American Psychiatric Association.]

Although not conclusive, the work of Puig-Antich suggests
that if blood plasma levels of imipramine, rather than just dosage,
can be monitored and controlled, one can achieve significant differ-

ences between medication and placebo groups (Puig-Antich and others, 1985a, 1985b).

If, during a suicide evaluation, the evaluator encounters a student that meets criteria suggesting a possible organic component, a referral for medication evaluation would be a necessary part of the intervention plan. Knowledge in this area is necessary for school-based professionals who conduct such evaluations.

Conclusions

In this chapter, we have discussed referral-oriented and treatment-oriented interventions with suicidal adolescents. We believe that school-based personnel have both an ethical and, as we discuss in Chapter Eleven, a legal responsibility to be able to evaluate the suicidal potential of their students. We do not, however, recommend that school-based personnel engage in treatment of suicidal adolescents. In fact, we believe the organizational structure of the schools to be counterconducive to treatment. However, we felt obligated to present treatment options to both help in making informed referral decisions and to provide further information for those who wish to pursue models of school-based intervention.

5

Postvention:
Coping with the
Aftermath of Crisis

This chapter examines interventions for people who are adversely affected by the suicides or attempted suicides of others. In spite of our best efforts at identifying and intervening with suicidal youth, and in spite of excellent prevention programs, some adolescents or others, such as teachers, will attempt or commit suicide, and their deaths or injuries will affect an entire school and community. What can be done to respond?

Hill (1984) describes a postsuicide intervention, or postvention, in a Cleveland, Ohio, school district, where, "after a sudden loss, feelings ran high; judgment was impaired, and guidelines for establishing protocol did not exist" (pp. 408–409). Given Hill's experience, our own experiences consulting with school districts, an experience following a colleague's suicide (Davis, Bates, and Velasquez, 1990), and the writing of others (Appel and Matus, 1984; Lamb and Dunne-Maxim, 1987), we have become strong advocates of the establishment of crisis intervention policies and teams to cope with crises and emergencies. These policies should provide principles to guide institutional responses following a suicide: In dealing with faculty, administration, students and their families, the family of the victim, and the media: (1) the suicide should not be glamourized or dramatized; (2) doing nothing can be as dangerous as doing too much; and (3) students cannot be best served unless the faculty is adequately coping (Lamb and Dunne-Maxim, 1987; Ruof, Harris, and Robbie, 1987).

Each school district should prepare its own crisis intervention plan to fit its particular context (school district planning is explored more fully in Chapter Ten). However, at least the following questions regarding suicide must be addressed by each district (Lamb and Dunne-Maxim, 1987, p. 247):

1. How and when should students and faculty be informed of the suicide?
2. How, when, and where should students be allowed to express their reactions?
3. What should be done about the victim's close friends?
4. What should be done about "high-risk" students?
5. Should the school hold a special assembly or memorial service?
6. Should there be a symbolic expression of grief, such as lowering the flag to half staff?
7. Should the school close for the funeral?
8. Who should go to the funeral?
9. What kinds of commemorative activities or symbols—plaques, memorial funds, and so on—are appropriate?
10. Should the victim's parents be contacted, and what help can be offered to them?
11. What should be done about the concerns of other parents?
12. How should the school deal with the media?
13. To whom should the school turn for outside consultation or help?

In the following section, we offer a set of guidelines for informing and responding to staff, students, and parents when a suicide has been completed. We also comment on possible responses to suicides by parents or school personnel.

Communication and Postvention Procedures

Although our proposal is by no means a developmental sequence, we suggest that postvention efforts in the schools encompass four phases: (1) initial staff communication and communication with the deceased's parents, (2) working with staff and crisis teams, (3) working with students and parents, and (4) follow-up. (Working with the media, which would be part of phase 3, is discussed in Chapter Ten.)

Phase 1: Initial Communications with Staff and the Victim's Parents

Administration, faculty, and other school personnel need to be informed when a suicide has occurred or is suspected. How these communications are to be made should be prearranged. Most often, the individual managing the crisis will start by using a phone tree to request administrators, faculty, and nonfaculty personnel to attend a planning meeting. Such a conference should be held within twenty-four to forty-eight hours (Hill, 1984); sooner is probably better than later as a general rule. The phone calls should inform people about who has been designated to respond to requests for information (often an assistant superintendent or principal) and tell them to refer calls, especially from the media, to that person. Besides communicating necessary information, the phone contact allows staff to begin processing the information on the "feeling" level so that they can be better prepared emotionally to help students.

Next, the school principal or a designee should contact the parents of the victim. The contact should focus on the expression of sympathy on behalf of the school and, if the parents seem receptive, information about community grief support groups.

Phase 2: Working with Staff and Crisis Teams

Continuity is important for the survivors. School should be held the day following a suicide if it is a normal school day (Ojanlatva, Hammer, and Mohr, 1987; Ruof, Harris, and Robbie, 1987). At a morning meeting, the principal or designee should provide the complete version of what is known about the event. This process may bring up questions and feelings that will need to be appropriately responded to. It can be very helpful to include an outside consultant with training and experience in suicidology, perhaps a worker in community mental health or the local suicide prevention center (Klingman and Eli, 1981; Kneisel and Richards, 1988). Such a consultant can help those who are part of a system in crisis not only to deal with the emotional upheaval that accompanies such a crisis but also to see beyond it (Davis, Bates, and Velasquez, 1990).

Lamb and Dunne-Maxim (1987) recommend that the consultant should focus on the feelings of the faculty as well as providing the psychoeducational experience usually requested by school personnel. For a large school, they suggest a "fishbowl" technique, with a volunteer inner circle of those capable of modeling expression of feelings asking group members to talk about their relationship with the student, often in a sequential fashion. "The major task of the consultant is to help faculty members with their own feelings about the suicide while simultaneously educating them on how they can be helpful to their students" (Lamb and Dunne-Maxim, 1987, p. 253).

Two other issues that may need to be dealt with are rumor and crowd control. After a suicide, rumors almost always spread throughout the school and community. When the school staff becomes aware of a rumor, it needs to be counteracted by an announcement clarifying the situation. Staff should be alerted to listen for rumors and to report them to the principal or designee so that they may be confronted. Opportunities for these confrontations will occur most commonly in media press releases and postvention counseling or small-group sessions.

Although not typical, crowd control can also become an issue. If, for instance, a student jumps from the top of the school building, the public at large and the student body may well develop a morbid interest in the site of the jump. The district will need to work with its security personnel to provide appropriate crowd control and to discourage sightseers. It would be a good idea to avoid releasing the exact location to the media or at least try to persuade the media not to print details. If mention of the location cannot be avoided, steps must be taken to prevent voyeurs from interfering with other activities at the school.

The preselected crisis intervention team, those school-based personnel who have received specialized training in crisis management, need to meet with the consultant to clarify and define the working plan for students and parents. Faculty, other school personnel, and crisis team members must also have opportunities to meet with the consultant to monitor their own reactions, evaluate their postvention efforts, and document and explore continuing concerns. An attitude that must prevail is that it is okay for helpers to ask for help.

Phase 3: Working with Students and Parents

As with the staff phase, the first part of this process is informing. How this will be done should be addressed in the overall crisis plan. It might be through an announcement to students over the school intercom, at a brief assembly (not a memorial), or in individual class sessions. The decision would depend on the size of the school, the philosophy of the staff, the comfort of the teachers with a particular method, and so on. Whatever method is chosen, an appropriate authority figure should present the facts, and the same message should be delivered to all students at the same time. The following is an example of the type of announcement that might be made:

> I have had a difficult time deciding what to say to you today about the recent suicide (attempt). As some of you may know, (state the known facts. Do not describe the means in any way.).
>
> As adults we are expected to have all the answers and control our feelings. Let me tell you, however, that I have no clear understanding of the reasons for this action, and I am as deeply affected by it as many of you.
>
> You will hear a great deal of speculation about reasons for a suicide from friends, families and the news media, but nobody will have all the right answers. Whatever the reasons for this incident, it did happen. Probably none of us could have stopped it. We may be asking ourselves why we did not foresee it or do something to stop it, but this is not a time for

guilt or second guessing. It did occur, we must learn from it, and we must continue on.

Another thing I know is that all of us will need to help each other for a time as a community. To help us with this, let me make some suggestions:

1. We need to respect each other's emotions, no matter how differently we feel or act. Each of us has our own way of seeing, feeling about, reacting, and coping with a death. That is good and as it should be. It is OK to cry, be angry, to do nothing, or even to joke.

2. If you are having problems and feeling confused or upset, please ask for help. You do this when you have a physical pain or problem and you should do this when you have emotional pain. To ask for assistance for yourself or others please contact your teacher, your counselor or (other resources at the school or known resources in the community, if appropriate).

3. It frequently helps to talk about your feelings, even if they seem weird or embarrassing to you. Someone else probably feels this way, too. We will give you a chance to talk during (details of when discussions will be held).

4. If you are having problems, they will probably be temporary and then fade away. You may always remember what happened, but will not have such strong feelings. If strong feelings persist, however, please talk to (school resource) [Colombo and Oegema, 1986, p. 38].

During the announcement, school personnel should appear to be relatively composed and should observe for signs of significant distress in students. Attending to reactions helps to spot at-risk students who may be intervened with quickly. Depending on when and where the suicide occurred, it may be important to inform intimate friends of the student and teachers who had close contact with the student before the general announcement is made (for example, if the suicide occurred on a Friday night, so that the announcement would not be made until Monday). Students' parents may already have been informed by reports in the media, but this should not be assumed, and the school should inform them through a letter. This letter should present the facts of the case, provide information about funeral and memorial service arrangements, and offer continued consultation, support, and referrals. Exhibit 2, adapted from Colombo and Oegema (1986), presents a sample of such a letter.

The second part of the phase 3 process is clinical intervention with students. There are three facets of this intervention: identification and monitoring, intervening with survivors, and suspending the normal routine.

Identification and Monitoring. The first step in the clinical intervention is the identification and appropriate monitoring (and immediate referral if necessary) of those students most at risk. Those most likely to be at risk include siblings, other relatives, a boyfriend or girlfriend, or best friends of the deceased. Less obviously but still potentially at risk are those who have recently experienced a major loss or separation or have a history of experiences somewhat similar to those of the deceased who have "pathologically identified" with that person (Sacks and Eth, 1981). Ruof, Harris, and Robbie (1987) provide a useful list of those who are probably at high risk:

1. Any adolescent who participated in any way with the completed suicide: helped write the suicide note, provided the means, was involved in a suicide pact, and so on
2. Any adolescent who knew of the suicide plans and kept them a secret
3. Siblings, other relatives, best friends
4. Any adolescents who were self-appointed therapists to the deceased child—who had made it their responsibility to keep that child alive
5. Any adolescent with a history of suicidal threats and attempts him- or herself
6. Any adolescent who identified with the victim's situation

Exhibit 2. Sample Announcement to Parents.

Date

Dear Parent:

As you may be aware, our school district has experienced a tragic suicide that has affected us deeply. Let me review the facts of the situation. [State known facts briefly; do not include information about the precise means or location.]

The students and staff will react in different ways to a suicide. We all should expect and try to understand that there will be a variety of emotions and responses to what has occurred. The most important thing we can do is to be supportive and encourage discussion about the event, the feelings it gives rise to, and what we can do about it if the subject comes up. At the school, we have implemented a plan for responding to this tragic event focused on helping our students and their families get back to regular learning and everyday activities. This plan has evolved from the district's experience with suicides in the past and the advice of mental health professionals from the community. Our teachers and counselors have been briefed on our plans and have received guidelines for discussing the incident and reactions to it. There will be district personnel available to students who need special attention and support. There is also help available from the community. We will try to maintain as normal a routine and structure as the situation and people allow, and we encourage you to do the same. If you feel that your child or family needs some assistance, please contact us, and we will do everything we can to help you. We will also hold a special meeting of the PTA [PTO, or other parent group] to review the facts, respond to questions, and provide support.

If you have any questions or concerns, please contact the school at [give preferred phone number]. We will keep you informed about funeral arrangements or memorial services as they are planned and pass on any other information we discover that will be of help to you or your child. We know you will join us in our concern and sympathy for the family. We appreciate your cooperation and assistance.

Sincerely,

Principal and Staff

---

7. Any adolescent who had reason to feel guilty about things that he or she had said or done to the student prior to the student's death

8. Other adolescents desperate for any reason who now see suicide as a viable alternative

9.   Any adolescents who observed events that they later learned
     were indicative of the victim's suicidal intent

All of these categories apply to adults as well as children. In addition, the following categories of adults are at high risk:

1.   Parents of the victim, especially if they had prior knowledge of
     the impending suicide and did not take it seriously
2.   School personnel who knew that the student had threatened
     suicide, did not take the threat seriously, and so did not take
     preventive action
3.   School personnel or other adults who had recently punished or
     threatened to punish the victim for some misdeed
4.   School personnel or other adults who had been too busy to
     make time for the student when the student indicated a need to
     talk

   Intervening with Survivors. The second part of the intervention is helping the survivors in the school to shed their identification with the victim, de-romanticize the act, and reduce real or
imagined guilt (Saffer, 1986). While some suggest intervening primarily with the peer network of the victim (Ojanlatva, Hammer,
and Mohr, 1987; Saffer, 1986), we recommend (as do Hill, 1984;
Lamb and Dunne-Maxim, 1987; and Singer, 1980) targeting those
most likely to be at risk but providing help for all students who
want to talk about what happened. Individual or group approaches
can be used; Hill (1984) recommends group counseling with groups
of five to fifteen students lasting from one to four sessions.
   Singer (1980), who provided counseling to about half of a
1,600-member student body after a cluster of four suicides over
eighteen months, found that the primary agenda for the students
was reassurance that suicide was not contagious; that is, that one
would not become suicidal as a result of physical or emotional
proximity to the victim. However, this does not seem to be the
major concern after isolated suicides. Hill (1984) has conceptualized
four phases that groups that he counseled went through. First was
shock, usually with either crying, silence, or withdrawal. Second
came the "why?" phase, an effort to make sense of and reduce the

anxiety caused by the suicide by understanding it. When understanding failed, there was a move to the third phase: trying to determine whose fault it was. The most typical responses were (1) "mine," which led to guilt; (2) "his or hers," which led to anger at the victim; and (3) "somebody else's"—for example, the school's—which led to anger and projection. Hill referred to these processes as overfocusing (guilt) and overgeneralizing (anger outward). The fourth phase consisted of survivors confronting each other or the group leader; these confrontations led to some relief and understanding that the causality of suicide is multifaceted and complex and that no one would probably ever know exactly how this particular suicide had come about. Lamb and Dunne-Maxim (1987) believe that not just those close to the victim but most of the students touch on those issues and feelings at some level.

Suspending Normal Routine. The general faculty and personnel must be willing to suspend normal class routine if necessary so that students may discuss their feelings, their memories, or the suicide itself without penalty. Ojanlatva, Hammer, and Mohr (1987) suggest that this suspension be extended for up to five days and that students who need to discuss these issues beyond that time be referred to counseling. We believe this to be a reasonable principle but can foresee many exceptions. The types of responses needed by the staff are succinctly stated by Lamb and Dunne-Maxim (1987) in Table 6.

Postvention with parents of the student survivors should be similar to that with the school personnel: dealing with the parents' feelings and educating them about how they can help their children. This is most often done at an emergency parents' and teachers' meeting, with parent group sessions or individual consultations scheduled as requested. With parents of students who were close to the victim, a more proactive outreach is appropriate.

Phase 4: Follow-Up

Not all people grieve in the same way or along the same time line. "Normal" grieving has its own ups and downs, and grieving complicated by a suicide can be more problematic (Hauser, 1987).

Table 6. The Postvention Process.

Student Reaction	Staff Response
1. Shock. Students may initially appear remarkably unreactive. In fact, they are in a state of shock and not yet able to accept the reality of the suicide.	1. Staff needs to assume a stance of anticipatory waiting, acknowledging the shock and showing a willingness to talk about the suicide when students are ready. Hill (1984) suggests waiting 24 to 48 hours before initiating more direct action.
2. Anger and projection. Students will look for someone to blame. Initially, this may be directed at important adults in the victim's life, including school staff. "Why did they let it happen?"	2. Some expressions of anger must be allowed. Staff members may share the similar feeling they have had. However, at the same time, reality must be introduced. There are limits on how much one person can be responsible for actions of another.
3. Guilt. Typically, students who knew the victim may move from blaming others to blaming themselves. "If only I had talked to him more."	3. Here, particularly, staff can be helpful by sharing their own similar reactions. And again, the reality principle is also introduced. One person cannot assume total responsibility for the act of another.
4. Anger at victim. This is a common reaction by students, even those not closely connected to the victim. "How could he do this to us?"	4. Staff needs to give permission for such expressions by normalizing them, perhaps tempered by questioning if the victim fully realized the impact of his act.
5. Anxiety. Students will begin worrying about themselves. "If he could kill himself because he was upset, maybe I (or my friends) could too."	5. Discussion should be guided toward helping students differentiate between themselves and the victim and toward other options for problem-solving.
6. Relief. Once the normal distortions of feelings are resolved, students can allow themselves to feel the sadness of the loss and begin the healing process.	6. Staff must guard against encouraging a pseudo-mourning process before students have worked at resolving their conflicts over the suicide.

Source: Reprinted from "Postvention in Schools: Policy and Process" by Frederick Lamb and Karen Dunne-Maxim from SUICIDE AND ITS AFTERMATH, Understanding and Counseling the Survivors, Edited by Edward J. Dunne, John L. McIntish, and Karen Dunne-Maxim, by permission of W. W. Norton & Company, Inc. Copyright © 1987 by Edward J. Dunne, John L. McIntosh, and Karen Dunne-Maxim.

Gould, Wallenstein, and Davidson (1989) also describe group grieving, a primarily adolescent and young adult phenomenon. Given
both this phenomenon and the possibility of clustering, it is important that there be follow-up and continued monitoring, especially
of students initially considered to be at high risk. Risk would be
further increased after another attempted or completed suicide in
the community, after the suicide of someone famous, on the anni-
versary of the suicide, and on other special dates, such as holidays,
birthdays, graduation, and homecoming.

If in-service training focusing on signs and symptoms of suicidality and ways to intervene in the process has not yet been provided, it should certainly be provided now. Even if such training has
already been provided, then reminders or refresher sessions may be
necessary. The attitude that "it can't happen again" is fairly common, so school personnel need to be made to realize that it can
happen, and that they must be as well prepared as possible.

Responses to Other Suicides and to Attempted Suicides

The intervention and postvention procedures dicussed above
are designed as a response to the completed suicide of a student.
Although the goals will be similar when the situation involves the
suicide of a parent or sibling of a student, the suicide of a person
working in the school district, or a suicide attempt, the procedures
will vary somewhat.

Suicide of a Parent or Sibling

The loss of a parent to suicide leaves a highly unfortunate
legacy. Although all children and adolescents in this situation need
to go through some form of initial grieving, the longer-term reactions may vary. Shepherd and Barraclough (1976) found that significantly more survivors suffered psychological problems than did
members of a control group. But some appeared to cope without
developing diagnosable problems, and a few even found relief from
"an insupportable situation" (p. 267). Cain (1972) and Dunne,
McIntosh, and Dunne-Maxim (1987) provide detailed discussions of
reactions to parental suicide. Literature on reactions to sibling sui-

cide is very scarce, and Rosenfield and Prupas (1984) suggest that
this may be a result of families wishes to "protect" the surviving
siblings. However, this unfortunate conspiracy can prove harmful,
the extent of the harm depending on the survivors' ages and circumstances (Herbert, 1987). Our main concern here with these children
is that they be reintegrated into the school system in a way that
enhances the social support available to them. This reintegration
can be difficult if, out of fear of potential stigma or denial, the
family or adolescent wants to keep the event secret. This may com-
pound the problem by further isolating one who is already in pain.
Although school-based professionals are ethically bound not to di-
vulge this information if they receive it confidentially, they do have
a few options.

First, they should always attempt to explore with the survivors their concerns about telling others. They may be helped to re-
evaluate their situation in a way that could open up opportunities
for support. For instance, a counselor spoke of a fifteen-year-old
female adolescent whose nineteen-year-old brother had completed
suicide. The girl attempted to swear the counselor to secrecy but
under gentle questioning revealed that she had been her brother's
confidant about the suicide and had not told her parents. Exploring
this issue allowed the counselor to move to the second option.

Second, the parent and/or adolescent should be encouraged
to seek counseling. Depending on circumstances, this may more
appropriately be offered by a school-based mental health worker or
by a person or agency that specializes in this kind of counseling,
such as a suicide prevention center.

Finally, since school-based professionals are bound to protect
adolescents at such risk, they should inform staff members that have
contact with those adolescents that they require monitoring. These
personnel must be reminded that this is confidential information
and that, even if other students ask about the situation, confidence
must be maintained. However, another student's questioning about
a survivor's situation may indicate that student's own suicidal ideation or other serious problems, in which case an evaluation of that
student might be appropriate.

Suicide of School Personnel

It is very clear that the suicide of a faculty member can have a strong impact on certain students and that most students who have interacted with that teacher will have feelings about it (Davis, Bates, and Velasquez, 1990; Kneisel and Richards, 1988). Perry and others (1988) also discuss students' reactions to the suicide of a school superintendent. In the case of the suicide of a school staff member who has had ongoing contact with students, particularly a teacher or counselor, while the standard postvention practices are followed, two additional issues must be addressed: who presents the facts to the suicide victim's students and who succeeds in that person's position.

Since loss will be an obvious issue for the students, we believe that the suicide victim should be replaced by either a long-term substitute, preferably to serve until the end of the school year, or a new permanent hire. This person should be well informed about the issues and sensitive to the multitude of reactions that might appear among the students. However, since it is unlikely that the new person will be familiar with the students, someone who is already a part of the school staff (perhaps a member of the crisis team but at least knowledgeable about handling crisis) should be assigned to present the facts of the suicide to the students and discuss it with them. Familiarity with the students would enable recognition of behavioral changes that might indicate students at risk and might enhance rapport with the students, although this may not be as important a factor. After the intensity of the first week following the suicide, this person should continue in a follow-up role, monitoring student's reactions, being available for consultation with the new person, keeping track of the high risk times previously mentioned, and perhaps conducting a review at the close of the school year.

Parasuicide and Suicide Attempts

As we noted in Chapter One, there are many more attempts at suicide than completions, and the majority of attempters do not become involved with medical, mental health, or school personnel at the time of the attempt. We can only hope that these attempters find some more productive way of asking for help or coping with their problems. As Hawton (1986) suggests, the attempt itself may sometimes change the dynamics of a situation in such a way that a problem will no longer be a problem or a different solution will emerge. When attempts are known of, however, definite postvention procedures should be initiated.

Ruof, Harris, and Robbie (1987) state that the nature of postvention should depend on how visible the attempt was. If it was highly visible—for example, occurring at and during school with many observers—the postvention should be as broad ranging as a completed suicide postvention because of the number of staff and students affected. If, on the other hand, the attempt was made at home and few people were aware of it, they suggest keeping the postvention quieter, working directly with the students affected by it and requesting that they talk to staff rather than to other students. Teachers and staff should be informed as needed and, as in other situations involving suicidality, asked to look for and refer potentially high-risk students. A crisis team member or members should make contact with the parents to offer sympathy, support, and encouragement to enter into or continue in treatment for their family members. If the student has been hospitalized for either medical or psychiatric reasons, the school should provide some form of outreach, such as homework, to lessen alienation, to deal with the student's probable shame or embarrassment about reentry, and to facilitate the return to school. All of these interventions assume cooperation.

What if the attempt is known of by more than a few people, but the attempter or the attempter's family does not want to recognize or talk about the situation? As previously discussed, a crisis manager needs to arrange the sharing of information with involved teachers, emphasizing the maintenance of confidentiality and exploring realistic ways of responding to students who ask questions about the attempt.

Conclusion

School-based professionals have an ethical, if not a legal, responsibility to understand and implement intervention and postvention strategies. There are five basic requirements for confronting adolescent suicide in the schools. First is recognition of the problem. The incidence of attempted and completed suicides varies according to age, race, and gender, but the problem exists in all groups. Second, school personnel must be motivated to want to know more about dealing with suicide crises, and the necessary knowledge and training must be made available to them. Third, each school district must create a crisis preparedness program and set of policies that fit that district's particular culture. The program should be negotiated and owned by as many personnel as possible. Fourth, the system must change enough to allow the policies and program to be implemented. It is not just another technique for people to add to their bag of tricks. Without structural change to allow its implementation and support, it is likely to fail. Finally, school districts must invest time, energy, and money to provide relevant training to their workers so that they are better able to cope with suicide crises in the schools.

Part Three:
Schoolwide
Prevention Efforts

6

Screening for
Students at Risk

The methodologies and instruments available to identify individual adolescents at risk are usually referred to as screening. Screening is not a new concept to school-based personnel. As a methodology, it is generally thought of as a low-cost procedure to identify those children at relatively high risk for developing a particular problem, such as academic failure, interpersonal problems, or dropping out of school. Depending on the target variable, interventions may be instituted with the screened group. More often, a second, more intensive, reliable, and valid set of procedures is implemented to confirm or disconfirm the presence of a problem and, if it is confirmed, to provide the appropriate diagnosis or classification and to begin treatment planning (Reynolds, Gutkin, Elliott, and Witt, 1984). The idea is to use finer and finer grades of screening for the sake of efficiency.

In this chapter, we present three potential ways to screen for students at risk for suicidal behavior. First, we review psychometric approaches that feature self-report questionnaire measures. Next, we discuss the use of peers as informants. Finally, we review what has been written about the use of school personnel as identifiers.

Psychometric Approaches

Most proponents of psychometric screening agree that screening for suicidal behavior is a two-stage process. The first stage consists of the administration of a psychological questionnaire designed expressly for this purpose to the general or a selected population of students. For screening the entire student body of a school, Reynolds (1986) suggests administering the test in small groups, no larger than the size of a classroom, toward the beginning of the week and the beginning of the school day. The screening should take place on a day when there are no academic special events, such as schoolwide achievement testing, that might interfere with the screening process and no special social events, such as homecoming, that could significantly influence the short-term emotional status of students. The project should be overseen by a coordinator who knows the material and procedures to be used and is competent to present an in-service training session to the teachers who will administer the instrument. On the day of the screening, the coordinator should also be in charge of disseminating, collecting, and scoring the instruments. An excellent outline of the questionnaire administration process can be found in Reynolds's (1988) *Suicidal Ideation Questionnaire: Professional Manual.*

The second stage of screening consists of thorough clinical evaluations of students identified as being at risk by the questionnaire. These evaluations are conducted by qualified personnel knowledgeable about psychological problems in adolescence and trained in the evaluation of adolescents for suicide. The evaluators are most often school social workers, psychologists, or counselors, but they may be other trained school personnel or nonschool mental health professionals providing service for screening purposes.

If, for whatever reasons, the district decides against schoolwide screening of senior and junior high school students, we strongly suggest that routine screening be done for at least selected groups of the student population who are at a statistically elevated risk to attempt suicide, including at least the following:

- Those who participate in prevention-oriented groups on topics such as substance abuse, children of alcoholics, divorce, or dropping out
- Those who approach school-based mental health personnel for individual or group work on personal problems
- Those who approach or are approached by counselors because of academic or behavioral problems

- Those who are being assessed by school psychologists for possible special education placement or reevaluation
- Those who are transferring from the regular high school program to another program, such as a continuation high school

Reynolds (1988) emphasizes the importance of the second-stage evaluators taking action quickly once the scores are obtained; we recommend that district crisis teams be available for further assessments on the day when screening is implemented (see Chapter Ten). We also recommend that in addition to whatever questionnaire is used, students should be asked whether they would like to speak to someone immediately about issues, thoughts, or feelings raised by the questionnaire. This can be done through a question either added to the instrument itself or asked by the person administering it. Second, the instruments should be scored that day or evening so that further interviewing can begin the following day, on the basis of some system of cutoff or critical-question scoring.

The parents and community should also be informed about the screening so that parents will know whom to contact if some concern or issue arises for which they feel they need help and community agencies or hot lines can prepare for the possibility of increased demands. Although it may seem that this is overly cautious or may create undue alarm, we believe that failing to take reasonable precautions could be highly risky and that if the notification is clear, direct, and reasonable, it should be more assuring than alarming. In addition, if any student who is identified as at risk by the screening does not come to school the next day, every effort should be made to contact that student and his or her parents. Although students generally perceive such screening as a caring intervention (Reynolds, 1986), there is a small chance that a student would become anxious about having revealed too much in the questionnaire and thus stay away from school.

Some studies suggest, rather than using psychometric instruments, simply asking students directly about their level of suicidality and even previous attempts (Harkavy-Friedman, Asnis, Boeck, and DiFiore, 1987; Ross, 1985). Although such a direct tactic might be considered as an adjunct or substitute to psychometric measures, psychometric measures will probably pick up more of the subtle indications of suicidality and allow districts and clinicians to better decide who can benefit from not only immediate clinical intervention but preventive programs as well. In addition, some students will probably respond better to less confrontive questioning, and these instruments provide a useful set of normative data.

Suicidal Ideation Questionnaire

Reynolds (1988) has developed the only instrument currently suitable for both a general screening of the student body and use with individual students, the Suicidal Ideation Questionnaire (SIQ). The measure consists of two forms, each entitled "About My Life." The high school form (grades ten through twelve) consists of thirty items; the junior high school form (grades seven through nine) consists of fifteen items. While we discussed the theoretical orientation, norms, and scoring of this instrument in Chapter Three, here we address its reliability and validity, user qualifications, validity checks, the use of a mail-in service, and limitations of the instrument for screening purposes.

Psychometric Properties. Reynolds estimated the internal consistency reliability of the instrument using Cronbach's (1951) alpha coefficient. This was done across developmental samples for subsamples by age and sex. The coefficients by grade were high, ranging from a low of .932 for seventh-graders to a high of .974 for seniors. Standard errors of measurement ranged from a low of 3.60 for seniors to a high of 4.69 for tenth-graders. When coefficients by grade and sex were computed, the values remained similarly high, with a low of .917 for seventh-grade males to a high of .978 for senior girls. Standard errors of measurement by gender ranged from a low of 3.55 for ninth-grade males to a high of 5.27 for eleventh-grade girls. Item-total scale correlations also support the homogeneity of item content, with the majority of coefficients computed for total samples by grades in the .60s to .80s.

Test-retest reliability is complex for a measure of suicidal ideation, since by its nature it is expected to fluctuate as a result of external and internal variables, and to do so in a short time. However, over a short period of time, with a large population, a mod-

erate degree of stability would be expected. Reynolds (1988) found
that with a sample size of 801 students from all grades, the test-retest
reliability over four weeks was .72, with no significant differences
between group means between the two testings.

Evidence for content and construct validity is also provided
by Reynolds (1988). He used a theory-based logical hierarchical continuum for suicidal thoughts to construct the measure, and the high
item-total scale correlations reported above support the instrument's content validity. Reynolds also reviews a number of studies
focusing on correlations between the SIQ and a variety of measures
of depression, hopelessness, anxiety, learned helplessness, and self-
esteem. All reported correlations are in the expected directions and
significant at the $p < .001$ level.

Reynolds also reports some exploratory factor-analytical
work on the development samples. Both the junior high and high
school yielded three factors, with some differences between them.
The analyses of the high school version yielded a strong first factor,
seemingly representing those components of suicidal ideation related to wishes and plans. The second factor consisted of those items
associated with "others," with the highest factor loading on the
statement "I thought that the only way to be noticed is to kill
myself." The third factor seemed to represent morbidity, with
strong loadings on "I thought about people dying" and "I thought
about death." The three junior high factors seemed to be related to
minor suicidal ideation, specific plans and desires for suicide, and
again a morbidity factor.

User Qualifications. Reynolds suggests that those who employ his measure for screening should be professionals who are
aware of the ethical guidelines for use specified by the American
Psychological Association (1985) and have appropriate training in
the use of psychological tests. Obviously, technicians could administer the questionnaire; the "users" would be those who interpret
and make recommendations from the data.

Validity Checks. Reynolds offers three possible ways of assessing the questionnaire's validity for an individual. First is minimum number of completed items (twenty-seven of thirty for the

high school form and thirteen of fifteen for the junior high form). Second is unusual patterns of responses, primarily all questions having the same reply. Third is pairs of items that should be answered in different directions. If they are not, and a pattern of inconsistent responding is revealed, validity must be questioned. Inconsistencies in response can result from a number of causes, such as reading problems or oppositional behavior, but they should be followed up with an interview with the student.

Mail-In Service. The publisher of the SIQ provides a mail-in service for those who use it. The service provides scoring, summary data, and at-risk student and invalid protocol identification by computer service for large numbers of protocols. The publisher states that the protocols are processed within twenty-four hours of receipt.

Suicide Probability Scale

Like the SIQ, the Suicide Probability Scale (Cull and Gill, 1982) is a fairly brief (roughly twenty minutes from administration to interpretation) self-report measure for evaluating suicidal risk. It is intended for fourteen-year-olds through adults. This age restriction makes it inappropriate for some junior high students, but it is appropriate for high school populations. The standardization sample is considerably smaller than that for the SIQ, consisting of 562 individuals from the San Antonio, Texas, area. Another weakness of the norm group is that only 10.3 percent of that population, or fewer than sixty norming subjects, were adolescents nineteen and younger (no specific number per age is provided). Therefore, it should be used cautiously by school-based professionals working with populations primarily twelve to eighteen years old (junior and senior high students).

Scoring. Scoring of the Suicide Probability Scale (SPS) is a matter of addition. It is set up similarly to the Western Psychological Services' Tennessee Self-Concept Scale (Fitts, 1964), with an oversheet to be filled out by the subject and an attached pressure-sensitive examiner's version. *T* scores and what the authors refer to as a "probability score" are retrieved from tables. A weighting system devised for the SPS allowed for the development of a probability score corresponding to a "presumptive risk" for suicide of high, medium, or low. Using a Bayesian probability procedure, the authors constructed a table of probability values associated with SPS total scores. These values are used to reduce the possibility of false-positive judgments. Clinically, the "high-risk" column would be used by those institutions, such as suicide prevention centers and crisis clinics, that draw from a high-risk population, the "medium-risk" column would generally be used by outpatient counseling centers, and the "low-risk" column would be used for assessments by schools that draw from the general population.

A profile form is also included. Unlike the SIQ, which is designed to measure the one construct of suicidal ideation, the SPS purports to measure four constructs and provides five scales: total score, hopelessness, suicidal ideation, negative self-esteem, and hostility. The authors provide a condensed personality inventory for the three major correlates of suicidal behavior: hopelessness, self-esteem, and anger or hostility. In this respect, the SPS is a somewhat more ambitious project than the SIQ.

Psychometric Properties. Cull and Gill also used Cronbach's (1951) coefficient alpha to estimate internal consistency reliability. The estimates were derived not for each age group but for the across-total sample. The reported total-scale alpha of .93 is certainly high; however, the fact that it is computed for all four scales together suggests that the subscales are highly correlated. Of the four subscales, suicidal ideation, with an alpha of .88, is the highest, only slightly lower than the total SIQ alpha. Test-retest for eighty subjects at three weeks yielded a correlation of .92, and the standard error of measurement for the total scale is 2.99.

Validity was examined by Cull and Gill in a variety of ways. First was a "qualitative study of the individual items within the subscales and by the theoretical rationale which led to the inclusion of these dimensions of suicide risk" (Cull and Gill, 1982, p. 45), which, when added to the reliability findings, they believe offers reasonable validity evidence. The second line of evidence, concerning content validity, was a study comparing the SPS items with an experimental MMPI scale for measuring threatened suicide (Farberow and Devries, 1967). Fifteen of their items correlated at .30 or greater with the scale, which was significant at the .05 level. The authors take this evidence to support the content validity and provide further data for construct validity. Further evidence for construct validity was generated by factor-analytical and multidimensional scalogram analyses. Finally, discriminate validity was supported by studies using the norming group (N = 562), psychiatric inpatients (N = 260), and a group of suicide attempters (N = 336). Correct classification rates ranged from 85.5 percent to 87.4 percent.

User Qualifications. Cull and Gill's (1982) recommendations about user qualifications are the same as Reynolds's (1988) for the SIQ.

Validity Checks. Cull and Gill suggest checking on the validity of a single score by a procedure similar to that of Reynolds. For their scoring system, using t scores, they suggest that a t score of less than 40 or greater than 85 should alert the examiner to possible faking or other problems, and their rule of thumb for further extended clinical evaluation is a score of 60 or more.

Criticisms of Psychometric Measures

As we have stated, the small norming population of adolescents used for the SPS is one factor that makes it weaker than the SIQ. However, Cull and Gill (1982) point out some weaknesses that are also applicable to the SIQ. First, both instruments are relatively undisguised and are therefore open to conscious manipulation as well as unconscious distortion. Second, there is presently no measure of current suicide level that can predict temporal changes in suicide risk, and it is unlikely that such an instrument will be developed. Third, and extremely importantly, predictive validity has yet to be established for either of these instruments. We have an additional concern about the use of such instruments, which is that they may be accorded inordinate power by school-based personnel who do not have sufficient psychometric knowledge to properly use them. The evaluator must always be more "knowledgeable" than the instrument.

The Use of Peers to Screen for Suicidal Potential

The use of peers has been a primary method of screening used by those interested in preventive intervention. As Ross (1985) has stated, "the persons most frequently contacted by adolescents contemplating or planning suicide, and who therefore would be their most likely rescuers, are their friends. As potential rescuers, they need to respond effectively to their suicidal friends" (p. 150). Although the data we have reviewed do not present as sanguine a view about how often suicidal adolescents actually reveal their suicidality, there are certainly a number of seriously suicidal adolescents who do tell their friends. Moreover, we believe that these friends can play a helpful role by responding in appropriate ways. Part of prevention then is educating youth to be better interveners or informers. Preventive efforts utilizing adolescents and the use of peer counselors as screeners are explored more thoroughly in Chapter Nine; here we focus on methodologies using peers to identify malfunctioning youth: sociometry, peer nomination, peer rating, peer ranking.

Sociometry

Sociometry is a procedure devised by Moreno (1934) to gather data on whom within a defined group, such as a classroom, a person would like to work with, play with, be with, and so on. These data can be used to trace patterns of friendship, communication, and interaction (Gronlund, 1959; Moreno, 1934) that can help school-based personnel to plan potential interventions for students. A "sociogram" is created by asking each member of the group to name one or more people for a role, task, or relationship. The number of times individuals are selected becomes one measure, but maps and diagrams of relationships may also be prepared from the group's responses.

Peer Nomination, Rating, and Ranking

Peer nomination, peer rating, and peer ranking are methodologies whereby group members judge characteristics of other group members such as leadership ability, most liked, best athlete, or virtually any personality or behavioral characteristic of interest (Kane and Lawler, 1978). For any of these methodologies to work, there must be two major preconditions. The first is a group of peers who know each other well enough to assess the criteria of interest; Smith (1967) found that at least ten per group were needed to achieve a minimum level of reliability. The second is an exercise framed in a way that elicits cooperation.

An important factor in this type of endeavor is the verbal construction of the characteristic of interest. In general, it is best to keep the characteristics positive. If the exercise requests negative nominations—for example, "Who are the three worst pupils in your class?"—it is likely that choices irrelevant to the criterion will be made. Positive factors, such as friendship patterns, do not seem to influence choices as much as negative factors, such as being annoyed with or not liking someone (Kaufman and Johnson, 1974).

Unfortunately, we have been unable to find any research linking these peer forms of assessment and suicide. The most closely aligned bit of research we found was by Lefkowitz and Tesiny (1980), who developed the Peer Nomination Inventory of Depression (PNID). Since it has already been established that 25 to 33 percent of those who complete suicides are depressed (Shaffer, 1985), this may hold some potential. Modifications of this instrument would be needed for junior and senior high school populations, since it was designed primarily for late elementary ages. Although it seems unlikely that one would ask adolescents who are the three most likely students to commit suicide, asking questions regarding the correlates of suicide—for example, "What three students do you think are the most depressed?" "What three students do you see as most lonely?"—may generate a list of students at risk for suicide. Currently, these questions are open to research.

The Use of School-Based Personnel to Screen
for Suicide Potential

Maag, Rutherford, and Parks (1988) have found that the ability of secondary school teachers to identify depressed students is limited. In the clinical experience of most school-based mental health personnel, "acting out" students are much more readily referred than others, although, as we have previously mentioned, if these students have a concurrent affective disorder, this is often not recognized. Nevertheless, as Ross (1985) and others state, frontline personnel are prime targets for preventive education aimed at increasing their knowledge and skills to enhance their diagnostic acumen. Ross (1985) reports an increase of referrals to a mental health center following a preventive intervention with school personnel, but how this increase came about is not made clear.

Out of a multitude of possible screening interventions, we believe that there is one primary approach that may be worth researching: a modification of the Lambert and Bower's (1974) Pupil Behavior Rating Scale screening instrument. The teacher's version of this multiperspective assessment is a behaviorally anchored interval scale for eleven selected attributes. Although it is focused on elementary-age children, it seems likely that this methodology could be used with junior and senior high school students if appropriate scales were developed to measure attributes that have high correlations with suicidality, such as depression and hopelessness. Thus, students could be reasonably quickly and efficiently screened with the use of ratings from teachers, counselors, and/or administrators. This method would allow for multiple perspectives on each student as well. One clear difficulty is the often heard lament of secondary teachers about how little they get to know their students. However, coupling this type of screening with prevention training may enhance its accuracy and power.

Conclusion

All or some of the approaches to screening discussed in this chapter could be used by any particular school district. Although there are no data that we know to suggest which technique is the most powerful predictor, we believe that student self-screening is the most likely to identify potentially suicidal students, peer screening next most likely, and teacher screening least likely. Nor do we know whether the use of some combination of two or three methodologies would yield better results. However, if one must face a district school board that is cautious about any kind of suicide screening, the least powerful method would probably be the most acceptable: Teacher screening would be less threatening to most school boards and administrators than peer and self-screening. It is clear from the data presented in this chapter that much research remains to be done on screening for suicide in the schools. However, whatever approach a school or school district takes to screening, it should not be seen as an isolated event but should be part of an ongoing crisis intervention policy.

7

Identifying
Suicide-Prone Populations

The measures and methodologies for screening an entire student population that we discussed in Chapter Six may not be acceptable to all school faculty, administrators, or school boards. When such resistance is encountered, professionals may be tempted to consider other preventive strategies. It may be possible, however, to continue screening but on a smaller scale, with selected high-risk, subpopulations rather than the entire student body. When no screening is possible, professionals should at least know which students may be at greater risk of suicide by virtue of their membership in a particular group known to be more at risk than the general population of adolescents.

Subpopulations that research has identified as particularly at risk for suicide attempts and completions include students who have substance abuse problems, those that have used running away as a coping strategy (usually to escape unbearable home situations), those who are dealing with sexual-orientation issues, those who have suffered from physical and/or sexual abuse, special education students, and continuation or alternative high school students. Although we organize our discussion in this chapter according to these categories, we by no means want to suggest that the categories are mutually exclusive. In fact, it would not be a surprise to find individual students fitting into more than one category. Although we know of no data that specifically support the notion that being a member of more than one of these categories increases risk, we suspect that this is the case, as it has been shown in comorbidity studies to be the case in psychiatric populations.

Substance Abuse

It is not news that substance abuse and suicide are related. Studies have revealed that 20 to 50 percent of suicide attempters or completers abuse drugs and 15 to 50 percent of suicide completers abuse alcohol (Murphy and others, 1979; Robins, 1982). At least 20 percent of alcoholics entering treatment programs report having made suicide attempts (Woodruff, Clayton, and Guze, 1972). Another sad statistic is that intoxication with drugs or alcohol often precedes suicidal behavior (Mayfield and Montgomery, 1972). One study reported 70 percent of male and 40 percent of female attempters as having elevated blood levels of alcohol (Paykel, Myers, Lindenthal, and Tanner, 1974). Drugs and alcohol can act as disinhibitors to increase impulsivity, can impair judgment, and can produce or exacerbate severe mood disturbances to the point of precipitating a suicidal depression (Schuckit, 1984).

Although the studies cited above dealt primarily with adults, studies of adolescents also confirm the link between drugs and suicide (Garfinkel, Froese, and Hood, 1982; McKenry, Tishler, and Kelly, 1983; Shafti, Carrigan, Whittinghill, and Derrick, 1985). An interesting study of adolescents by Harlow, Newcomb, and Bentler (1986) found that "men may turn more automatically to drugs in response to psychic discomfort than women; whereas women may turn more automatically to suicidal thoughts given psychic discomfort. This may help explain why others have found that women tend to have more frequent suicidal ideation than men, and males more often use drugs than do females" (p. 18). Obviously, the combination of drug use and suicidal ideation may create a person at high risk regardless of gender (Schuckit, 1984).

Given these figures, efforts aimed at reducing adolescent drug use and abuse could well be a component of a suicide prevention program. Most substance abuse programs, however, are not coordinated with suicide prevention programs. For example, a fairly comprehensive evaluation questionnaire used in a pilot program in California aimed at reducing drug abuse included no questions about depression, hopelessness, suicidal ideation, or previous attempts. Nor have the school-based implementers of the drug prevention program received any specific training in suicide awareness

or intervention. We believe this to be extremely short-sighted. As substance abuse and suicide are related, so should be programs aimed at the prevention of these problems. Prevention efforts need to be well thought out and integrated. Anyone being trained in substance abuse prevention should be trained in suicide prevention as well, and if only limited screening for suicidality is to be implemented, substance-using and -abusing students absolutely should be one of the targeted groups. The best resource we know of for help in planning in-school drug prevention programs is the National Association of State Alcohol and Drug Abuse Directors, 444 North Capitol Street, N.W., Suite 520, Washington, D.C. 20001, (202) 783-6868.

Runaways

In a list of eleven questions that he developed to help identify suicide attempters, Robins (1989) has found that the single question that adds most to the identification of attempters is whether the respondent has ever run away from home. Furthermore, Shaffer and Caton (1984) report that 33 percent of all the runaway youths seeking assistance from a New York City shelter had seriously contemplated suicide and that 15 percent of the males and 33 percent of the females had made suicide attempts. It is clear that runaways are at increased risk and can be identified by a direct question. It is also important to note that these statistics come only from those youth who are served by youth centers. Since these centers see slightly less than 10 percent of the runaway youth population, the problem must be much larger (Bucy, forthcoming).

Running away from home represents a variety of potential negative life experiences, including physical and sexual abuse, psychiatric problems, and, very clearly, severe relationship problems among family members (Janus, McCormack, Burgess, and Hartman, 1987). Running away is not an overnight adventure. One major problem faced by school-based personnel attempting to identify and work with runaway youth is their lack of school attendance. One study found that only 34 percent of a sample of runaway youth had completed high school (Westat, Inc., 1986). For obvious reasons, it is extremely difficult to work with nonattending students.

The implications of these findings are that to have any success with runaway youth, even to evaluate them, requires collaboration with social services and youth centers and most probably some type of school outreach program. Any time multiple system interventions are necessary, the complexity of the interventions increases, and case management becomes more problematic.

Given the potentially dire consequences associated with runaway youth, not only increased risk of suicide but also increased levels of drug abuse, increased possibility of prostitution, and so on (Janus, McCormack, Burgess, and Hartman, 1987), successful interventions with members of this group would have a high return in terms of both societal and economic gains. However, it is also very clear that a high level of diligence and commitment is necessary for working with these youth and that school systems are not well designed for serving them.

Gay and Lesbian Youth

Hunter and Schaecher (1987), from the Institute for the Protection of Lesbian and Gay Youth in New York City, have written about many of the kinds of stresses and traumas faced by gay adolescents in schools. Unfortunately, the stress is considerable. For instance, the National Gay Task Force (1984) found that about 45 percent of gay males and 20 percent of lesbians had experienced some form of verbal or physical attack in secondary schools. Rofes (1983) suggests that as many as 30 percent of gay males and lesbians may suffer from substance abuse problems, although the San Diego Suicide Study (Rich, Fowler, Young, and Blenkush, 1986) did not find significant differences in the prevalence of substance-abuse disorder between gay and straight males who completed suicide. Gibson (1989) estimates that as many as 25 percent of youth living on the streets are gay male, lesbian, bisexual, or transsexual.

Given these statistics, it is plausible that gay and lesbian youth are at increased risk of suicide attempts and therefore completions. The often cited works of Saghir and Robins (1973) and Bell and Weinberg (1978) support this conclusion. While the findings of the San Diego Suicide Study do not support the premise of increased risk, the authors of the study believe that their findings would have been statistically significant given a slightly larger sample size of gays exhibiting the same attempt ratios. In addition, the members of the study sample were all age twenty-one or older; since the average age of "coming out" has been found to be eighteen or nineteen (Dank, 1971; Harry and DeVall, 1978), and this is considered to be the time of greatest risk, the San Diego study may well have missed important data.

Since estimates of homosexuality are about 10 percent of the male population (Kinsey, Pomeroy, and Martin, 1948) and 2 to 6 percent of the female population (Diepold and Young, 1979; Kinsey, Pomeroy, Martin, and Gebhard, 1953) roughly 15 percent of our junior and senior high school population are struggling with this intensely emotional issue and the social difficulties that they encounter. They are clearly in need of support and guidance. To prevent suicidal as well as other adverse outcomes, the schools should make information on homosexuality available through sex education or other means, lessening the stigma of homosexuality through school or district interventions, and increase opportunities for socialization (Canaday, 1987). We recognize that these are very difficult tasks. Systemic changes will require work with school personnel, school boards, and the community to expand sex education and reduce stigma. Alternative kinds of socialization experiences require sensitive selection of school personnel to lead activities such as art, music, dramatics, and academic clubs and ongoing consultation to ensure a tolerant climate for homosexual students (Harry, 1982). They may also entail the use of or development of community resources, including those from the gay and lesbian community.

In counseling or crisis intervention work with a gay student, part of the interview should include a suicide evaluation. In counseling or crisis intervention with any suicidal adolescent, if it appears that coping with the issues surrounding homosexuality may be connected to the suicidal thinking, the question of homosexuality should be broached. Gibson (1989) suggests asking very directly but sensitively about sexual orientation, while Kremer, Zimpfer, and Wiggers (1975) suggest a less direct approach, indicating an openness to issues and feelings about homosexuality. Regardless of one's approach, it is clear that if the resulting intervention focuses on changing sexual orientation rather than helping the client and family resolve the conflict, conditions are likely to worsen (Gibson, 1989).

As Canaday (1987) and Ross-Reynolds (1987) point out, one can tell by how little is published on adolescent homosexuality how taboo the subject has been and how much more we need to know. School-based personnel must become knowledgeable and influential in this area.

Victims of Abuse

At least among clinic populations, it is clear that physically abused (Green, 1978; Kosky, 1983) and sexually abused (Briere and Runtz, 1986; Lanktree, Briere, and Zaidi, 1989) children and adolescents are at an increased risk of suicidality. In their study at a Canadian community mental health center, Briere and Runtz (1986) found that 55 percent of their sexually abused group had made at least one suicide attempt, whereas only 23 percent of their clinical control group had made an attempt. At the most extreme in this population, they found that of the 14 women who reported a suicide attempt prior to age thirteen, 92.3 percent (thirteen out of fourteen) had been victims of sexual abuse. Yet none of the methodologies we reviewed in Chapter Five suggested broaching the subject of abuse with the child or the child's family. In fact, Lanktree, Briere, and Zaidi (1989) found that if molestation was not specifically asked about, it probably would not be uncovered. In their study, they found that a review of randomly selected outpatient charts revealed reported sexual abuse in 6.9 percent of the cases. After clinicians were instructed to directly ask about sexual abuse, they found that 31.4 percent of the next patients seen had been sexually abused. Similar studies have also found problems in reporting sexual abuse (Briere and Zaidi, forthcoming; Cavaiola and Schiff, 1988).

Given this kind of evidence, it seems clear that the issue of sexual abuse should become part of a thorough suicide evaluation, and visa versa. Among the many excellent books and articles on abuse, four that we have found particularly useful are Haugaard and Reppucci (1988), Kempe and Heyfer (1980), Kempe and Kempe (1984), and Wolfe (1987).

Special Education Students

Learning disabilities have been documented as a significant correlate of suicide in adolescence. Some of the original work by Jan-Tausch (1964) and Shaffer (1974) found significantly more children and adolescents labeled as learning disabled than youth not so labeled in their samples of suicide completers. A high ratio of learning disabled to non-learning disabled children has also been found in an acutely suicidal group of hospitalized preadolescents (Myers, Burke, and McCauley, 1985). Both ideator and attempter groups have disproportionate numbers of learning disabled students.

Further evidence that special education students are at particular risk is provided by several studies of the problem-solving capabilities of suicidal adolescents. Kenny and others (1979) found that a sample of adolescent suicide attempters had greater problems with visual-motor coordination than did a control population; Kaslow and others (1983) found deficits on the WISC-R Block Design subtest and an anagram test; and Levenson and Neuringer (1971) found deficits on the WAIS Arithmetic subtest.

Rourke proposes that there is a specific subtype of learning disability that predisposes these students to adolescent and adult depression and suicide risk (Rourke, Young, Strang, and Russell, 1986; Rourke, 1988; Rourke, Young, and Lenaars, 1989). He refers to this subtype as a "nonverbal learning disability" (NLD) and suggests that the various characteristics of an NLD result in four generalized kinds of adaptive difficulties. The first set of problems manifests as psychomotor clumsiness and some problems with tactile sensitivity. A second set of deficits is in visual-spatial organization, as also found by Kenny and others (1979). This deficit in turn can produce difficulties in understanding body language or reading the demeanor or mood of others from postural or facial expressions. A third set of difficulties can arise in dealing with novelty. Instead of orienting to and engaging flexibly with new situations, NLD adolescents experience failure in new situations and become prone to withdraw from the new. An extreme reaction can lead to social isolation. Finally, Rourke suggests that problems in intermodal integration can lead to "problems in the assessment of another's emotional state through the integration of information gleaned from his or her facial expressions, tone of voice, posture, psycho-motor patterns, and so on" (1988, p. 171).

Rourke strongly advocates identification through diagnosis of these students so that specific cognitive-behavioral interventions can be planned to help the NLD student better cope with his or her environment and therefore reduce the risk of social withdrawal, depression, and suicide. Although more data are needed in this area, and some may question the validity of Rourke's position, it does seem clear that special education students are at an increased risk.

Alternative and Continuation High School Students

Few studies have dealt with the question of whether nontra-ditional high school students are at particular risk for suicide. An example from our own experience illustrates the dilemma faced by professionals working in this area.

An intern in a continuation high school and his field super-visor were attempting to place a student with emotional problems in the county self-contained classroom for Severely Emotionally Disturbed (SED) students but could not get approval to do so from the head of the county's special education programs. It was clear from the intern's description that the student could easily be diag-nosed as conduct disordered, but California, the state in which he worked, provides no categorical funds for students exhibiting these types of behaviors, and SED programs are not devised to work with conduct-disordered youth. The intern was asked where students like this tended to be placed in his district; the answer was continuation high school.

While we believe that at least a significant minority of the students attending a continuation high school could be diagnosed as conduct disordered, many states have no provisions or codes es-tablishing formal evaluations for students that are transferred from a main campus to an alternative school. If our premise is correct, this population is being underserved, and perhaps dangerously so. Conduct-disordered youth, especially those who are clinically de-pressed and/or suffering from a substance-abuse disorder, are at particular risk for attempting and completing suicide. Unfortu-nately, for many of these youth, the conduct-disorder symptomatology draws our attention, and other highly relevant data go unnoticed.

Conclusion

A common characteristic of all the groups of students we have reviewed in this chapter is alienation. They do not "belong" in ways that are generally recognized as health promoting. Schools as institutions typically exacerbate the problem of alienation. We must find ways to reach these students even though they are frequently the most difficult types of students for us to reach. Because they have internalized alienation processes and can use them extremely well to keep themselves aloof and seemingly protected, they are resistant clients. Major process and structural changes for school-based professionals must be focused particularly on special education and alternative high school populations, where the institutional processes can unintentionally foster the alienation that these adolescents feel.

We end this chapter as we started it, highly recommending that substance-abusing, runaway, gay and lesbian, abused, special education, and continuation and alternative high school populations be screened for suicide potential. However, identification of students at risk of suicide is not in and of itself a solution. It is only the beginning of a process that should lead to prevention and intervention. The final two chapters of this part explore programmatic interventions and the systemic changes needed to support them.

8

Educating the
School Community

The goal of the educational programs discussed in this chapter is primary prevention. Primary prevention efforts are directed at the entire population, not simply those at risk of developing problems or those who are already experiencing suicidal ideation. Primary prevention involves educating the entire school population, administrators, teachers, children, and parents, about the phenomenon of adolescent suicide. The most economical method for doing this is to include a program on adolescent suicide in the regular curriculum of the school or make it a topic for presentation to parents' and teachers' organizations.

A number of model curricula have been developed, and numerous programs are under way nationwide (County School Board of Fairfax County, Virginia, 1987; California State Department of Education School Climate Unit, 1986; Ruof, Harris, and Robbie, 1987; Poland, 1986; Cole and Brotman, n.d.). This chapter describes the elements of a model curriculum, focusing on the curriculum program developed for the California public schools, one of the most comprehensive in the country. It is also highly desirable to integrate information about suicide across the curriculum, so we also describe alternate educational approaches and a model for classroom-based prevention. We conclude the chapter by addressing some of the unresolved issues in suicide education.

Classroom Programs for Adolescents

Most programs designed to introduce the concept of suicide and suicide prevention to adolescents are included as part of a

122

course in a broader topic taken by large numbers of students. The program developed in California fits within the framework of health education and was designed to be integrated with content on mental and emotional health and on the use and misuse of substances. Its lessons, however, may be included in courses in social studies, language arts, physical education, home economics and consumer education, or psychology.

The California course, like many others, is most effective for high school freshmen and sophomores, but some curricula have been developed for the junior high school level and even for the upper elementary ages. While the foundation for suicide prevention should be laid during the elementary grades, where children should be explicitly encouraged to discuss problems with caring adults, the most appropriate time to introduce the specific curriculum is at the beginning of high school, since this is when students are cognitively sophisticated enough to deal with many complex issues and to imagine how others might view the world (in the Piagetian system, when they are most likely to have begun the development of formal operational thought) and are most likely to be in contact with peers who are considering suicide. As we have mentioned, suicides under the age of twelve are rare, so introducing an explicit and detailed program focused on suicide before grade six may not be efficient.

Trained personnel should be available to respond to potential student self-referrals while the curriculum is being presented. Thus, the curriculum should not be taught just before a vacation and, if possible, should be taught early in the day so that there will be an opportunity for students to identify themselves for counseling following presentations or discussions.

Curriculum Content

Most curricula on suicide focus on increasing students' awareness of the danger signs that indicate that a person may be contemplating suicide: a suicide threat or other statement indicating a desire or intention to die; a previous suicide attempt; depression; marked changes in behavior, including changes in eating and sleeping patterns, acting-out behavior, hyperactivity, substance abuse, or high-risk-taking behavior; and making final arrangements, saying goodbye, and giving away possessions (Ross and Lee, n.d.). The warning sign of substance abuse is given specific emphasis, since recent studies reveal that many suicides in adolescents are attempted while the teen is abusing drugs or alcohol (Shafti, Carrigan, Whittinghill, and Derrick, 1985). Additional objectives of such curricula include (1) increasing the students' understanding of suicide and its causes, (2) helping students to appreciate the fact that depression is a natural and transitory part of life, (3) helping the students to understand the relationship between suicide and stress, (4) developing the students' skills for coping with stress and depression, (5) developing the students' skills for assisting friends who are suicidal, and (6) increasing the students' knowledge of school and community resources for suicidal individuals. The following list, adapted from Garland and Shaffer (1988), presents topics covered in most suicide prevention curricula and for whom the information is meant.

Topic	*Intended Audience*
1. Factual information about suicide	Students, teachers, administrators
2. Suicide warning signs	All
3. Treatment resources	All
4. Referral procedures	All (but procedures differ according to audience)
5. Confidentiality	All (but different content for different audiences)
6. Disclosures and discussion of suicidal thoughts	Students
7. Problem-solving skills	Students
8. Stress reduction	Students
9. Legal issues	Teachers, administrators
10. School policy	Teachers, administrators
11. Crisis management	Administrators, guidance staff
12. Crisis intervention	Guidance staff
13. Causes of suicide	Guidance staff
14. Suicide identification	Guidance staff

The California curriculum, written by Lisa Hunter and Donna Lloyd-Kolkin and based on content provided by Charlotte Ross (1980, 1985), consists of five separate lessons (California State Department of Education School Climate Unit, 1986). These lessons are outlined below.

Introduction. The first lesson introduces the topic of suicide and exposes common misconceptions of suicide and its causes. Among the myths exposed are that people who talk about suicide never kill themselves; that if suicidal persons really want to die, there is no way to stop them; that a person who is determined to complete a suicide will continue until he or she succeeds; and that talking to a person about suicidal feelings will inevitably cause that person to commit suicide.

The lesson begins with a general introduction, including the ground rules for discussion. The students then take a sixteen-item quiz on suicide facts and myths. Ten of the questions are true-or-false, and six are open-ended. A sample true-or-false question is "Suicidal persons really want to die, so there's no way to stop them." A discussion of the answers serves as a vehicle for communicating information and uncovering misconceptions. Finally, the students are given an assignment to gather information about community agencies that may serve as resources to adolescents who need some kind of counseling help. Each student is assigned a different agency and asked to complete a work sheet with information about the agency, such as hours, service provided, and whether parental permission is required.

Understanding Depression and How to Help. The goal of the second lesson is to help students understand the universality and transient nature of depression, to identify its symptoms, and to learn how to be helpful. In this lesson, the suicide warning signs are explicitly discussed. The relationship between depression and the abuse of drugs and alcohol is also part of the lesson. The students are asked to recount their own experiences with depression to illustrate the point that it usually passes. They are usually asked to recall a time in their life when they felt "down," depressed, or "blue." This inquiry can be conducted in open discussion, or alternatively, the students can be asked to record their experiences on a work sheet. The teacher then elicits the thoughts, feelings, and behavioral changes that occurred at these down times and may point out that behavior changes during periods of depression are observable to others and that the reactions are universal and transitory. It should be noted that the curriculum does not make a distinction between pathological or diagnosable depression and "normal" depression. Once the teacher has listed the observable behaviors of depression, these behaviors can be related to the suicide warning signs. The lesson closes with a discussion of a vignette illustrating an encounter between two adolescent peers, one of whom exhibits warning signs. The students are led to speculate about what would be helpful to the possibly suicidal character in the vignette.

Substance Abuse and Stress. The goal of the third lesson, "Understanding Substance Abuse and Stress," is to help students recognize the roles of substance abuse and stress in the development of suicidal feelings and to teach them some skills for coping with stress and depression. One coping skill that is emphasized is how to identify people to whom they may turn during a time of crisis.

The lesson begins with a reference to the vignette from the first lesson and a request that the students list the various stresses present in adolescents' lives. In the discussion of stress, a distinction is made between positive and negative stress: Positive stress, such as experienced when a student appears in a school play, may be life enhancing and motivating, but negative stress, such as the stress brought on by the loss of a loved one, can lead to illness and feelings of being overwhelmed. The discussion centers on two kinds of individuals who are at most risk for high stress levels: those who are having difficulty with school and peers and those who are perfectionists and set too high standards for themselves. Next, the teacher turns the focus to ways in which individuals react to stress, pointing out that drugs and alcohol use is a way of trying to escape stress but that this "escape" also exacerbates the problems. Alcohol use creates depressive reactions as well as risk-taking behavior, which are in turn connected to suicidal behavior. The objective is to impart an understanding that periods of stress and depression will come to an end at some point and that it is possible to examine a stressful situation and devise ways of attacking it, thus counteracting feelings of helplessness and hopelessness. Students learn that regular exercise, relaxation techniques, and talking problems over with others are ways of managing and overcoming stress. They next identify on a work sheet specific individuals they could turn to in times of stress and what the characteristics of such individuals are. Finally, students are helped to formulate responses to peers who they suspect are abusing drugs. They are shown that awareness of the possible outcome of drug abuse—suicide—can lead to honest messages about concern for the friend's well-being.

Helping Skills and the Conspiracy of Silence. The fourth lesson is directed specifically at giving students the skills necessary to be helpful to friends who are suicidal. This lesson is predicated on the assumption (verified by Nelson, 1987) that teenagers in time of stress are most likely to turn to a friend for assistance. The helping skills stressed in this lesson are listening to others, being honest about one's feelings, sharing feelings, and getting help from an adult who can support the person in need.

The lesson begins with a review of the suicide warning signs and the presentation of a listening-helping model based on the Rogerian tradition (Benjamin, 1987). The instructor emphasizes the importance of taking talk about suicide seriously. Next, students are given practice in making specific helping responses to peers. Finally, a vignette is presented, following up on the first one, in which a friend engages a suicidal adolescent in an appropriate and exemplary way. Included in the vignette and highlighted in the ensuring discussion is a simple approach to assessing the urgency of the suicide by which the students are taught to ask: (1) Have you thought about suicide? (2) What method have you thought of using to kill yourself? (3) When do you think you are going to do this?

The emphasis in this lesson is that adolescents can be most helpful to peers by establishing a contract that they will not take immediate action and hurt themselves and by referring their friend to a professional. The teacher points out strongly that keeping a friend's suicidal thoughts and actions secret and confidential is really not in the best interests of that friend and, in fact, can be very dangerous.

School and Community Resources. The final lesson is entitled "You Are Not Alone: All About Helping." The goal of this lesson is to continue the student's introduction to helping skills and to increase students' understanding of appropriate and available school and community resources. The lesson starts with a review of the helping skills covered in the previous lesson. Next, the discussion turns to ways to get a friend who is at high risk of suicide to someone who can help. As a follow-up on the first lesson's assignment, the available community resources are explicitly listed and discussed, and procedures for contracting them are presented. Much of the time during this lesson is devoted to general discussion so that students' questions about suicide can be answered.

Teacher Training

Whether the person delivering the suicide curriculum is a counselor, a school psychologist, or another kind of pupil services worker, his or her role here is that of a teacher. Those assigned to teach this curriculum should receive special training in teaching about mental health issues and should be interested and concerned about this particular problem. Teachers should probably volunteer for this instructional assignment and expect to do extra preparation. Release time should be made available for such teachers to attend training sessions at suicide prevention centers or other mental health training grounds. The teacher should have close relationships with the guidance staff and be supported with information and consultation during the teaching of this and other sensitive units.

In training sessions, teachers are led through the lesson plans that have been developed to teach about suicide and are helped to plan a curriculum. They are given sufficient background information to elevate them to the status of relative expert and may be provided with role playing and other devices to make them comfortable with teaching the curriculum. An important part of the curriculum is getting teachers to understand their own feelings and attitudes about suicide as an act and toward suicide attempters and completers. Creating ease with this highly emotionally charged curriculum is not always easy. Teachers should be supervised carefully during their first attempts to teach this curriculum and should have adequate resources, both human and media, to support them. One effective strategy is to team teach the unit with a mental health expert or an experienced and skilled teacher.

In training sessions for teachers, it should be emphasized that instruction on a topic that is emotionally laden requires more time for discussion and assimilation than does instruction on other types of topics. The importance of a nonjudgmental attitude cannot be over-stressed (Jones, 1968). Because of the sensitive nature of the topic, the training should also include some discussion of confidentiality, its limits, and how to discuss this with students. Such discussions are particularly important because one of the concepts presented in the curriculum is that students should not keep peers' secrets when they involve suicide. The guidelines for the California program suggest not requiring names on papers for some of the exercises, although this practice may create a problem if a student in the course decides to communicate dangerous suicidal thoughts via the class assignments. Perhaps a better practice is to be sure that the papers handed in are carefully collected by the teacher and kept secure from casual glimpses by peers.

Training might also emphasize that the teacher must be prepared to monitor discussions carefully and to intervene in them by interrupting skillfully when particular students reveal too much about themselves. Students sometimes get swept up in a discussion and say things that they later regret. Even worse, some students may withdraw and pull back after too much exposure. Teachers also must be comfortable in disclosing some of their own feelings and experiences during the course of the program. This self-disclosure must be made with a reasonable degree of comfort and naturalness, since it serves as a model for the students' own disclosure. Finally, training should emphasize that the obligation of teachers is to inculcate knowledge and attitudes about personal problems, not to substitute for counselors or therapists (Ross, 1985).

Educational Materials and Resources

Films. Many curricula make use of films, filmstrips, and videotapes to stimulate motivation and interest. Resource A at the end of this book provides a list of such materials that may be used for student programs, school staff training, or parent groups. Some of the films listed are intended to be used for a particular purpose, such as training teachers and guidance staff prior to undertaking a curriculum unit on suicide; others may be used with multiple audiences.

Media must be selected with care, since films vary in their quality and application to a particular population. In addition, films that sensationalize or romanticize suicide should be avoided. The presentation of any film needs to be accompanied by sufficient time for questions, answers, and general discussion of reactions to the film. Many of the resources, particularly filmstrips, come with teachers' guides and lesson plans to assist in the discussion.

Written Materials. The material in the California program includes a number of work sheets, quizzes, and simulation games to facilitate discussion. Examples of these are contained in the implementation guide (California State Department of Education School Climate Unit, 1986). Another source of well-developed supplementary materials is the guide produced by the County School Board of Fairfax County, Virginia (1987). This booklet even includes samples of schoolwide memos issued on various aspects of the suicide prevention program, as well as handouts for use in the classroom.

For most classwork, supplemental reading material on the topic should be available. Resource B includes a list of pamphlets that present information about suicide in a brief form, reading materials that follow up and supplement lessons, and curriculum packages.

Consultants. An important resource for any program is individuals from outside the school available to assist in the instructional program. Both community agencies and professionals in private practice are often willing to cooperate with public schools in putting on a special program. It may be particularly useful to have knowledgeable therapists available to help students discuss their experiences and to answer their questions. When a guest speaker or consultant is to be included in the curriculum, he or she should be oriented to the information that will be covered in the course and should be given a copy of the curriculum before meeting with students.

Other Curriculum Approaches

Substance-Abuse Prevention. Suicide prevention may be addressed indirectly in the context of another course or subject matter, for example, as part of a substance-abuse prevention program. Since suicide is often the outcome of other kinds of social problems, such as drug and alcohol abuse, or of failed adolescent attempts at identity formation (see Nelson, Farberow, and Litman, 1988; Garfinkel Froese, and Hood, 1982), it may be equally effective to address these precipitating problems directly, realizing that, as a secondary effect, suicide may be prevented. Other programs that could have a direct effect on the contributors to suicide are programs on drug education and social studies courses featuring human relations, training, and development. Botvin's (1983) Life Skills Training Program is an example of a drug education program that provides adolescents with skills necessary to resist drug involvement and supplies them with alternative coping strategies so that they may be able to avoid excessive drug experimentation. The program consists of eighteen lessons divided among three components: personal skills, social skills, and substance abuse–specific information and skills (Botvin and Dusenbury, 1987). The personal skills, which are based on social learning theory, are developing a general decision-making strategy, recognizing social influences affecting decisions, recognizing persuasive tactics, formulating counter-arguments and other cognitive strategies for resisting advertising pressure, and developing techniques for coping with anxiety. During the personal skills phase, the students use the principle of self-change and self-reinforcement to improve a personally selected skill or behavior.

The social skills taught are communication skills, recognizing the causes of misunderstandings and guidelines for avoiding them, overcoming shyness, initiating social contacts (including those with the opposite sex), basic conversational skills, and assertiveness skills (see also Rotheram-Borus, 1988, on assertiveness). As-

sertiveness in resisting peer pressure to smoke, drink, or use mari-
juana is emphasized.

Specifically related to substance abuse are sessions devoted to
the negative short- and long-term consequences of drug use, as well
as other information on drug abuse. Included in the curriculum is
a laboratory demonstration using a biofeedback device to illustrate
the negative physiological effects of cigarette smoking.

Many of the same elements of listening skills and communication skills covered in this and other programs are covered as part
of suicide prevention programs. What is missing in these programs,
of course, is specific information of suicide warning signs, information about community agencies and other resources relevant to suicide, and the special injunction to break promises to keep suicidal
thoughts and plans secret and to seek adult help.

Competence Enhancement Programs. Another indirect approach to the prevention of suicide is competence enhancement
programs (Cowen, 1985). These programs teach general coping
skills and stress-reduction procedures. They are intended to help
adolescents to be more aware of the changes and pressures in their
lives and to develop positive ways to address them. This approach
to prevention seems particularly appropriate, since it is clear from
the research reviewed in Chapter Two that suicidal adolescents lack
important social skills and coping strategies.

One particularly important set of competencies is social
skills (Matson and Ollendick, 1988). Exemplary programs are Spivack and Shure's (1974) Interpersonal Cognitive Problem Solving,
Elias's Improving Social Awareness—Social Problem-Solving
(Elias and others, 1986), and Gesten and Weissberg's Social
Problem-Solving (Gesten, Weissberg, Amish, and Smith, 1987). The
latter program, for example, consists of thirty-four lessons designed
for children in grades two through five that teach an eight-step
social-problem-solving process: (1) look for signs of upset feelings,
(2) know exactly what the problem is, (3) decide on your goal, (4)
stop and think before you act, (5) think of as many solutions as you
can, (6) think ahead to what will probably happen next after each
solution, (7) when you think you have a really good solution, try
it, and (8) if your first solution does not work, try again. The process

is taught in the general context of conflict resolution and results in improvement in attitudes, behaviors, and adjustment (Gesten, Weissberg, Amish, and Smith, 1987). The skills developed through this type of program enable children to cope more effectively with social problems and stresses that may result in suicide and thus serve to prevent suicide. Other programs in the general category of competence enhancement involve relaxation training, meditation, and self-hypnosis (Woolfolk and Richardson (1987). A popular program by a prominent cognitive behaviorist is Meichenbaum's (1985) stress inoculation training.

The skills fostered in competence enhancement programs are also often covered in suicide prevention programs. These programs are for younger children, however, and may be preventive in a different way, in that they address some of the causes of suicide before a student becomes actively suicidal. However, one major correlate of suicide, psychopathology, is perhaps outside the scope of any educational program.

Teachers teaching these and other kinds of programs and curricula need to be aware that suicide and suicidal ideation may come up in the course of the program and should be prepared to address them as they occur. The fact that suicide is not a focus of these programs does not mean that the topic will not spontaneously arise. Another key element not covered in these programs is the imperative to break confidentiality when a friend is talking about suicide.

Bibliotherapy. Another way of integrating suicide prevention information into the curriculum is through a structured program of reading. *Bibliotherapy* may refer to a variety of practices, from the careful individual selection of books for a patient by a psychotherapist to informal activities using literature for growth and adjustment purposes (Bernstein, 1977). Reading about other adolescents' experiences with problems, coping with depression, rejecting suicide as an option, and the aftermath of a suicide can offer a number of benefits. If the book is a good one, it will foster the opportunity to identify with others or with new ideas. The identification process allows readers to perceive their own problems more clearly and to use the figure in the story to talk and think about problems that they themselves have. Reading about others also lets adolescents know that they are not alone in their feelings and that others have coped with similar feelings and situations in the past. Reading expands horizons and introduces the reader to alternative ways of framing problems and alternative solutions. New skills may also be learned about and copied.

Although we have not located a school-based bibliotherapy program specifically directed at suicide prevention that has been carefully evaluated, there are a number of excellent resources on the general topic (for example, Bernstein, 1977; Fassler, 1978). Bibliographies such as the one listed in Resource C appear in many curriculum materials. The types of works range from fiction and biography to science and other nonfiction. Popular films, too, may be used with care.

Successful bibliotherapy is characterized by *excellent materials* in which the author communicates important human truths; a *good match* between the material and the student's abilities (reading and cognitive), needs, and personality; and a *skilled discussion leader* (therapist, librarian, teacher) who is able to make the match, monitor attitudes, and create self-awareness in students (Moody and Limper, 1971). Making a match between the student and the book does not imply that specific books need be assigned. Bibliotherapy seems to be most effective when students select their own books from among a pool (Bernstein, 1977). This practice keeps bibliotherapy from becoming too intrusive, creating defensiveness, or intensifying a difficulty, since students can choose books that are appropriate to their emotional status and level of interest. Creating a collection of materials on suicide prevention is not easy. Although one might start with the books listed in Resource C, the bibliotherapist should read all the books chosen, judge each on its merit as literature, check its factual content, estimate its reading difficulty and interest level, and consider the religious or moral values put forward.

Besides creating a collection of books on appropriate topics, the adult guide's responsibilities include conducting a discussion of what has been read. During the discussion, the guide should listen actively, clarify what is being said, and highlight some of the specific coping skills used by protagonists. Quizzing the student about details, conducting literary criticism, and asking why the book was selected are not usually appropriate or necessary, assuming that the book is a good one. The specific training of bibliotherapists should be similar to the training of teachers preparing to teach a set suicide curriculum.

Integrating the Topic of Suicide into the Entire Curriculum. As we have observed earlier in the chapter, information on suicide should not be confined to a single unit. Important topics such as sex education and driver safety have a way of losing their impact when they become isolated in the curriculum. We do not wish to have this happen to a unit on suicide. Some courses, particularly those dealing with social studies or literature, will be more logical places than others to bring up topic. Is the English teacher prepared to discuss the role of suicide in *Romeo and Juliet?* we might ask. A comprehensive program would involve all teachers in some kind of training about suicide so that they will be more comfortable when the topic comes up in academic discussions and so they can aid in the identification process. We turn to these training programs next.

Programs for School Personnel

For many reasons, it is important to orient school personnel to the problems of suicide prevention. School personnel are gate-keepers or potential "rescuers" who are in contact with most ado-lescents and, with training, can intervene to get help for those who are suicidal. Separate programs may be prepared for administrators, teachers, counselors, and school psychologists, or they can receive a common set of training experiences.

Administrators

Programs for administrators often stress the need for policy statements about suicide prevention and for contingency planning and are designed to help administrators think through ways of im-plementing programs in their particular schools, including for staff training and supplemental assistance in counseling. The kinds of school policies discussed in Chapter Ten could form the nucleus of an in-service program for administrators and policy makers. The legal and ethical issues discussed in Chapter Eleven may also be addressed in programs for administrators.

Guidance Staff

Guidance staff also need extra training in suicide prevention. A number of films listed in Resource A have been produced specifically for mental health workers rather than for children. Programs for guidance staff should provide detailed coverage of such issues as the causes of youth suicide and ways of identifying children at risk and facilitating referrals. This volume, particularly Chapters Two, Three, and Four, is intended to form the basis for a program in staff development, but reading these chapters alone will not be sufficient. We recommend that a training program include a workshop component in which role playing or other simulation activities may take place so that the skills in interviewing, intervening, and referring may be practiced before a program is implemented.

An unusual resource for training school mental health professionals is the computer-controlled videodisc curriculum developed for medical students by the National Institute of Mental Health and the National Library of Medicine. Entitled *"The Suicidal Adolescent: Identification, Risk Assessment, and Intervention"* (see Resource A), the program requires an IBM personal computer and a videodisc player. The user controls the video screen by selecting options. The program presents case studies and asks the user to make decisions during the process of conducting a time-limited interview, attending to user attitudes and considering practical realities, assessing suicidal risk, and intervening with a variety of options. At any time during the program, the student can refer to critical reference materials in the computer text files.

Teachers

In programs for teachers, the stress is on the myths, signs, and symptoms of suicide, responding to suicidal crises (making a referral), and knowledge of referral sources. Mental health personnel from community agencies are often invited to participate in the awareness training and to provide a personal bridge between school and outside resources. Programs may use a variety of training strategies, including lectures, audiovisual materials, self-evaluation exercises, small-group discussions, case histories, and role playing (Ryerson, 1987).

All of the available programs for school personnel cover generally the same topics addressed in the programs for children. Information about such issues as suicide dynamics and warning signs is at the heart of the curriculum; it also presents ways to respond to a child at risk and to see that the child gets help from an appropriate source. The difference is usually in the depth and sophistication of the information presented.

Research and Evaluation

The American Association of Suicidologists Committee (Smith, Eyman, Dyck, and Ryerson, 1987) has surveyed the suicide prevention programs available in the United States and Canada. They have found that most programs are conducted in the public school classrooms, although a substantial number are conducted in community-based crisis centers. The programs that they surveyed might begin as early as kindergarten or as late as the eleventh grade, but most were designed for children above the sixth grade. One-third of the programs included a component directed at school personnel. The training time averaged five hours. The committee rated relative emphasis of various content areas for all classroom educational components on a four-point scale, from 0 (not emphasized) to 3 (vital to program), as shown in the following list:

Content	*Mean Rating*
Myths, signs, facts, and symptoms	2.84
Learning about referral sources	2.78
Identification and acceptability of feelings	2.70
How to respond to a suicidal crisis	2.65
Stress management, coping, and problem solving	2.47
Communication skills	2.42

The nature of ambivalence 2.35
Motivations for suicide 2.34
The nature of depression 2.21
Risk assessment 2.17
Mourning and bereavement 1.46
Philosophical issues (for example, the right to die) 0.86
The realness of death 0.63
Religious and moral injunctions 0.47

One-third of the programs used integrated printed materials. The programs for teachers were more likely to feature the lecture format (47 percent), although many featured discussion (37 percent), experimental exercises (14 percent), and films (12 percent).

Conclusion

Many excellent curricula on the issue of suicide among adolescents are available, and it has been estimated that more than 400 programs are in operation in the United States and Canada. However, a number of issues with respect to educational programs on youth suicide are still to be resolved. Until more evaluative research is done, we will not know what aspects of these programs are most effective and what their anticipated as well as unanticipated outcomes are. (Issues related to program evaluation are discussed in greater detail in Chapter Eleven.) Those involved in school programs are proud of their efforts and feel that it is worth while; nevertheless, issues about the dangers of romanticizing or deemphasizing the aberrant aspects of suicide must be seriously considered.

In addition to program effectiveness, two other general issues must be settled: the appropriate place for suicide prevention in the curriculum and whether suicide or social skills should be the focus. As more and more subjects are introduced into the curriculum, it is becoming more and more crowded, and many reformers point to the fact that the amount of time spent on basic skills either has been declining or is not comparable to that among competitor industrial nations, such as Japan. In general, those who wish to add to the school curriculum must justify any addition in the strongest terms, because it will imply the dropping of some other course to the curriculum. A strong argument can be made, however, for the importance of adding a few hours in the academic year devoted to this serious problem.

There is also controversy surrounding the issue of whether the program should focus on specific information about suicide or be more generally oriented toward social skills and coping with stress. It has been argued that a skills orientation will allow for intervention earlier in the chain leading to suicidal behavior. Felner, Jason, Moritsugu, and Farber (1983) argue persuasively that our efforts should take into account our research and knowledge about the casual chains leading to the problems that we are attempting to address. They believe strongly that efforts should be directed toward base causes rather than symptoms, such as suicidal behavior. On the side of offering an explicit curriculum on suicide is research suggesting that information does not always transfer as one hopes and that specific instruction in context is needed. There is no substitution for knowledge of community resources and information about the warning signs of suicidal behavior. This debate might be resolved by a comprehensive suicide prevention program including both elements explicitly directed at adolescents' knowledge of suicide and elements directed more generally and earlier in a child's life toward providing social and coping skills that can be used in times of stress.

An aspect of school programs that was not discussed in this chapter is peer counseling programs. While one goal of the educational approaches described here is to enable peers to be more supportive and to facilitate referral, peer counseling programs are special programs in themselves. Chapter Nine discusses these programs and other preventive activities with peers as a dominant component.

9

Involving Peers
in Suicide Prevention

Given a choice of who would be the recipient of a suicidal message from a distraught adolescent, 91 percent of a normal high school sample indicated that if they were to tell someone, they would first confide in a friend rather than a parent, teacher, or other adult (Ross, 1985). When Shaffer, Garland, and Bacon (1987), however, interviewed a group of disturbed adolescents, they found that only 59 percent believed that they would confide in their peers. Although this difference in numbers is dramatic, the fact remains that peers are the group most likely to know about suicidal ideation and intention. Other researchers, such as Friedman, Asnis, Boeck, and DiFiore (1987), found that about two-thirds of a group of attempters did not tell anyone prior to their attempt, and fewer than two-thirds told anyone about the attempt after they had failed. These data suggest that if adolescents confide in anyone, it is most likely to be a peer, but that they do not confide in others as often as helping professionals would like.

Developmental theorists, of course, point out the importance of age mates for the important work of adolescence, the formation of an identity. As Erik Erikson states, adolescents use other adolescents as a sounding board to discuss their thoughts, feelings, and plans for the future in an effort to create their newly changing identity (1962). Any discussion of suicide prevention among adolescents thus must include a focus on peer relations. It is clear that adolescents need to be educated about suicide, especially about the signs of suicidal intention and what to do if a friend begins to exhibit these signs, but there are also other preventive activities using peers that may be undertaken. For example, peer screening activities and counseling programs can assist in the identification of suicidal youth. In addition, a school climate that fosters the development of friendships and contacts between adolescents may decrease the feelings of isolation and loneliness that contribute to depression and suicidal behavior. Many of the stressors that exacerbate this depression and trigger suicidal behavior can be modified or ameliorated through the creation of a positively oriented youth community. This chapter discusses both peer counseling programs and the creation of an adolescent peer community in the schools.

In Chapter Two, we reviewed a number of factors that have been associated with suicide and can be used to generate a causal model of suicidal behavior. We acknowledged the importance of biological predisposing risk factors and the contribution of various psychopathologies to the explanation of suicidal behavior. We also suggested other influential contributing factors, such as hopelessness, stress (particularly stress related to sexuality, achievement pressure, and personal loss), and family attitudes about suicide. We reviewed the evidence that a lack of interpersonal problem-solving capacity contributes to the likelihood of suicide. These factors combined with various precipitating events, such as disciplinary crises, sudden losses, or relationship difficulties, round out a complex model of suicidal behavior that can be used to guide preventive activities. As many of the significant others in most adolescent lives are peers, it seems reasonable that efforts at prevention should be directed at variables related to conditions in the student's school environment by creating structures in the schools that improve communications, lead to better interpersonal problem solving, and create a sense of purpose, direction, and community. We believe that a focus on peer groups in schools might prevent many suicidal actions by interrupting the causal chain. The programs reviewed in this chapter are not explicitly designed to prevent suicidal behavior; there are other valid reasons for offering these programs. Nonetheless, it seems logical that a comprehensive program aimed at improving the peer culture for adolescents may also reduce the number of suicide attempts and completions.

Peer Counseling

A number of secondary schools have developed peer counseling programs. From a survey in California, Wilson (1986) estimated that 22 percent of the high schools and 6 percent of the junior high schools in that state had peer counseling programs. A program developed in Palo Alto, California (Varenhorst, 1976), is typical. Volunteers from the student body, juniors and seniors in high school, are offered an eighteen-hour training course in counseling skills. After the students have been trained, a professional coordinator assigns them to students or situations that are appropriate for receiving help from trained peer counselors. The problem areas dealt with are alcohol abuse, school attendance, drunk driving, academic achievement, new students, social problems, sexuality, and peer relationships (Wilson, 1986). The peer counselors receive continuing supervision and training in weekly practicum groups. In addition, there is a training course for adults to prepare them to function as supervisors and trainers of future peer counseling training groups. A part-time coordinator and adult supervisor-trainer administer the program. The program is intended to serve students who are new to the school and community, students who are lonely and isolated, and those with physical and mental handicaps. It is not intended to serve severely disturbed students, students involved in the drug culture, or other students clearly in need of counseling from adult professionals. It is recognized, however, that the peers might become a bridge between troubled students and professionals who can better serve the troubled students' needs.

During training, peer counselors are taught communication skills, alternatives for dealing with common problems such as family relations, breaking into cliques of students, health problems, peer relations, and the strategies and ethics of counseling. Included in the training are how to make referrals to adults, the importance of confidentiality, and the limits of the peer counseling relationship. One of the most comprehensive and helpful discussions of peer counseling training is found in Fulmer (1978).

Outcome studies of peer counseling programs suggest that they can be successful in serving a large number of students and that they are as beneficial to the peer counselors themselves as they are to the peer clients. Peer counseling programs are perhaps more common at the college and university level, where they have also been evaluated as successful (Giddan and Austin, 1982). Most originators of peer counseling programs do not intend that peers should deal with suicidal students, and we certainly do not recommend that suicidal students be referred to peer counselors, but we do note that these resources may be available in a school. We concur with Ruof, Harris, and Robbie's (1987) recommendation that suicidal students not work only with peer counselors. Obviously, part of the training of peer counselors should be a clear emphasis on recognizing suicidal ideation and signs and making explicit referrals for suicidal students.

To the extent that helping a lonely and isolated peer is an objective of many peer counseling programs, however, they may be perceived as being preventive. Peers may be able to help one another break through some of the social barriers that exist in secondary schools. In any case, these programs supply some human contact that may otherwise be missing in large, impersonal institutions. Also, peers can help other peers develop good friendship skills and assist with other dilemmas, such as dating. Much of what peer counselors are learning and teaching is interpersonal and social problem-solving skills, and these are undoubtedly helpful for adolescents at risk. Peer counselors may have contact with students who in turn are in contact with suicidal individuals. A peer counseling program in a secondary school may be an effective way of providing a network of watchful students on the lookout for potentially suicidal individuals. It is likely that peer counselors provide a resource that is unavailable in any other form.

An example of this was provided by one of our students. An intern school psychologist was called to her senior high placement one morning because Cindy, a senior that the intern had supervised in the peer counseling program at the school, was crying and upset and asked to see her. It turned out that the afternoon before, Cindy was asked by a counselee to keep confidential the fact that the counselee had stocked some of her mother's medications and was contemplating suicide. Cindy agreed to maintain confidentiality if the counselee agreed to meet the following day. The counselee did not come to school the next morning, and Cindy panicked. After clarifying the issue, the intern called the counselee at home and discovered that she was at home with her mother and had not attempted suicide. A member of the school crisis team was dispatched to the home to conduct a suicide evaluation and review the situation while the intern debriefed the peer counselor. Not only is this a useful example of how peer counselors can "screen" for peer suicidality, it also illustrates both the need to continue stressing the limits of confidentiality and the potential risk that a peer counselor could become a "survivor" traumatized by a suicide.

The key to any successful peer counseling program is effective supervision and coordination (D'Andrea and Salovey, 1983). Programs cannot be set up and left to run themselves. Supervisors must be on the lookout for signs of suicidal intent missed by their supervisees and be available to receive and act on referrals for suicide. In addition, if there is a district crisis intervention team, they can be used as an additional resource. Contacts between peer programs and district programs should be explicitly structured and maintained.

Conflict Resolution Programs

A number of schools around the nation have instituted "conflict resolution" or "conflict management" programs, which are similar to peer counseling in some respects and different in others. These student-staffed operations are intended to take the place of adult intervention in disagreements and disputes that arise in the school. As do peer counseling programs, conflict resolution programs select students, usually natural leaders in the school, and train them in listening and problem-solving skills. The students also receive some kind of formal designation as conflict managers and badges of office at the conclusion of their training. In elementary schools, they may wear "conflict manager" T-shirts or otherwise be identified to their peers. Conflict managers are called in to help when there are disputes between children on the playground, between classes, or during instruction. The idea is to avoid the escalation of a conflict into a full-blown problem calling for serious disciplinary action. Conflict managers intervene early to help students express their problems clearly and reach their own resolutions of disputes. Often, disciplinarians on the school faculty, such as deans or vice-principals, offer students a choice between traditional discipline by adults or referral to a conflict resolution team. In addition to disputes between students, conflict resolution teams are also sometimes used to resolve disputes between students and teachers.

In one school with a conflict resolution program, a fight that occurred after one girl accidentally bumped another was sent to a conflict resolution team. As the conflict manager unraveled the events and, more importantly, the thoughts that had led up to the fight, it became clear that one of the students involved was a social isolate who believed that she was being rejected by the other girls because of her immigrant parents' behavior in the community. When it turned out that a number of other girls were actually interested in and attracted to the isolate but repelled by her distant, "stuck-up" behavior, the result of the conflict resolution process was not only to clear the air around the fight but also to correct a number of mistaken ideas. This resulted in the isolate becoming integrated into a group at school, which enhanced her social status and self-concept.

The establishment of conflict resolution programs in schools has been facilitated by the National Association for Mediation in Education (NAME), founded to serve as a clearinghouse for information about conflict resolution programs. The organization publishes a number of helpful publications (for example, Cheatham, 1989). Outcome studies on conflict resolution programs have shown a decrease in the incidence of violence and fighting and improvement in attitudes toward conflict, in the personal and emotional development of the peer mediators, and in measures of "consumer" or disputant satisfaction (Lam, 1988). Programs have been evaluated throughout the country, particularly the prominent ones located in New York City and San Francisco. In most evaluations, the qualitative and anecdotal evidence is stronger than the quantitative evidence; nevertheless, the latter does indicate positive effects on student mediators, the general student body, and teachers.

To the extent that suicide is correlated with undirected and strong feelings of anger, conflict resolution programs will serve a preventive purpose. Not only can disputes be settled, but negotiat-

ing and problem-solving strategies are explicitly taught and practiced in real-life situations. Feelings of hopelessness engendered in
a student faced with seemingly insolvable problems can be dissi-
pated with skillful peer negotiation. On the other hand, conflict
managers need to be helped to recognize that students who are ha-
bitually in conflict and who may show signs of emotional instability or depression are at risk for suicide and should be referred to an
appropriate adult. With awareness of the signs of suicidal intent,
they can be frontline resources in an identification network of peers.

Extracurricular Activities

Another contributor to (or at least correlate of) teenage suicide is a sense of isolation and hopelessness about the future. One
way to combat isolation in a large secondary school is to make sure
that there are a variety of extracurricular activities available to students and that students are encouraged to participate in them. Extracurricular activities include athletics, student government, and
various interest-oriented clubs. Such clubs and activities can improve the peer culture of the institution by creating a setting where
like-minded individuals may form friendships. In many secondary
schools, faculty are paid for their time after hours as coaches or as
sponsors of clubs and other kinds of activities, such as drama and
stagecraft. The danger is, of course, that clubs and groups of students can become very cliquish and set up an atmosphere of exclu-
siveness so that some students may be very deliberately discrimi-
nated against and thereby isolated. The existence of extracurricular
activities by itself does not guarantee that there will be preventive
outcomes. In addition to creating the activities, guidance personnel
must be willing to help sponsors and others supervise the programs
carefully so that they remain open to all who are interested and to
develop additional venues to ensure a variety of options for
students.

Faculty sponsors are often closer to the peer culture or a
subset of the peer culture than are other school staff members and
thus will more often hear rumors or be the confidants of troubled
youth. This group of teachers will need to be particularly well

informed about suicidal potential and skilled at facilitating referrals.

Work Experience Programs

Perhaps the most important socioemotional task of adolescence is gaining a sense of identity (Erikson, 1962). Much of an individual's identity is gained through finding a satisfactory occupation, as well as through close interpersonal relationships. One solution to meeting the vocational needs for a wide variety of students is to create work experience programs, particularly for noncollege-bound youth. By giving them an introduction to the broader world outside of school and an opportunity to do meaningful work that may not be of an academic nature, a work experience program may improve the self-esteem and mental health of many students. Those students who are not oriented to academic matters and find the academic emphasis in school unmotivating and alienating can find peer connections in these settings. In addition, work experience programs introduce youth to caring adults in the workplace. They may become mentors and a source of support for alienated youth that is lacking in the peer culture. A number of individuals who have been vulnerable to later developmental problems have overcome severely limited backgrounds by forming an attachment to an adult outside of the family (Werner and Smith, 1986). There is evidence to suggest that work experience programs may be more important for males (who are at higher risk of completed suicide) than for females. In an interesting study of 407 high school students, Simons and Murphy (1985), using a sophisticated multivariate path analysis, concluded that "for males, employment problems were the best predictor of suicide ideation" (p. 431). These results strengthen the case for the preventive effect of vocationally oriented programs.

Student Advocates

Similar to a conflict resolution program is one that establishes a student advocate or ombudsman in the school to act as a mediator in problems between students and faculty. Although student advocates are often adults, they may be student peers. Having such a mediator who is clearly not identified with the administration or faculty of the school can permit a number of problems to surface. Typical problems include conflicts related to achievement or practices fostering undue anxiety or competition in the classroom. These kinds of conflicts, of course, may precipitate suicidal ideation if they are perceived as unfair and students see no hope of a reasonable outcome. Usually, an ombudsman helps manage more ordinary disputes but any reduction in student-teacher conflicts can be helpful in improving the school climate. Once again, because of the position, the student advocate may be one of the first to hear of suicidal behavior and must be sensitized to and prepared to act on any information received.

Assessing the Peer Culture

One tool for assessing whether a school's climate is conducive to good mental health is Gottfredson's (1984) Effective School Battery, a set of questionnaires designed to be given confidentially to students and teachers to provide objective measures of a school's strengths and weaknesses in such areas as safety, morale, race relations, and administrative effectiveness. It provides two kinds of information: (1) the students' and teachers' perceptions of the climate of the school and (2) the characteristics of the students and teachers. This battery was developed at the Center for the Social Organization of the School at the Johns Hopkins University and has been well researched and validated.

Another school climate assessment device is the Classroom Environment Scale, second edition, by Moos and Trickett (1987). This instrument focuses on the teacher-student and student-student relationship and on the organizational structure of a junior or senior high classroom and yields nine scales. It was produced as part of an attempt to measure a number of social climate scales in various institutions, such as schools and hospitals, and has been used fairly extensively in research. Walberg and Thomas (1974) are the authors of another such scale that can be used with the early grades, although their focus is on the "openness" of education rather than classroom environment.

If the results of these assessments suggest that peer culture is an unfriendly one or that the school climate is not facilitative of learning, then a number of steps can be taken to correct the situation, not the least of which would be the establishment of peer programs such as those described in this chapter.

Conclusion

This chapter and others have highlighted the importance of peers in the identification of, intervention in, and prevention of youth suicide. Peers may be used in screening and in facilitating referral to school personnel. More importantly, perhaps, they can be helped to create a school culture that reduces the stressors that lead to suicidal ideation. The notion of school spirit is an old-fashioned one, but there is little question that the social environment of a school can be improved by caring adults. We strongly believe that creating a climate of openness and acceptance in a school, where students are involved in meaningful activities, is one of the strongest preventive activities available to school personnel.

We are not suggesting the creation of a number of new or innovative peer programs, although we have outlined programs in this chapter that may not be operational at a school. Rather, we recommend that current programs be reexamined, evaluated, and modified, if need be, with an eye to improving the social milieu for *all* members of the school community. Particular attention should be paid to the at-risk populations discussed in Chapter Seven. Traditionally, school programs are overbalanced toward setting up competitive relations between peers rather than cooperative interactions. Some competition cannot be avoided and is, indeed, necessary, but too much emphasis on "winners" and "losers," especially for some adolescents, can prove hurtful. Peer programs in a school must be designed for everyone, not just a clique of successful students. The programs must reach potential dropouts, drug users, and other alienated youth, who, as we have noted, are most likely to consider suicide.

In so many ways, peers are the key ingredient to a successful response to the suicide challenge. They are central to identification, prevention, and reparation. The more students are empowered within the system rather than objects of the system, the more the system will be aware of and able to meet the needs of the student body.

Part Four:
Influencing the System

10

Making Institutions Sensitive to Suicide

There are limits to the effectiveness of efforts directed at individual children and their parents and teachers. The institutions in which the children and their caregivers function must also be a focus of intervention if suicide is to be prevented and the impact of completed or attempted suicides lessened. The school as social system must be emphasized, because it is the single social institution through which all children pass and certainly the one that occupies the majority of their waking hours. Most of this chapter is devoted to exploring ways in which the school as a system can be sensitized to the problem of adolescent suicide and prepared to cope with this wide-ranging problem. Other institutions are not exempt, however, and the mental health system, the criminal justice system, and organized religious institutions can also be involved in suicide prevention. Ideally, the various systems could collaborate and support each other's interventions. Beyond the local community, in the broader society, some interventions and activities need to take place to bring about more effective policies that will assist in preventing or at least reducing the frequency of adolescent suicide.

District Preparedness

Creating a District Policy

Most school district leaders and boards of education are aware of and concerned about adolescent suicide. Although few districts have gone so far as to create a districtwide policy on suicide, such a policy can focus attention on the problem and lead to careful planning and thought about local problems and needs. Another purpose of developing a districtwide suicide policy statement, besides helping to ensure the safety of students, is to protect the staff and school from charges of negligence.

An effective policy statement documents the school staff members' responsibilities, affirms the district's intention to be aware of the suicide problem, prepares individuals to cope with the problem, and clarifies the district's stance on the issue. It is an institutional record of guidelines that can be communicated to the public and can be used to hold the district accountable. An example of a brief policy statement on prevention and intervention is the following: "Staff members are expected to learn how to recognize students at risk for suicide, to identify warning signs, to assess the degree of the risk, to take preventive precautions, and to report suicide threats to the appropriate authorities. Staff members who have been issued a copy of the District Suicide Prevention Policy and Procedures are responsible for knowing and acting upon them." Such a policy statement should be backed up with a policy and procedure manual that expounds on and concretizes it. A more detailed and concrete policy is offered by Heiman, Lamb, Dunne-Maxim, and Sutton (1986):

1. Upon receiving information that a student has threatened or actually attempted suicide, staff members or students shall notify school crisis coordinator or building principal.
2. The crisis coordinator or principal shall
    a. Designate a Crisis Intervention Team Member to talk to and remain with the student.
    b. Notify and talk with the student's parent or guardian.
    c. Notify the District Crisis Intervention Team and convene if necessary.
3. The Crisis Intervention Team will make an initial assessment of the student and determine the proper referral agency for services. It will assist the parent or guardian, if contacted, to deliver the

student to the agreed upon agency or private practitioner.

4. If the parent or guardian cannot be contacted, and the situation is deemed serious, the student will be hospitalized.

5. If the parent or guardian declines to cooperate, an appropriate child protective services agency shall be contacted and asked to intervene and follow-up.

6. If the Crisis Intervention Team and the principal decide there is no imminent danger, the principal will:

   a. contact the parent or guardian and refer them to a member of the crisis intervention team;

   b. refer the student to the school child study team who will monitor and follow up as needed.

It is no longer enough simply to have a policy. The entire district, from the board of education and superintendent on down, must make a strong commitment to suicide prevention and crisis response and recognize that time and resources must be given to support the policy. The cost of preparedness activities is primarily staff time, but planning time is also an essential component. And staff must be allowed to contribute their expertise by being given release time from other duties.

Supporting Staff Training

One of the first things to be done to increase school district readiness is to arrange for staff training on suicide prevention (Chapter Eight describes a number of programs that can be used for staff training). One individual or a small committee needs to plan for this training. Initially, the entire staff of the school district, including noncertified personnel, should receive some form of training. A local consortium made up of district guidance staff, community mental health professionals, and clergy might conduct the training activities. Of course, outside experts from universities or more distant locations might be brought in to conduct the training, but this would increase the cost and perhaps decrease sensitivity to local customs and needs. Resources A and B list a number of materials that can be useful to whoever may conduct the training.

The time and location of the training sessions, both the initial sessions for the existing district staff and annual sessions thereafter for new staff members, must be clearly established. Plans for refresher courses are also a good idea, since one-shot training may not be sufficient, and people tend to forget information when they do not use it often. Some districts use regular in-service days for the training, while others involve everyone during orientation sessions before the beginning of the school year. New employees might be regularly required to receive the training as part of their orientation to the district, or, if the number of new employees is too small for training to be efficient, neighboring districts might join together in preparing their new employees to deal with suicide. The location chosen should match to the type of presentation: auditoriums for large lectures, and smaller meeting rooms for small-group discussions or role playing. Rather than one set of presentations for the entire district, the training might be conducted school by school, if space and time are available.

School District Crisis Teams

A comprehensive district plan implies crisis teams at the district level and at each school site, or at least in each secondary school. The crisis team created to respond to suicidal crises can also be used to respond to other emergencies or crises in a district: events such as homicides, accidents resulting in severe injury or deaths, deaths of teachers or students, or other incidents that have the potential to traumatize children. Any such team, however, should have special and particular training in responding to suicide.

A first step in establishing a crisis team is to assign individuals to the various roles indicated in the plan: a district crisis coordinator, a school site crisis coordinator, crisis managers, police and security liaison, and a media spokesperson. A job description and list of responsibilities may be developed for each person. These people should establish communication links with others both within and outside the district and keep them up to date. For example, the district coordinator should set up telephone trees so members of the crisis team could be reached twenty-four hours a day and establish links with local mental health organization, hospitals, and other community agencies. Similarly, the security coordinator would meet with police personnel and the media spokesperson should hold meetings with local newspaper editors and reporters and keep lists of names and phone numbers.

In addition, all members should prepare materials for use during times of crisis. The district coordinator should prepare forms to assist in coordination and a district handbook; the crisis managers should establish referral procedures at their schools and locate space where counseling or other activities might take place during a crisis; the security coordinators should distribute identification cards and develop crowd control plans and other procedures to ensure student safety; and the media spokesperson should prepare prototype press releases and plan for a media center to be used during times of heavy press interest.

Crisis preparation can emphasize districtwide teams or school-site teams; both are needed to some extent. In large districts with a number of school psychologists, nurses, social workers, and counselors, those with special skill, interests, and training can be identified and formed into a team to be drawn from their regular assignments and sent to the school where a suicide or other traumatic event occurs. However, even though they may have more expertise than that particular school's personnel, they will still need the assistance of those personnel who know the children and the parents affected. Consequently, the school must also have a team in place. Small districts may not have enough mental health workers on staff to create a mobile team. Nevertheless, some districtwide planning and coordination will need to be done, and, even though each school may not be able to have its own team, each should designate at least one person, such as a teacher or principal, as crisis manager.

An optional adjunct to a districtwide crisis team is an external team composed of experts from the community, either from a single mental health agency or from a number of agencies or private practitioners. The district may contract with the outside team to provide services during a time of crisis. If such an arrangement is made, the district will still need a designated district liaison to coordinate the work of the team and some site-level preparation and training. The district will need to be sure that the personnel sent into the schools are appropriately prepared to work with children, adolescents, and their families and are appropriately licensed. Another possibility, of course, is to create a joint districtwide team composed of both school and community personnel.

Elements of a Suicide Preparedness Plan

Although a district might use a model such as those listed in Resource B to develop its preparedness plan, the plan must be tailored to the district's particular needs. The plans of large districts will be different from those of small ones because of their larger, often more specialized staffs; urban districts' plans will be different from those of rural districts because of differences in the availability of community resources; and so on. But each district should prepare a procedural manual outlining the elements discussed below.

Who Is in Charge. The plan should indicate who is to be in charge in the case of an attempted suicide, a completed suicide, or an individual on the brink of suicide. Coordinators should be designated at the district level as well as at the individual school level. The district coordinator might be the director of psychological or counseling services or the district superintendent. The coordinator for an individual school would probably be the school principal or vice-principal. Routine referrals need not be immediately brought to the district-level person's attention. However, in times of emergency, one person should be empowered as the final decision maker. The district-level crisis coordinator would decide whether to delegate the authority to the school-level coordinator, probably depending on the magnitude of the crisis. There should always be at least one and preferably two backup people with authority to act in the absence of the person in charge.

Whom to Contact with Concerns About Suicide. The manual should indicate the lines of communication in the district and at each school site. Everyone working in the school district, from bus drivers to the superintendent, should know which staff member to inform if they learn about a suicide or an attempted suicide or suspect that a student may be suicidal. Someone at each school—a mental health specialist such as a guidance counselor or a school psychologist, if assigned to the school full-time—should be designated as the suicide crisis manager, to be informed when a student is thought to be suicidal, to pass the information on to the crisis coordinator, quickly if it is an emergency, and to otherwise manage the case. The suicide crisis manager should receive additional training in facilitating referrals and collaborating with referral sources and advanced training in working with suicidal youth in the schools.

How Training Will Be Conducted. The plan should detail how the staff members in the school district will be trained to recognize students at risk and to take appropriate action. The procedure manual need not go into detail about the content of training but should indicate that such training will take place, how often training will be updated, and how new staff will receive their training after initial districtwide training.

Community Resources. The crisis plan should address how community resources will be used during times of crisis. The procedural manual should include a list of community resources, including local suicide prevention or crisis centers, hospital emergency rooms, private psychiatrists or psychologists who specialize in adolescents, police and protective services personnel, and others who can provide expert assistance and who may need to be summoned by the school suicide crisis manager. The list should also include those to whom the student and parents can be referred. It is critically important that these resource people be identified and interviewed in advance so that school personnel are sure that they are appropriately trained and can become familiar with the agencies' policies and procedures. These community resources may be identified by name, location, telephone number, hours of operation, and other pertinent details.

Parent Communications. The plan should consider when parents should be notified, how they should be informed of events,

and by whom. Parents who are known to be concerned and cooperative should be notified at once by the person in charge during
a crisis. In routine cases, it will be enough to make a referral. If it
is suspected that the parents will be uncooperative, it may be pref-
erable to contact the community resource agency or mental health
specialist first, so that they can assist when the parent is contacted.

Hospitalization Policy. The plan should include contingen-
cies for a child who poses immediate danger to him- or herself and
thus requires hospitalization. The policy and procedure manual
should also indicate whether and how the student will be taken to
an appropriate agency, such as a hospital emergency room or suicide prevention center, if necessary. Once again, if the parents are
cooperative and available, they might transport the child. If appropriate, a member of the school staff may wish to accompany the
parents and student. If the parents are uncooperative or unavailable,
the police would transport the student, preferably accompanied by
a staff member. If the police are contacted, it should be requested
that a juvenile officer be sent since such officers have usually received suicide prevention training. A useful inclusion in the implementation manual would be a copy of state laws relevant to
preventive detention. The district plan should also indicate who is
responsible for maintaining liaison with the police and protective
services.

Informing Students. The district plan should also include
details on how the student body is to be informed of a suicide event.
A plan implementation manual should also indicate how the other
students in the school will be told of a completed or widely wit-
nessed attempted suicide. (This topic is covered more extensively in
Chapter Five.)

Informing Others. The plan should also indicate how others,
including reporters from the news media, are to be informed and by
whom. First and foremost, the teachers and staff must be informed
(these procedures are also discussed in Chapter Five).

Working with the Media

Working with the media is a somewhat specialized skill, and the district might designate one person with good communication skills to be a media spokesperson. A school administrator or school staff person might deal with routine inquiries, but he or she should work from an established protocol.

Often a student suicide or attempted suicide becomes a newsworthy item. Effective communications with the media can reduce the interference from the media, can serve to inform others appropriately, and can serve some of the preventive goals of the school by informing the public about where to go for help.

The media are motivated to report events that editors and reporters believe will be of interest to the general public. The events of the day and the news value of those events determine the kind of coverage that the media give to a suicide. On "slow news days," a local newspaper might devote the front page to a relatively trivial event, such as unusually hot weather, while on other days, when there is a great deal of national or international news of importance, student suicides may not even make the newspaper.

Journalists who follow Rudyard Kipling's old formula of who, what, where, when, why, and how when contacting the school will request this information first, if they do not already have it. A newspaper will obviously be interested in the most unusual and bizarre aspect of a case, although reporters will usually try to tie the particular situation into a more general societal issue. For example, a story on a student suicide might be tied into growing national trends related to drug abuse.

Different media will compete with one another to learn more about an event than the others. Reporters will vie with each other to gather data or speculation about an event. Thus, members of the media will badger school contacts to get more information than previous reporters obtained. School secretaries will have to know what to say and when to pass a request for information on to others. Having one designated spokesperson for the school to whom others may refer questions will help reduce confusion. Still, the spokesperson may well be deluged. One solution to this problem is to read a prepared press release, giving each member of the media the same amount of information. The following list presents guidelines for preparing a press release and communicating with the press:

1. *Report what happened.* Avoid sensational or romantic accounts of what occurred, and omit precise information on methods used in the attempt or the suicide so that impressionable individuals will not be able to copy the tragedy. For example, one might announce that a suicide was committed by carbon monoxide poisoning but not go into details about how a hose acquired from a local store was connected between the tailpipe of a car and the driver's window and the individual then sat in a running car in a closed garage.

2. *Report who was involved in general terms.* Use general terms and not names of individuals, unless this information is public knowledge and next of kin have been notified. A victim may be described in terms of sex and grade in school and other relevant demographic facts but usually not by name. If others were involved, that fact can be generally indicated without identifying data.

3. *Report when the suicide or attempt occurred or was discovered.* Give this information as precisely as known.

4. *To the extent relevant, report where it happened.* The location of the suicide or attempt can be reported, although addresses of private residences or businesses should not be released. If the location could lend itself to sensationalism, it would be best if it could be omitted, played down, or only vaguely mentioned.

5. *If someone is injured, report what the prognosis is for those involved.* Prognosis and status can be given as long as they have been verified. This information can often be left to the hospital.

6. *Indicate what the district will do or has done.* The emphasis should be on positive actions taken by school personnel or students. Communicate the fact that the district is concerned about the health and safety of all students and will provide resources as well as work with other community agencies to help the student body recover from the event and return to the basic tasks of learning.

7. *Indicate where troubled individuals in the community can get help.* Indicate what counseling services will be available to

those upset by the event or who are also having suicidal thoughts. The phone number of the suicide hot line, for example, might be listed.

8. *If asked, provide other sources of information.* The reporter may wish to consult with other individual experts or organizations who can supplement the story. Resource B includes a list of national groups concerned with suicide.

9. *In interviews, avoid "no comment" answers.* These sorts of statements suggest that the spokesperson has something to hide. If you cannot make a comment, you might respond "I have not had enough time to talk to others" or "We have just received the information and must study it before giving an answer."

The constant quest for information on the part of reporters often creates problems by tying up telephone lines. If the school has the resources, it may wish to designate a specific line for media information and refuse any media calls on other than that line. The information line may also be attached to a recording device, which would free an individual from having to answer the same questions again and again.

One problem facing the press information officer is knowing what information to release. Various state and local information regulations may affect this decision, but by and large schools are governed by the provisions of the federal Buckley Amendment, which outlines what types of information are considered public information. In most cases, the name of a minor attending a school is *not* public information. In most states, probably only a child's sex, school grade, and age are public information.

In addition to wishing to talk with a school spokesperson, reporters will also want to interview individuals directly involved—teachers, students, particularly those close to the suicide victim, and parents. It is impossible to prevent reporters from talking to individuals, but it is not appropriate for a school spokesperson to give out a list of teachers and students involved. It may be appropriate, given the inevitability of a reporter contacting other individuals, for the school's spokesperson to act as a broker, introducing the reporter to both students and teachers who volunteer ahead of time to talk to the media. Before a reporter may be given a student's name, the student's parent must give his or her permission for the contact to take place and must be willing to sign a release. The importance of the media in working with the community is discussed later in this chapter.

Rumor and Crowd Control

Following a suicide or other traumatic event, districts must be prepared to undertake crowd and rumor control. First, they will need to work with their security personnel to prepare for crowd control. The district will need to prepare identification badges, crowd control barriers, and so on that can be quickly brought to the site of an emergency. Second, they will need to be prepared to deal with rumors. Following suicides and attempted suicides, a number of rumors spread throughout the school community. Although it is difficult to control rumors, one way to reduce their impact is to make announcements as information is collected. Staff must be prepared to meet and deal effectively with rumors as quickly as they surface with an announcement clarifying the situation. Staff should be alerted to pick up rumors and report them to the crisis coordinator so they may be rectified quickly.

Creating Comprehensive Counseling Services

Almost all school districts have counselors and other pupil personnel workers, such as school psychologists and social workers, who are trained in counseling techniques and theories. Counseling services to students can be effective both in prevention and after a suicide attempt or completion has taken place. Counseling personnel in the school district must have training in suicide awareness and intervention, training in referral skills, and time and space to practice these skills. School counselors who are involved only in educational planning, vocational planning, or student disciplinary matters and are not provided time to offer general counseling will not be able to serve the district suicide program as well. During the hiring process, district personnel should look for personal counseling knowledge and skill, particularly skills in recognizing and responding to suicidal ideation and depression, in applicants for counseling positions. In addition, school districts need to provide the time and space for counselors to serve the mental health needs of district adolescents. Lowering student counselor ratios to a manageable level, such as 1:500, would make a district more ready to deal with the problem of adolescent suicide.

Supporting the Staff During Times of Crisis

School districts need to be prepared to respond not only to the needs of children but also to the needs of the staff when a suicidal emergency occurs. Since school personnel do not usually treat staff members, it will be important to make outside contracts with mental health service providers so that counseling services are available to teachers, administrators, and other school personnel who may react strongly to an adolescent suicide. Employee assistance programs could be modified to allow for counseling following the occurrence of traumatic events in the district.

Assisting Guidance Personnel Following a Crisis

Everything in the previous section concerning support for teachers and administrative staff is applicable here. Helpers who have responded to a suicidal crisis also need opportunities to be debriefed. Everyone is affected by working closely with children who are suicidal or with students who have been affected by a suicide. Issues of personal mortality, guilt, and helplessness come up for helpers. They, too, must have some backup and opportunities to debrief following a particularly stressful or difficult intervention.

Sensitizing Staff and Altering Stressful Practices

Requiring staff to receive training in recognition of the signs of suicide and potential suicide and depression can go a long way toward preventing suicides, since the schoolteacher is one of the few adults who sees children daily. In addition to sensitizing staff to suicide itself, the district might work at being alert to and changing procedures and practices in classrooms that may contribute to suicide. Teachers should be educated by supervisors about the consequences of using classroom practices that embarrass or belittle the student, such as extreme sarcasm and "put-downs." Teachers might be sensitized to extreme competition in their classrooms and the rewarding of student perfectionism. The risk of suicide is increased by stressful environments, and we believe that reducing high levels of stress on students can be part of a useful preventive plan. On the positive side, school classroom environments that reduce isolation of pupils from one another and that stress communication and create friendship may be preventive. Thus, the creation of student clubs, extracurricular activities, and vocational preparation in a school is likely also to enhance prevention. School curricula aimed at the prevention of drug and substance abuse, as well as curricular efforts aimed at providing students with social skills (see Chapter Eight), are also important school district activities.

Testing the System

Even after school policies and procedures for dealing with suicide have been developed and the crisis team has been established, a school district's job is still not finished. It is important to test any system, and from time to time drills should be conducted to make sure that the procedures that have been set up work as anticipated. These drills can be realistic, with a student role playing a suicide or a suicide attempt on the school grounds, or they may be more intellectual, with staff called together, presented with a scenario, and asked to review what their activities would be. Although suicides are rare events in schools, such a drill should be conducted once a year, at the very least. Much can be learned following a suicidal emergency. School district staff should take time following an event—for example, after three weeks have passed— to review what occurred, both facts and feelings, so that flaws in the planning and response mechanism can be identified and improvements made to the system.

Community Preparedness

Working with the Media

The groundwork for media relations must be done prior to a suicide. Local editors of media should be made aware, either through meetings with school district personnel or meetings with other mental health professionals in the area, of the roles that the media can play in preventing suicidal behavior in young people. The editors of newspapers and news editors of radio stations should be sensitized to the issues of contagion and youth suicide (Davidson and Gould, 1989). Research suggests that nonfictional media coverage of suicide is associated with an increase in the observed number of suicides over the number expected, although this association may not be uniform over all age and sex groups. It is not clear, however, whether news media coverage works to create new suicides or to accelerate suicides that would have occurred anyway. In general, social learning theory makes it clear that people will imitate and model their behavior on another person if that person is held in high regard and if there are clear rewards associated with the behavior. It follows, then, that if a suicide is portrayed in the media as gathering a great deal of attention, or other kinds of rewards emerge from the manner in which the report is presented, reportage might encourage some imitative behavior. Therefore, the news media should be encouraged to avoid romanticizing suicidal acts and making celebrities out of adolescents or other individuals who die by suicide. Rather than presenting the act as a response to stresses and strains, the press should emphasize its pathological aspect. In addition, the means should not be reported in precise detail, lest the suicide be imitated. With some persuasion, newspapers might refrain from carrying the news of a suicide in prominent locations in the paper and from running pictures with the story. Particularly, they should refrain from displaying pictures of the aftermath of the suicide, especially violent images, such as a wrecked car. If a photo must be run, it might be best to use a yearbook photo or possibly a photo of a grieving parent. The underlying text of the story might emphasize the maladaptive, inadequate aspect of suicide, and any story should include information about what community resources are available for assisting those with suicidal inclinations or thoughts. Close work with reporters and editors can create positive voluntary guidelines for reporting suicides.

Creating Links with Mental Health Agencies

While a community may be served by a number of mental health agencies, the most relevant of these is likely to be a suicide prevention agency. Usually these agencies are funded by charitable organizations such as the United Way and work to prevent suicide in the community, operating twenty-four-hour crisis lines and conducting suicide training for crisis-line volunteers. They also maintain educational programs, which may include outreach to the public schools. While the focus of this book is on school-based prevention efforts, we fully acknowledge that a powerful resource in many communities is the suicide prevention program. Many school districts rely heavily on such an agency in both preventing and responding to suicidal emergencies, and any school planning should include the participation of local suicide prevention program personnel.

Another agency found in most communities is a community mental health organization. Such community mental health centers are mandated and funded by the federal government to provide general mental health services to the community. A given agency may or may not be interested in and provide programs on suicide prevention, but all of them are staffed by professionals trained in dealing with depressed and suicidal individuals. In times of crises, the personnel from a mental health center might be brought into the school or serve as consultants to school-based helpers. Mental health agencies can also provide backup for the school staff and school staff helpers by providing counseling services and undertaking the debriefing of school professionals working with children. To the extent that the agenda of a community mental health center can be shifted to youth suicide, it will devote resources to working with this problem.

Other mental health resources may be found through local

private and county public hospitals. Most hospital emergency rooms have access to professionals who can assist in intervening with suicidal patients. Private psychiatric hospitals may be persuaded to undertake community outreach in the area of child and adolescent suicide as a way of making a contribution to the community and as a way of introducing their staff to the community so that they will be kept in mind for referral. It is best if all the mental health agencies within the community are collaborating so that they can respond to a crisis without tripping over one another. During the planning stages, school and agency personnel should meet together and conduct follow-ups at least once a year to clarify roles and lines of communication with one another. The school can take a leadership role in this networking and coordination and must do so in the absence of initiatives taken by community agencies.

Creating Links with the Clergy

Another group of professionals found in most communities is the clergy. Many clerics are trained as pastoral counselors in their seminary work. They may have a great deal of experience in providing pastoral counseling services to their congregation, which may include youth and young adults. Although different religious denominations may take different theological positions with respect to suicide, and theology may dictate particular responses to suicidal ideation or to a completed suicide, organized religion has a role to play in suicide prevention and intervention. With the separation of church and state as a guiding principle, school time and space cannot be given to clergy for religious purposes except in emergencies, but they can support school programs with their congregations, and they may be an appropriate recipient of a referral.

Creating Links with the Criminal Justice System

The final institutions in the community that intervene and have some interest in suicide prevention are the police and court systems. These institutions are charged with implementing preventive detention laws and are involved in responding to both suicidal attempts and completed suicides. Although they do not do primary prevention, the police are often called on to deal with an adolescent threatening suicide, especially if the adolescent possesses some type of a weapon. Many police are trained in intervening in these kinds of crises, and on large staffs, at least, there are individuals who have expertise in talking to individuals in these kinds of situations. In work with all of these agencies, ultimately the effectiveness of coordination and school agency contacts will depend on the quality of personnel.

Using Community Resources

Just as school personnel vary in training, skill, and sensitivity, so do newspaper editors, employees of mental health agencies, the clergy, and the police. Prior to a crisis, it is absolutely imperative that communication and meetings with the people involved in the various community agencies take place. The school district must determine who on the various staffs have the requisite training and can work effectively with adolescents. Most of the personnel are trained to work with adults; fewer receive explicit training on and supervised practice in working with young people. Moreover, these agency personnel need to be educated to the special needs and circumstances of the public school system and vice versa. Clergy are usually aware of the delicate position they are in and the delicate position of education with respect to religion and are aware of their limitations. Nevertheless, some screening of the personnel by the school system will be necessary in order for them to feel comfortable in calling on community resources and establishing a network of qualified individuals to intervene in times of crisis and to participate in staff awareness and training activities as well as educational programs.

Societal Prevention

Some prevention efforts need to be aimed at the broader society. As public citizens, school district staff can work to effect changes in the media and in the availability of suicidal means and risk factors to contribute to preventive efforts.

Fictional Accounts of Suicide

As further discussed in Chapter Eleven, there is a raging controversy over whether fictional accounts of suicide contribute to youth suicide. There is some evidence that imitative suicides do follow from films and television plays, although this relationship has not been established as strongly as the relationship between nonfictional media accounts and suicide. Given the possibility that a fictional program may stimulate suicide, it may be important to include at the beginning of such a program a warning indicating that the program might adversely affect people viewing it and advise parental discretion. The television networks and Academy of Motion Picture Arts and Sciences should also recognize their responsibility not to romanticize suicidal acts. Unfortunately, popular movies such as *The Dead Poet's Society* that contain an underlying theme of romantic adolescent suicide are still being released without warnings to parents or information about referral, although we are beginning to see these addenda more and more.

Eliminating the Means of Suicide

The three means that adolescents and young adults most frequently use to kill themselves are (1) firearms and explosives, (2) hanging, strangulation, or suffocation, and (3) ingestion of poison (Holinger, 1978). These are followed by jumping from high places, carbon monoxide poisoning, and automotive "accidents." The elimination of access to these popular methods of choice will reduce the likelihood of an impulsive suicidal action. Thus, working for gun control laws or even raising the age at which it is legal to drive might have a preventive effect in reducing the number of suicidal fatalities. Working for legislation that would achieve these ends might be a preventive activity.

In a nationwide experiment in England, where the method of first choice for suicide was suffocation by means of cooking gas, natural gas was "odorized" to facilitate the detection of leaks and to make the use of this means more unpleasant and difficult. The outcome of odorization was a decrease in the number of suicides not only by this means but also by any other means. To the extent that suicide is an impulsive act, reducing the likelihood that individuals have the means at hand might have some success. Unfortunately, it is practically impossible to limit the availability of poisons in our environment and will probably never be feasible.

Conclusion

There is much to be done on a systems level to prevent suicide and ameliorate the effect of a suicide once it has occurred. There is work to be done at the school, school district, community, and societal levels to mount a comprehensive attack on the problem of youth suicide. Our own ethical codes and courts of law will not allow us to ignore this problem any longer.

Concerned pupil services workers must take leadership in helping a school district, a community, and our entire society to be aware of the need for preventive action. There are a number of models for constructive policies and procedures available for the professional to use as a basis for local action. There is no excuse for remaining idle. Although the problem can be attacked on many levels, guidance personnel should first inventory their own skills, knowledge, and practices and those of their co-workers. From this inventory, lacks can be quickly identified so that resources may be immediately brought to bear to educate the professional, and programs may be started to capitalize on the strengths in an appropriate way. If a school psychologist is an effective organizer, he or she may begin discussions of a district crisis team. If a counselor is good at working with groups of students, he or she may begin to examine ways to improve the peer culture of the school. Everyone can do something and can learn to do more.

11

Legal and Ethical Issues

Perhaps the first question that school district personnel might ask about suicide prevention in the schools is whether they are obligated to use schools' resources and time to mount a suicide prevention program. As is so often the case, school policies and procedures are dictated by decisions made in courts of law, but legal considerations are not the only ones that must be considered when a school suicide prevention program is being planned. The execution of such a plan must take into account various ethical considerations. Many prevention activities create ethical dilemmas for practitioners, and these should be identified and faced before a prevention program is planned. We have discussed some of the issues related to confidentiality previously in this book, but other issues remain and manifest themselves during preventive activities. This chapter examines a number of legal issues involved in a suicide prevention program, such as obtaining parental permission for screening and preventive counseling activities. Next, we discuss a number of ethical issues that arise in mounting prevention programs, doing screening, and providing group counseling services. Finally, we discuss the need for continued research and program evaluation to answer important questions of legal and ethical responsibilities, particularly questions dealing with the major issue of suicide contagion.

Legal Issues

Obligation to Provide a Suicide Prevention Program

One day, fourteen-year-old Brian Kelson brought to class and revealed to the teacher a .38 caliber revolver. He brandished the gun and forced the teacher to hand over a small amount of cash. After giving him the money, the teacher persuaded Brian to accompany him to the vice-principal's office. On their way to the office, Brian placed the weapon in the waistband of his pants. During discussions with the vice-principal, Brian revealed a suicide note he had prepared and asked to speak with his favorite teacher but did not receive permission to do so. While this conference was going on, the school contacted the local police, who in turn called Brian's parents and informed them of what had happened. When Brian and the vice-principal left the office, they were met by a police officer, who told the boy that he was "in trouble with the law." After a further conference with the police officer, Brian asked to go to the rest room. He received permission, entered the lavatory, and shot himself with the gun, which had never been taken from his possession. These are the facts in the case of *Kelson* v. *The City of Springfield*, 767 F. 2d 651 (1965).

The *Kelson* case was the first brought to a federal court in which the parents of a child who had committed suicide were able to bring an action against their child's school on the grounds that the death resulted from the school personnel's inadequate training in suicide prevention. This case was most noteworthy because it was the first in which the court permitted a lawsuit when there was no intentional act to harm the child on the part of school district employees but the child's death could be linked to the inadequate training of district employees. The complaint specifically charged that the school district had a duty to provide suicide prevention training to its employees and that it had failed to do so (Slenkovich, 1986). This case established the precedent that schools may be held monetarily liable for the on-campus suicide of a student, although the case has not yet been completely resolved.

While the *Kelson* case concerned a suicide that took place on school grounds, another type of case is that of Gregory Brown. Gregory, an eighth-grader in Milford, Connecticut, received a number of failing grades on his report card. On his way home, he turned to a group of children playing on a playground and announced, "Hey, guess what I'm going to do? I'm going to kill myself." When he arrived home, he took his life with a shotgun that he used for duck hunting.

On the day of the suicide, Gregory's friends had noted that he was acting strangely, and when they heard his suicide threat, one called the police, who sent a team to the child's home to talk with him. They left after receiving his assurance that he had no intention of killing himself and after looking through the house unsuccessfully for a weapon (Hildebrand, 1987). He killed himself shortly after the police left. Gregory's parents filed a lawsuit against both the school and the police, accusing school personnel of failing to identify Gregory's suicidal intent and to refer him for counseling. This case, too, is still unresolved.

Both of these cases are directed at the inadequate preparation and training of the school staff, teachers, administrators, and guidance personnel for identifying a suicidal student. The implication is that a school district should provide the staff with some training in suicide prevention, and the staff should take action when faced with a potentially suicidal child. Suicide should perhaps be treated similarly to child abuse, in that all personnel having contact with children and adolescents are obligated to report suspected suicidal tendencies.

No suit has yet been filed claiming that a school has an obligation to provide a program directed at students, although some state legislatures have enacted requirements for school districts to offer such programs. In California, for example, the state legislature passed a bill in 1983 calling for the development of a statewide suicide prevention program that included teacher training, parent awareness, and a student curriculum. The bill did not, however, require school districts to implement such a curriculum.

Standards for Training Programs

Given that a school district must at least provide a program of training for school personnel, it follows that the program should be an effective one. Anyone with a duty to care for others is held to the standard that they must perform in a way similar to how a reasonably prudent person under similar circumstances would perform. In other words, we are all held to normative behavior. Professionals may be charged with negligence or malpractice if they fail to perform in a way that is recognized as standard in the profession.

Although school district personnel should intervene whenever a child threatens suicide or manifests signs of the intent to commit suicide, most courts have recognized that schools are not equipped to do the necessary in-depth counseling and treatment of children. Rather, the courts hold that school personnel are in a position to make referrals and have a duty to secure assistance from others, with parent involvement, when a child is at risk. The grounds for a suit against school personnel in the event of a completed suicide would be that the school personnel had a duty to prevent a suicide and that it did not meet that duty. We all have a duty to show "due care" in our daily actions, but health care providers, such as school psychologists and counselors, have a greater obligation to prevent suicide because of their superior knowledge and training. A professional must exercise "reasonable professional judgment." Such judgment is validated by the testimony of expert witnesses (McWhirter and McWhirter, 1987). A jury will decide whether school personnel used reasonable professional judgment to the degree that the suicide attempt was foreseeable. *Foreseeable* in the legal sense means that a reasonable school personnel member should have predicted the suicide and should have done something to prevent it from occurring.

It can be argued that professional standards would require that, at a minimum, school personnel recognize the warning signs of suicide and know how to report their suspicions of suicidal behavior. Presumably, a district should establish some kind of reporting mechanism so that, at the very least, suspicions may be acted on. Just as with suspected child abuse, each school should have designated reporters and a clear set of procedures. Usually, as chief administrative officer at a school site, the principal would have responsibility, although he or she could delegate the suicide management role to someone else. The suicide or crisis manager in the school would receive reports from anyone in the school and act on them. In some instances, the crisis manager might be someone at the district or county level or in a community agency. Arrangements might vary, but *someone* must be clearly identified for the role of receiving and acting on reports from teachers and others about a child who is perceived to be a threat to him- or herself. School district employees should understand their liability in the case that they do not report their concerns about a child who is a danger to him- or herself or other people. Once again, since school district employees are made aware of their reporting obligations with respect to child abuse, it may be efficient to combine policies and training for the two areas.

Another legal difficulty yet to be tested is whether participants in a suicide prevention program who later become suicidal and/or are injured in a suicide attempt have a cause of legal action. When prevention is seemingly unsuccessful, has there been a breach of contract? Can the originators of a suicide prevention program be sued if one of the participants later commits suicide? In California, the threat of such litigation has held up a program on suicide prevention (Davis, Sandoval, and Wilson, 1988). Tort actions have not yet been taken in situations in which crisis counseling and intervention have not proved successful in the schools.

Although it seems obvious, it should be made clear to school personnel that aiding and assisting in a suicide is a criminal act in most states. Counselors and teachers must not help in planning a suicide, provide the means, or in any other way actively assist a student to engage in self-destructive behavior (McWhirter and McWhirter, 1987). There are a few documented cases of this occurring. It is, of course, possible to bring a civil action against someone who acts in such a way as to "cause" a suicide. There have been workers' compensation cases where an injury in the workplace was shown to lead to a worker's later suicide and the relatives were awarded compensation. But since suicide has been traditionally viewed as an individual's intentional and willful act, courts have not been quick to assess third-party blame (McWhirter and McWhirter, 1987), and cases are seldom brought against mental health or other care givers on the basis of causing an injury. Rather, suits are brought on the basis of a duty to prevent suicide.

Another strategy for avoiding charges of malpractice or negligence is to ensure that a school's suicide prevention program is regularly evaluated and tested. Such testing may include unscheduled drills and simulations to ensure that the staff is ready to act. For example, during a scheduled in-service training day, instead of the announced topic, teachers might be presented with a suicide scenario and asked to play it out. The hypothetical problem might begin with a child presenting suicidal symptoms and proceed on to a suicide attempt and then suicide. At each stage, the teachers would be asked what they would do with their students and with whom they would coordinate their actions at the school site and the district level. Opportunities for discussing and reinforcing correct responses and procedures would be scheduled throughout the simulation. At the same time, participants would be alert for weaknesses in the current system and ways to improve the school's response. At a minimum, school districts should provide training for new employees and refresher courses for veteran teachers, guidance personnel, and administrators.

Labeling a Child as Suicidal

A number of legal issues arise when one takes active steps in the school to identify students with suicidal ideation or potential for committing suicide. A proactive program of suicide prevention would include such screening procedures. However, attempts to identify potentially suicidal students will create a problem if this screening procedure results in some students being given a special label or otherwise identified to the school as a whole so as to cause them embarrassment. If such a labeling procedure results in the unfair treatment of a student, it may also deprive the student of his or her constitutional rights to due process and equal protection. Any screening program must be valid and lead to interventions that are in the best interests of the students with a minimum of negative side effects. A good way of reducing the possibility of negative outcomes of screening and identification is to keep the information obtained confidential and to be sure that the screening procedure automatically leads to a reasonable and effective intervention.

Giving a child a label that has unpleasant or embarrassing connotations brings up the issue of defamation. Defamation occurs when an individual is libeled or slandered; that is, when information is circulated that is injurious to the reputation of the individual. Falsely labeling a child as suicidal may cause this kind of injury. While there have been few defamation cases brought against school mental health workers, one should nevertheless be careful with this practice, particularly with using jargon. In one case, a psychologist was sued, although unsuccessfully, for reporting that a child was a "high-grade moron" (McDermott, 1972).

Testing

It goes without saying that any test used in screening will have to meet generally accepted test standards, most likely the *Standards for Educational and Psychological Testing* (American Psychological Association, 1985). These standards identify a number of specific criteria that should be met by all tests before their use with children in schools. Among them are specific statements about the need for appropriately established reliability and validity related to the purpose for which the test will be used. The test also must be appropriate for all students tested and not racially or in other ways discriminatory. All tests used in screening should be subject to the increasingly efficient means to detect and eliminate test bias (Reynolds and Kaiser, 1990). The screening devices reviewed in Chapter Six are reasonably well constructed, but they probably do not meet all the stringent standards. Since they are relatively new, evidence on their validity is still accruing.

Another necessity, related to both testing and the invasion of privacy, is to make sure that any assessment or screening devices is restricted to obtaining the minimum amount of information necessary from individuals and nothing more. Although it is important to have valid measures to identify children at risk, it is also important to collect no more information than is necessary and not to push students into self-confrontation or into revealing any information about themselves that is not strictly necessary. Many personality testing batteries contain questions and stimuli that are provocative and intrusive and not related to depression or hopelessness.

Privacy and Parental Permission

Children in school have rights to privacy. The most sweeping laws that have guaranteed this privacy are the Buckley Amendment and the Hatch Amendment, both of which require that parental permission be secured before any kind of testing takes place and before any information is released to a third party. The Hatch

Amendment explicitly requires permission if the purpose of the screening or testing is to reveal information concerning "mental and psychological problems potentially embarrassing to the student or his family." Assuming that suicidal tendencies are potentially embarrassing to the child's family, if not to the child, it is reasonable to assume that screening for suicidal tendencies is governed by the Hatch Amendment. Therefore, if a screening measure includes potentially embarrassing questions, parental permission should be obtained for its use, and copies of the screening questions must be made available for inspection. Best practice calls for fully informed, written parental consent prior to screening and the right of adolescents to refuse to participate. It should be noted that in their survey of school-related suicide programs, Smith, Eyman, Dyck, and Ryerson (1987) found that none of the four programs located that emphasized screening required parental permission. Future programs should address this issue directly.

As DeMers and Bersoff (1985) point out, informed consent has three elements: knowledge, voluntariness, and competence. To give true informed consent, an individual must understand what will be done, why it will be done, and how it will be done—that is, must have a complete knowledge of what he or she is agreeing to. Furthermore, consent must not be obtained under duress. Group and other pressures must not be applied to parents to force them to go along with a decision. In schools, the threat of suspension, lowered grades, or stigmatization for refusal to consent to a procedure is unethical and illegal. Individuals also must be competent to give consent, and school personnel must often make a careful determination of whether a child or parent is incompetent by virtue of low intelligence or emotional disturbance. When securing informed consent, psychologists must work hard to explain their procedures in language that parents or children can understand (Pryzwansky and Bersoff, 1978).

Parents must also give permission for counseling related to suicide, although, as we discussed in Chapter Four, parental permission can be temporarily waived when someone feels that a child's life is at stake. State law regarding consent should be consulted, as the need for permission and restrictions may vary. After the crisis has been addressed, parents must be informed as soon as practical. In using counseling for preventive activities where an emergency is not at hand, it will be necessary to secure parental permission before initiating a contact.

Counselors and school psychologists who encounter children whom they suspect of being suicidal have a duty to warn the children's parents of their suspicion. And school mental health personnel who discover evidence that a child is suicidal have a duty to warn even though they have not met with the child personally. For example, if a school counselor hears from a student that the student's friend is on her way home with a gun and is planning to shoot herself, the counselor should contact the parents as well as the authorities. Or a screening procedure might turn up a student whose scores indicate that he is at extraordinarily high risk, but there may be no time to see the youngster with a follow-up interview. In these instances, psychologists still have an obligation to contact the parents with their concerns about the adolescents.

Another issue that has not been adequately determined is at what age a child is capable of giving his or her own consent for screening or counseling (Grisso and Vierling, 1978; Melton, Koocher, and Saks, 1983). Psychologists, legal theorists, and religious authorities disagree on an appropriate age, and there are obviously great individual differences in intellectual competence at any given age. The age of eighteen is most often cited in legislation (for example, the Buckley Amendment), but to keep within the spirit of good legal and ethical practices, one should give children the option to consent to a procedure whenever they seem able to rationally understand the request. Some forms of consent for testing can be obtained for children as young as two years old (Sandoval and Irvin, 1990). Child consent does not substitute for parental consent in minors; rather it is an additional requirement. Table 7 offers some guidelines for obtaining consent in various situations related to suicide prevention and intervention.

Privacy and School Records

The Family Educational Rights and Privacy Act of 1974 (Public Law 380), commonly known as the Buckley Amendment, guarantees the rights of parents to inspect, review, and amend all

Table 7. Guidelines for Obtaining Permission for Prevention Activities.

Activity	Child's Consent	Parental Consent
1. Screening	Yes	Yes if screening likely to "embarrass"
2. Screening follow-up	Preferred	Yes, duty to warn
3. Contact with student mentioned by peer	Good idea	Yes
4. Contact with student referred by teacher or other staff	Good idea	Yes, unless emergency or "imminent danger"
5. Counseling of student immediately following attempt	Not necessary	As soon as possible
6. Hospitalization	No	As soon as possible

educational records pertaining to their child. Any records kept in a district related to the outcome of screening must be available for inspection by the parents.

The Buckley Amendment allows psychologists or others to keep private notes that need not be disclosed to parents, but any information that is shared between school personnel should be available for inspection by parents. This is not to say that information must be shared with all school personnel; information of a sensitive nature should be shared on a need-to-know basis only, and the results of screening for depression or suicide should have very limited distribution in a school setting. The results of this screening, for example, should not be routinely included in files that are open to any interested staff member.

Ethical Issues

One of the main ethical and legal issues is the need to maintain confidentiality while doing preventive work. While one can never assure children of total confidentiality, since issues related to potential death or injury may come up, a client needs to know that other matters will be kept strictly private and that he or she will be consulted when confidentiality is breached. In breaking a confidence, a professional must limit information revealed about children to those who need to know about it. Students who wish to discuss personal issues with individuals following a suicide prevention curriculum should be assured to the greatest extent possible that their thoughts and concerns will be kept confidential. Any counseling should take place in a private location where the counselee cannot be seen or heard by anyone other than the counselor.

In addition, test security should be enforced. Screening materials should be kept under lock and key, and other counseling records should be filed securely as well. When confidential information is shared with other school personnel, it is appropriate to remind the recipient of the status of the information, although the psychologist has little control over another's behavior.

Religious Beliefs and Suicide

One of the problems in doing suicide prevention work is that differing religions and cultures have different positions on suicide and treat it differently. The Catholic church, for example, has declared suicide a sin and forbids the burial in consecrated grounds of individuals who have taken their own lives. Judaism considers suicide a dishonorable act. In Asian systems, such as in Japan, suicide is still sometimes considered an honorable and admirable act, for adults, at least. Because of religious attitudes, teachers or counselors may be more or less comfortable in talking about suicide, and pupils may feel uncomfortable during an open discussion.

There have been few national attempts on the part of religious leaders, however, to oppose suicide prevention activities; churches usually support prevention efforts. Objections to prevention programs may occur at the local level, however. Resistance from parent or religious groups is usually based on the notion that talking about a subject "puts ideas into the head" of an "impressionable" child. There is no good evidence that this is the case; in fact, as we discussed in Chapter Eight, the opposite is more likely to be true: Not talking about suicide makes it more "forbidden" and potentially romantic. As a result, objections based on the idea that prevention leads to the act should be met head on. It is also often a good idea to inform local clergy of prevention activities and to involve them as appropriate.

Client Welfare

Another ethical consideration is that of client welfare. In working with student who are at risk, there is always the possibility that a particular adolescent will actually commit suicide. Secondary prevention is based on working with individuals at risk. Because we are dealing with probabilities rather than certainties, it may be inappropriate to automatically impose a program of counseling for an individual who happens to fit a particular actuarial profile. It would be unwise, for example, to automatically include a Native American youth or a drug abuser in a program simply because he or she belongs to an at-risk group. Further evaluation following screening is appropriate before adolescents are assigned to treatment. One must proceed with caution, not treating signs of suicidal risk as automatic indicators. Rotheram-Borus's (1988) "imminent danger" would be one way to conceptualize the issue. Following an evaluation, if the answer to "imminent danger" is yes, we might be more confident of proceeding with a particular program than if the answer is no.

Preventive activities proceed on the basis of the probability of an occurrence. As a result, there will be a number of false positives (those believed to be suicidal who are not) and false negatives (those not believed to be suicidal who are) in any population. Erroneously involving in suicide prevention programs students who will not encounter or experience depression or suicidal thoughts may be wasting time. When the cost of programs is weighed against the probability of helping someone or the magnitude of the negative impact of the crisis on even a single child, there may not be a justifiable trade-off for the small number of individuals helped. Making such a determination, of course, is very difficult, and in the case of suicide, it seems to be reasonable that prevention activities take place.

Another ethical issue, although it will be encountered exceedingly rarely, is the belief that suicide is a legitimate solution to an individual's problem. This solution is often related to extreme and painful terminal illnesses or cultural situations where extreme transgressions against societal norms have occurred. Szasz (1986) argues that suicide is a moral act of an individual who is alone responsible for it. The helping professional should not consider prevention a professional responsibility, according to Szasz, although he or she should offer some sort of help. Szasz's remarks were made in the context of helping adults, not children, however, and he has not commented on adolescents. It is reasonable to conclude that adolescents are not sufficiently mature to make some of the philosophical decisions mentioned by Szasz, but there may be cases (although we cannot imagine any) where a counselor may find him- or herself siding with this position.

Professional Competence

An important component of most professional codes of ethics is the concept that professionals should actively assess their own competence and objectivity before taking on a professional activity. Practice should be limited by training, previous supervised experience, and opportunity for peer review. Before becoming involved with suicidal youth, a school-based professional should seek appropriate training and supervision and weigh personal competence and institutional role against the availability of other qualified help so that the client is best served.

Research and Program Evaluation Issues

While there is both an ethical and a legal need for effective suicide prevention programs, too few suicide prevention programs have been carefully and systematically evaluated. There are good reasons for this state of affairs, but good program evaluation is entirely within the capabilities of school personnel. We present some of the difficulties first.

Methodological problems plague the use of actuarial data in demonstrating program effectiveness for suicide programs (Shaffer, Garland, and Bacon, 1987). Suicide is simply too rare an event to be documented effectively, and it is often difficult to know whether an adolescent's death should be classified as accidental or suicidal. A possible way around the problem is to record a more prevalent index, such as suicide attempts. Ross (1985) used as an index of program effectiveness an increase in the numbers of referrals of self and friends to suicide crisis centers and hot lines under the assumption that awareness brought about by the prevention program would bring about increases in referral rates.

Shaffer, Garland, and Bacon (1987) point out that using suicide rates as a base line to evaluate change after the implementation of a program is also dangerous. Programs are most likely to be implemented after a suicide cluster, in which case the suicide rate will be artificially high unless a long base line for the community (such as three decades) is used. A better solution might be to use a control community for comparison purposes, but the community must be carefully matched to the program community on such factors as ethnicity and social class.

Garland and Shaffer (1988) also criticize evaluation researchers for failing to take into account confounding reasons for suicide rate changes, such as sudden influx into a community of older adolescents who are more suicide prone. Evaluators often have problems defining what the intervention was and what the period of exposure was for participants because of the haphazard way that programs start up and change over the years.

Most program evaluations that have risen above the level of case study description have been limited to a study of knowledge and attitude changes in participants. An evaluation of the California program, for example, demonstrated significant improvements in knowledge and attitude toward suicide, and the evaluators were pleased with the program (Nelson, 1986, 1987). The improvements included increased participant knowledge of community resources and of warning signs and better attitudes toward seeking help and the possibility of taking action. Measuring such short-term changes at the end of the program is the usual method of program evaluation, where there is one. Published accounts are rare; we have relied on one published report by Nelson (1987), unpublished reports such as those of Shaffer, Garland, and Bacon (1987) and Garland and Shaffer (1988), and related studies, such as that of Abbey, Madsen, and Polland (1989), which focused on college undergraduates. The situation is not much better for evaluations of community center-based programs. Dew, Bromet, Brent, and Greenhouse (1987) could locate only seven good quantitative studies of suicide prevention centers. Program implementers often lack evaluation skill and the funds needed to conduct an evaluation component, and programs are often put together under emergency conditions, with little thought given to evaluation.

In their well-designed study of a comprehensive school program, Shaffer and Garland (1987) found little change in either knowledge about or attitude toward suicide. Students who held sound views and had comprehensive knowledge prior to the program's inception did not change. Those who started with unsound views, who made up approximately 20 percent of the participants, also demonstrated little change. The 8 percent of the participants who had admitted a prior suicide attempt reported a clearly negative effect of program participation: They stated they would be less likely to reveal suicidal thoughts to others, that they believed more firmly that they could not be helped by psychotherapy or counseling, and that they viewed suicide as a reasonable course of action in some situations. Thus, there is some question as to whether suicide prevention programs are effective with their intended audiences. In fact, they may make people feel good about suicide prevention and let down their guard. If one considers the intended audience for these programs competent and well-informed adolescents who will subsequently guide peers to help, then Shaffer and Garland's findings are not so discouraging, since these are the adolescents we wish to reach.

In any case, it is important to learn in program evaluations whether certain groups of students at risk respond differentially to treatments. Will aptitude-treatment interactions emerge in our preventive activities? For example, how successful are programs designed to prevent suicidal outcome from occurring in those students who are at risk because of substance abuse or a particular predisposing factor? Perhaps programs focusing on students who are substance abusers can be fine tuned to the point where they may be more successful, say, than programs aimed at students who are at risk because of extreme guilt or emotional instability.

Prevention and Contagion

Another issue that Shaffer raises is the portrayal of suicide in most suicide prevention programs. In the California program and others, suicide is presented as a reaction to normal adolescent stresses or pressure; it is not portrayed as a function of mental illness in the child. The problem with this view, according to Shaffer, Garland, and Bacon (1987), is that students are more likely to imitate suicidal actions when suicide is portrayed as a tragic, heroic, or romantic response to stress and pressure imposed by an uncaring adult world. If it is labeled as a deviant act by someone with a mental disturbance, it may be less likely to be copied and emulated. However, most program designers want to encourage self-initiated referrals and believe that labeling suicidal behavior as a symptom of mental illness will encourage stigmatization and prevent students from referring themselves or others. These two views may be reconciled if the curriculum material stresses the multicausal nature of suicide outlined in Chapter Two of this book. Any program evaluation should include a component checking qualitatively on how the program is delivered to determine whether the program romanticizes suicide or the educators unwittingly make suicide attractive to adolescents.

Another important issue in suicide prevention, particularly in presenting films and other materials in an effort to add to education, is the issue of contagion. Social scientists have long been fascinated by the "Werther" effect, named after the sensation caused by Goethe's enormously popular novel of 1774, *The Sorrows of Young Werther*. In this novel, one of the first in the romantic period, the attractive protagonist, faced with the many problems of young people of the time, ultimately committed suicide. The youth of the day made the book a best seller and began to emulate the hero, and the suicide rate among youth skyrocketed. Authorities across Europe banned the book in an effort to counteract the loss of life (Eisenberg, 1986). The Werther, or contagion, effect is demonstrated by the observation that suicides cluster when spectacular cases of suicide are brought to the public's attention (Coleman, 1987). Although multiple simultaneous suicides or a series of suicides occurring closely in time and space may account for only 1 to 5 percent of all youth suicides (Gould, Wallenstein, and Kleinman, 1987), a community should take such an occurrence seriously and intervene. The Centers for Disease Control have prepared a set of recommendations for a community plan for the prevention and containment of suicide clusters that should be helpful to state and local agencies, including school districts (O'Carroll, Mercy, and Steward, 1988).

Whether or not clusters are significant, the fundamental question is whether preventive efforts or information about suicides contributes to the phenomenon. Can prevention stimulate contagion and clustering? Gould and Shaffer (1986) have examined the impact on suicide rates of four television programs with a theme of suicide. They note that the incidence of completed suicide increased following the showing of three of the four programs. Thus, Gould and Shaffer suspect that an unanticipated effect of a suicide prevention program is stimulating individuals to complete suicides.

The one exception in the Gould and Shaffer study was a program that was accompanied by a distinctive educational and preventive adjunct program. The program depicted the suicide of a high school senior following several interpersonal crises. However, the majority of the film focused on the reactions of the surviving family members and did not romanticize the act. Perhaps responsibly done mass media presentations are not dangerous.

An alternative view, originally put forth by Durkheim (Eisenberg, 1986), is that whereas suicide rates may increase directly after much publicity, sensational accounts of suicide stimulate only those who are on the verge of suicide to completion and, shortly after the publicity, suicide rates actually go down, evening out over time, so that Gould and Shaffer overestimate the problem.

Save for the Gould and Shaffer (1986) and Phillips and Carstensen (1986) studies, the research that has been conducted on the contagion theory of suicide has not supported the notion. A review in 1973 by Lester (1974) suggested there was no conclusive evidence that the rate of suicide would increase because mention had been made of suicide in a television program. Ross (1985) believes that where the attitude is projected that suicide should not be talked about but should be denied and buried, students are more likely to be made anxious and concerned. Klagsbrun (1976) does not believe that young people will be incited to suicidal behavior by hearing about it. Rather, she firmly believes that they will continue to be prevented from helping themselves and others if they are falsely "protected" from the subject. Others have challenged Gould and Shaffer's research, and a lively debate has ensued (Berman, 1988).

Guidelines for Program Evaluation

Special services personnel have an important research role to play in enabling the relatively new programs of prevention to become successful, and good evaluation is a key. Here, we briefly set forth some guidelines for practitioners.

First, the designers of programs should clarify their goals and objectives. If stated in behavioral terms, the objectives will be more easily and accurately communicated to others and will more readily lend themselves to being measured.

Second, it is important to consider both formative and summative evaluation. Some evaluation efforts should be directed at collecting data throughout the implementation of the project. The purpose of this formative evaluation is to collect data that will help the program to be changed in midstream, if need be, or to fine tune the delivery of various components. Summative evaluation, in contrast, takes place at the end of the program, is directed at the achievement of outcomes, and leads to decisions about the overall worth of the program.

Third, it is vital to check on whether the program is delivered as intended. If the summative evaluation indicates that the program is working, everyone will want to be assured that it is for the correct reason and that the program was implemented as planned. If the program is not working, everyone will want to know how well each program element was delivered. For example, an evaluator may wish to know whether the unit on community resources allowed sufficient time for students to learn about using such resources should the evaluation show this objective was not met.

Fourth, it will be useful to have an appropriate design. The usual approach is to collect base-line data before the program is initiated and then comparable data after it has been implemented. Another design is to use a control group, either randomly selected or carefully matched, to compare the performance of program participants with that of individuals who have not had the program. A number of other experimental and quasi-experimental designs are available to the evaluator.

Finally, a good evaluation depends greatly on the quality of the measures. There will be one or more measures of effectiveness for each of the program outcomes. Suicide prevention programs are usually evaluated by questionnaires, tests, or actuarial data. The questionnaires and tests should be carefully constructed. A few tests and surveys have been used in more than one study. The following list summarizes the outcomes that can be measured through a program evaluation and cites some model measures that might be adapted to local needs:

1. Student knowledge (Knowledge of Suicide Test and Suicide Prevention Questionnaire, Abbey, Madsen, and Polland, 1989)
    a. Warning signs
    b. Available resources
    c. Referral procedures
2. Student attitudes (Nelson, 1987)
    a. Positive
        i.   Toward mental health professionals
        ii. Toward seeking treatment
        iii. Toward suicide as a solution
    b. Unanticipated negative (Shaffer and Garland, 1987)
3. Staff knowledge (Suicide Intervention Response Scale, Neimeyer and MacInnes, 1981)
4. Staff attitude
5. Staff comfort and confidence
6. Staff performance on drill or stimulation (Abbey, Madsen, and Polland, 1989; suicide-related vignettes, Dew, Bromet, Brent, and Greenhouse, 1987)
7. Lowered suicide and attempt rates
8. Increases in referrals for suicide (Ross, 1980)
    a. Self-referrals to counselors
    b. Peer referrals

Conclusion

We have seen that the law strongly supports the development of effective suicide prevention programs in the schools. School personnel have a number of obligations for suicide prevention and intervention, just as they do for the identification of and intervention with victims of child abuse. Moreover, the ethical standards that most practitioners subscribe to, such as the Ethical Principles of Psychologists (American Psychological Association, 1990), emphasize their responsibilities toward the consumers of their services. To assist their clients, they must be competent, honor children's and parents' rights to privacy, and act ethically.

Further, if they are to act in the best interests of children, it is important that they monitor their own behavior through program evaluation and by other means so that they can eliminate ineffective behavior and constantly improve their services to others. This chapter has reviewed these issues and provided some guidelines for effective action. If mental health professionals are ever to live up to the promise of helping children and adolescents grow into competent adulthood, it is clear that they must learn to work in programmatic ways.

12

Conclusion: Toward a Better Understanding of Adolescent Suicide

At the beginning of this book, we presented data demonstrating that youth suicide is a leading cause of death in the adolescent population. Depending on the race and ethnicity of the adolescent, suicide is usually the second or third leading cause. Among children of high school age, suicide and attempted suicide have increased dramatically over the last few decades. It is clear that suicide is a serious mental health issue, yet few institutions other than the school are capable of mounting effective identification and prevention programs. Nevertheless, our experience indicates that a knowledge and expertise gap remains in the public schools and that school personnel have not been able to do as much as they should to assist suicidal youth.

Suicide rates vary substantially among different groups in the population. As more studies are done, we will know which groups are at most risk for suicidal ideation, suicide attempts, and completed suicides. Such information will permit us to focus our energies in the schools on high-risk individuals and the adults (teachers, counselors, and administrators) who are in most intimate contact with them. Adults and peers must be continually sensitized to the issues and symptoms of suicide.

We already know that a number of groups, such as various special education populations, must be studied more comprehensively because there is a suggestion that suicide rates are unusually high among these adolescents. The future may bring focused prevention programs for these and other at-risk groups, in addition to new general programs directed at the entire student body.

Causes of Suicidal Behavior

Although each suicide is as individual as the person who attempts or completes it, a number of models have been constructed to explain suicidal behavior. Clearly, there are genetic and other biological correlates of suicide. Moreover, it is often useful to view suicidal behavior as an expression of psychopathology. Nevertheless, we currently find the most useful model for conceptualizing suicide intervention and prevention to be the Blumenthal and Kupfer (1988) threshold model, which brings together a number of variables.

According to this model, biological factors and personality traits predispose children for suicidal behavior. But it is the presence of risk factors, such as hopelessness and psychopathology, linked to or found in conjunction with stress that increases the probability of suicide. Stress in adolescence may result from emerging sexuality, achievement pressures, family problems, attitudes about suicide, and the experience of personal loss. In addition to the stress, however, the students may have deficits in coping and problem-solving strategies that lead them to turn to suicide in the face of life problems. Critical events or life problems encountered by youth may become precipitating factors in a suicide. Precipitating factors are perhaps most productively thought of as problems for which the child either has not developed appropriate coping skills or has exhausted his or her coping resources. According to this model, then, suicide is thus multiply determined.

This explanatory model gives us a way to direct our identification and referral efforts as well as to plan for preventive interventions in the schools. As complex, multi-varied models such as this one are validated and expanded, we hope that new ideas for responding to suicidal emergencies and prevention programs will naturally follow. No doubt the future will bring an expansion of this model both as social factors change and as we learn more about human biochemistry.

Evaluating a Child's Suicide Potential

Although school personnel may not wish to take on in-depth suicide evaluations as one of their responsibilities, they still need to know about this process and how to make an appropriate referral. Generally speaking, the best way to determine whether an adolescent is suicidal is to ask him or her directly. Structured interviews may be used to help guide a school-based evaluator's suicide assessment. Structures such as Corder and Haizlip's (1982) or Bradley and Rotheram's (n.d.) can guide a suicide evaluation.

School personnel can also become more sensitive to potentially suicide-provoking situations and look more closely at an individual's problem-solving and coping skills. Tools such as a "no-suicide contract" can be used by school personnel as part of the process of helping the adolescent to contain the suicidal impulse until he or she can be referred to someone more expert. As more such tools, interview protocols, and questionnaires are developed, school-based personnel's ability to identify and refer suicidal youth to effective interventions will be improved. The future must bring more preservice education in these identification procedures for the special service personnel who will be serving our schools.

Following up and Intervening with Suicidal Youth

The major school intervention for suicidal youth is establishing the level of imminent danger and then, depending on the outcome of this evaluation, deciding between immediate hospitalization and referral to a mental health care provider for further evaluation and treatment. Mental health personnel in the schools should learn and internalize the procedure for initiating a hospitalization or having one initiated and should establish a set of contacts in the local community so that this intervention may be carried out as quickly and smoothly as possible. If a nonemergency referral is in order, school-based personnel should know how to present a referral to an adolescent and his or her family to increase the chance of its success. In order to make an effective referral, the school-based personnel should be familiar with the various options for treating a suicidal child. They must also be able to provide parents with options available in the community, taking into consideration both the child's and the parents' needs. This includes sensitivity to the family's values and traditions.

As new techniques are learned about making effective referrals, and as effective treatments for suicidal youth continue to develop, school personnel will need to keep abreast of both new interventions for suicidal youth and new ways of increasing the probability that children and their families will get access to effective treatment. Pharmacology will continue to expand as new treatment options are discovered. We fervently hope that the current trend away from funding community-based mental health treatment centers will be reversed.

What to Do After a Suicide

We estimate that every school in the United States will experience at least one suicide every few years. Knowing how to respond to the suicide of either a student, a teacher, or a parent will be important in heading off clusters of suicides as well as other mental health problems. Districts should develop procedures to deal with issues such as suicide and communicate these procedures to the school community and to parents. How the staff should be prepared to work with children following a suicide and how to implement and mobilize resources to work with students and their parents should form part of a district's suicide or crisis management plan. Individuals at high risk for mental health problems following a suicide should be identified, and special procedures should be drawn up for intervening with the survivors of the suicide.

More and more school districts and consortia of school districts are preparing contingency plans for school district personnel to follow in times of crisis or disaster. Routine in such crisis planning is the creation of teams that can respond to suicidal events. We look forward to research on how such crisis intervention teams may best be structured and implemented in public schools.

Identifying Students at Risk

An important strategy in preventive work is identifying individuals at risk for the condition to be prevented. With respect to identifying students at risk for suicidal behavior, three methods of screening have been developed: self-report questionnaire measures, the use of peers as identifiers in a screening procedure, and the use of school personnel as informants in efforts to screen suicidal youth. Any of these methods can be directed at populations that research has identified as being particularly at risk to commit suicide. Screening should take place, however, only when it is possible to follow up with a referral or other kinds of programs for those identified.

A number of screening devices have recently been identified (Cull and Gill, 1982; Reynolds, 1988). The future, no doubt, will see the development of new generations of screening measures for use with children and staff. Because of the importance of the decisions that will be made on the basis of the screening measures, it is critical that the measures meet the standards for psychological tests put forward by the Committee to Develop Standards for Educational and Psychological Testing of the American Educational Research Organization, the American Psychological Association, and the National Council on Measurement in Education. The area of measurement most ripe for development is the use of teachers as informants about suicidal behavior, since teachers as raters are most acceptable to school boards and using them is least invasive of privacy, and most efficient in time usage.

Prevention Efforts for High-Risk Populations

In addition to demographic factors correlated with a higher suicide incidence, it is also clear that substance use and abuse, runaway behavior, gay and lesbian conflicts in adolescents, a history of sexual abuse or physical abuse, and special education problems have been identified as signs of risk for suicidal behavior. In the future, new at-risk groups may be identified. It remains to be seen whether special screening devices for particular populations can be developed.

Education-Based Prevention Programs

A primary effort in suicide prevention involves educating the entire school population about the phenomenon of adolescent suicide. A number of model curricula have been developed to be taught in the public schools with the goals of alerting adolescents to the problem of suicide, helping them to identify the warning signs of suicidal behavior, developing skills for coping with stress and depression, and enabling them to help friends who are suicidal. These curricula may be taught as part of social studies or health education programs or may stand alone. The lesson plans in the curriculum may be supplemented by films, filmstrips, or videotapes. Experts from community agencies can often be brought into the public schools. Less direct efforts at suicide prevention have been implemented under the label of "competence enhancement programs." These programs teach general coping skills, the reduction of stress, and assertive behaviors to help children deal with peer pressures.

As these programs are being implemented and evaluated, we are learning more about effective program features and are attempting to resolve such controversies as whether prevention programs may contribute to an increase rather than a decrease in suicidal behavior. Research on curriculum intervention programs continues, and there will be much to be learned in the future years about how to mount programs in the schools.

We would like to see developed in the schools some experimental secondary prevention programs for students. As we improve our ability to identify students at risk, we will be able to take the next step and develop educational programs specifically designed for particular groups, such as students who have suffered a personal loss. An educational program focusing on loss and grieving issues and providing students with coping skills appropriate to overcoming a loss might be particularly effective. Such programs could be more efficient than primary prevention programs, although they would not be a substitute for them, since peers are such effective identifiers. In our review of the literature, we found no such program, but as the use of screening procedures becomes more common, it will be natural for programs to be developed for those identified as being at risk.

Peers as a Focus for Prevention

Although peers are a focus for prevention in curriculum-based programs and are used as informants for screening programs, peers can serve as a focus for prevention in other ways. Facilitating the development of a positive peer culture in the secondary schools may result in a number of positive outcomes, including a reduced rate of suicide. Suicide prevention may be enhanced by peer counseling programs, conflict-resolution programs, a well-rounded set of extracurricular activities within the school, and work-experience programs. School personnel may develop the student body as a general force to both prevent precipitating events and encouraging the early identification of suicidal behavior. We hope that the future will see a renewed emphasis on student development in the secondary schools. A number of ills besides suicide can be prevented by the creation of a positive peer culture in the schools. Good peer programs can have a positive influence on rates of dropping out and substance abuse.

Other Ways of Changing the Schools

A number of other preventive activities can take place in schools to reduce the impact of suicide. First, the district can develop a districtwide policy and plan for suicide prevention and intervention. By creating school district crisis management teams, the district can prepare itself to better respond to a number of disruptive events in addition to suicide. A number of models for an effective suicide preparedness plan can be adapted and adopted by local school districts.

Besides preparing themselves, schools may work with community leaders to help them prepare for suicidal events. They may work with the media, community mental health agencies, suicide prevention agencies, the clergy, and the criminal justice system to prepare for a coordinated response when a suicidal emergency occurs. Reaching beyond the community, school district personnel may direct their efforts at the national media and how they portray suicide. They can also work at eliminating the means for suicidal behavior by supporting gun control legislation and other initiatives, as well as positive legislation to implement suicide prevention programs and activities.

As prevention efforts are under way and school people involved in prevention develop networks, they will meet and share experiences. In time, a whole new generation of preventive activities will be developed and implemented.

Why Suicide Prevention in the Schools?

Increasingly, school districts seem to be under a legal obligation, as a result of either court cases or legislative mandates, to create effective suicide prevention programs. In implementing such prevention programs, school personnel must pay attention to legal principles requiring that they protect children's privacy and guarantee them equal protection under the law. School personnel must be particularly aware of their duty to warn parents and others of the potential for suicidal behavior. In conducting suicide prevention activities, district personnel must act within their range of competence and not exceed their training and knowledge. Awareness of legal and ethical issues can ensure a high-quality suicide prevention program.

As the future brings new court decisions and legislative initiatives, school districts will increasingly need to designate personnel to implement suicide prevention programs and assist them with in-service education. This book and others may serve as resources.

A Last Word

It has been our intention in this book to detail what is known about current suicide prevention and intervention programs, thereby facilitating the implementation of new programs from which more may be learned. We hope this volume will stimulate preventive activities as well as the discovery of ways to improve intervention and prevention programs. Our children deserve our best efforts.

Resource A:
Films, Filmstrips, and
Videotapes on Suicide

The following films cover topics related to suicide in adolescence and youth. Listings include the format (F = film; FS = filmstrip; V = videotape), the running time (if known), a short description of the content, and the distributor. The addresses of the distributors are provided at the end of the list. The films have not been rated for quality, which varies widely. Any film used in a program should be previewed to determine its suitability. Sufficient time should be set aside after the showing to answer all audience questions and provide a forum for discussion under the direction of an expert.

ABC Notebook: Teen Suicide. F, 20 minutes. This ABC adjunct to the television movie *Surviving* deals with the pressures and stresses of teenage lives and includes interviews with teachers, parents, and teenagers. Coronet/MTI Teleprogram.

Adolescent Suicide: A Matter of Life and Death. F, V, 39 minutes. Vignettes from the viewpoint of adolescents explore the emotional impact of quarreling parents, death of a loved one, juvenile detention, teenage pregnancy, joblessness, academic suspension, and other situations surrounding or leading to adolescent suicide. The film discusses the myths of suicide and steps toward prevention. Leader's guide included. American Personnel and Guidance Association.

Amy and the Angel. F, 30 minutes. Depressed about her lack of social life and her parents' divorce, seventeen-year-old Amy considers suicide. Then her guardian angel shows her how dismal life would have been if she had never been born. This dramatization seeks to convey the message that things are never as bad as they seem and that obstacles can be overcome. Coronet/MTI Teleprogram.

Before It's Too Late. F, 20 minutes. Designed to teach students in grades nine through twelve how to spot suicidal behavior and what to do if someone they know is suicidal. Walt Disney Media Company.

But He Was Only Seventeen: The Death of a Friend. FS. The death of a seventeen-year-old killed in an auto accident evokes questions about death and mourning, including reactions and the stages of grief. Three-part filmstrip. Part I: "Stages of Grief"; Part II: "Learning to Mourn"; Part III: "Reinvesting in Life." Sunburst Communications.

But Jack Was a Good Driver. F, 15 minutes. A funeral is ending. As Bob and his classmate Ed move to their cars, the conversation reveals both boys to be secretly and painfully preoccupied with the possibility that their friend may have taken his own life—that he may have deliberately driven his car off the road at high speed. As they explore their feelings, Bob and Ed explore the subject of suicide. McGraw-Hill Films.

A Case of Suicide. F, 30 minutes. This British documentary presents the recollections of the mother and husband of an eighteen-year-old woman who committed suicide, as well as the clues preceding the act and the woman's family background. Michigan Media.

Childhood's End. F, 30 minutes. A Canadian film that focuses on a bright young man who kills himself. The film includes interviews with his family and friends. Filmmakers Library.

Cry for Help. F. Useful for parents and school personnel. Hospital and Community Psychiatry Service.

Dead Serious. F, V, 24 minutes. Explores case studies of teenage suicide, identifies warning signs, and prescribes listening skills for teens as a response to peers in crisis. Based on the book by Jane Mersky Leder. Coronet/MTI Teleprogram.

Depression: Blahs, Blues, and Better Days. F, 20 minutes. Narrator Joseph Campanella explores the range of emotions from blues to depression. Shows the difference between normal and abnormal reactions to crises in three case studies. Directions Unlimited.

Did Jenny Have to Die? FS, 35 minutes. An analysis of a case of teen suicide reveals some of the causes and warning signs of and ways of preventing adolescent death. Students view the details of the tragedy through the eyes of family members, friends, teachers—and the victim herself. Part I: "Road to Nowhere"; Part II: "Behind the Smiles"; Part III: "A Foundation for Living." Sunburst Communications.

Everything to Live For. F, V, 24 minutes. This documentary tells the stories of four young people who either attempted or completed suicide. The film seeks to increase awareness of the family and social pressures that often force teenagers to the brink and of the warning signals that usually precede a suicide attempt. Viewers also learn about the various organizations founded to help teens deal positively with their problems. Coronet/MTI Teleprogram.

Family of Winners. F. Drama of one boy's stressful life situations and subsequent suicidal depression. Paulist Productions.

Getting Through the Bad Times: Teenage Crisis. FS, V. Three film-strips—*Understanding the Problem, Handling the Problem,* and *Using the Crisis Technique*—devoted to providing students with coping techniques for emotional crises. Sunburst Communications.

Gifted Adolescents and Suicide. V, 26 minutes. Specially adapted Phil Donahue program featuring two parents of intellectually gifted adolescents. The program points out how parents and teachers need to recognize the pressure of expectations on superachievers and know when to leave a youngster alone and when to intercede. Films for the Humanities and Sciences.

Hear Me Cry. F, V, 30 minutes. In this drama, two boys develop a close friendship as a result of serious difficulties that each is experiencing in relationships with his parents. But their mutual unhappiness only heightens their feelings of despair. When a suicide pact results in the death of one boy, a tragic moment of truth confronts all concerned. Coronet/MTI Teleprogram.

Help Me! The Story of Teenage Suicide. F, 28 minutes. SL Film Productions.

In Loveland: Study of Teenage Suicide. F, V, 28 minutes. Why would an average boy take his own life at age fifteen? This film reconstructs the tragic course of events that ended in the death of Mark Cada of Loveland, Colorado. Interviews with Mark's family and friends underline the importance of attending to warning signs and becoming more sensitive to the needs of troubled teenagers. Produced by ABC News. Coronet/MTI Teleprogram.

Inside, I Ache. F, V, 30 minutes. Explores the reasons for suicide, the warning signs, and places to seek help and urges friends of those in trouble to "tell." For high school, college, and adult audiences. *NFTY* (16 mm. rental) and UAHC Television and Film Institute (video purchase).

Is Anyone Listening? and *Hearing Between the Lines.* V, 30 minutes each. *Is Anyone Listening?* focuses on Alberta, Canada, where the teenage suicide rate is the highest among the provinces and where there has been a far-reaching and effective approach to the problem. *Hearing Between the Lines* examines issues of teen suicide from the perspective of a serene upstate New York farmland community and the frenetic life-style of New York City. Youth Suicide National Center.

Keeping Your Teenager Alive: Theory, Prevention and Treatment of Adolescent Suicide. V, 110 minutes. Carl Tishler, Ph.D., examines the problems of teenage accidents and suicide. Describes the factors essential to teenage care, the symptoms of depression, elements of loss, and treatment factors when working with adolescents. Vidcam, Inc.

A Last Cry for Help. F, 32 minutes. Unable to talk with anyone about her feelings of depression, a seemingly popular teenage girl attempts suicide. When her parents deny that any problem exists, a psychologist helps the girl understand that things won't change until she takes control of her own life. Offers illustration of how family therapy is conducted and how it works. Coronet/MTI Teleprogram.

Learning to Cope. F, 14 minutes. Dr. Hans Selye offers suggestions on avoiding stress and provides insights into our unique abilities to handle the problem. American Educational Films.

Let's Stop Teen Suicide. F. The upbeat theme "Talk it over, talk it out" dramatically shows teens what they can say and do when they have a suicidal friend. Neighborhood Service Organization, Suicide Prevention Center.

Preventing Teen Suicide: You Can Help. FS. Tells the story of Jennifer and explains why teens commit suicide, signs and symptoms, myths that surround teen suicide, and prevention techniques. Of special interest is the filmstrip *Did Jenny Have to Die?* included in this series. Sunburst Communications.

Reach Out for Life. F, 11 minutes. A cartoon that addresses possible motivations for suicide. Filmmakers Library.

Ronnie's Tune. F. Through the eyes of an eleven-year-old girl, one sees the effects of a teenager's suicide on her family. Wombat Productions, Inc.

The Suicidal Adolescent: Identification, Risk Assessment, and Intervention. Interactive videodisc program. A comprehensive curriculum for professionals, developed for medical students, delivered through state-of-the-art teaching technology. Four case studies are presented. The user conducts interviews and attempts intervention techniques interactively with a personal computer while viewing a videodisc. At any time during the program, the student can look up critical reference materials in the computer text.

Suicide at 17. F, 18 minutes. Why did Bobbie Benton take his own life? He had friends, popularity, a record of achievement in the classroom and the gym, loving and conscientious parents and teachers, and a coach who cared. A film documenting the suicide of one teenager. Lawren Productions, Inc.

Suicide: Causes and Prevention. FS, 35 minutes. Seeks to evaluate the causes of suicide in our society and suggests ways to help a suicidal person. Sunburst Communications.

Suicide: It Doesn't Have to Happen. F, 21 minutes. Illustrates the intervention role of the adult in the prevention of youthful suicide by presenting an actual case in which a girl is guided to a rap group by a high school teacher who himself once attempted suicide. Negative feelings precipitating suicide and methods of dissipating them as well as symptoms are discussed. BFA Educational Media.

Suicide Prevention and Crisis Intervention. F (12 films, 6 tapes). Useful for mental health professional and counselors. Charles Press Publishing.

Suicide: Teenage Crisis. F, 10 minutes. The film explores the problem of teenage suicides and includes descriptions of a variety of community and school programs. McGraw-Hill Films.

Suicide: The Warning Signs. F, 24 minutes. The film combines dramatic enactment with documented remarks from a recognized authority on youth suicide. There are three dramatized vignettes: Greg, the class clown; Carol, a determined achiever; and Curtis, who has experienced loss of a girlfriend and poor grades. Through narration and interviews, the film brings out a number of clues that may indicate that a person is considering suicide and what parents, teachers, and teenagers themselves can do. Coronet/MTI Teleprogram.

Suicide: Who Will Cry For Me? FS, 26 minutes. Filmstrips and recording seek to provide information and put the subject into perspective, aiming toward the particular problems of young people. *Dancing with Death* introduces the subject of suicide by portraying a fourteen-year-old girl who takes her own life, *Dangling Their Feet in the Pool of Death* analyzes teenage suicides and suicide attempts, and *You Can Always Die Next Thursday* discusses various ways of preventing suicide. Audio Visual Narrative Arts.

Suicides. F, V. Useful for mental health professionals and counselors. Behavioral Sciences Media Laboratory, Neuropsychiatric Institute.

Suicide Survivors. V, 26 minutes. This program explores the special needs of suicide survivors, the role of suicide survivor groups in helping to cope with the bereavement process, and the changing societal attitudes that are enabling suicide survivors to come out of the closet. Films for the Humanities and Sciences.

Teen Suicide. F, V, 28 minutes. This Phil Donahue show featuring Heather Locklear of "Dynasty" seeks to find ways to stem the tide of increasing suicide rates among teens, to help youngsters and adults recognize the signals and warning cries of potential suicides, and to show what kind of help can be offered. Films for the Humanities and Sciences.

Teen Suicide: Who, Why and How You Can Prevent It. V. Videotaped interviews with people who have faced the tragedy of teen suicide. Helps young people recognize critical signs of trouble in themselves or friends and where and how to seek help. Avna Media.

Teenage Blues: Coping with Depression. FS, V. Introduces students to the concept of depression, some common causes and symptoms, and where and how to get help. Offers specific advice on how to get a friend to "open up," how to spot suicidal tendencies, and where to get help. Sunburst Communications.

Teenage Suicide. F. Narrator Timothy Hutton explores the lives and deaths of four teenagers. Films, Inc./PMI.

Teenage Suicide. F, V, 22 minutes. Interviews with teens offer insights into their view of suicide as a viable option. Professionals in the field alert viewers to the warning signs that often precede a suicide attempt and emphasize the need for parents to listen to what their children are saying. Coronet/MTI Teleprogram.

Teenage Suicide. F, V, 19 minutes. This documentary explores some of the reasons why teens commit suicide and the recent increase in suicide and describes some of the behavior patterns to which family and friends should be alert. A young man who failed in a suicide attempt describes his calls for help and how he hoped they would be heeded. Films for the Humanities and Sciences.

Teenage Suicide: A Cry for Help. FS. The reasons for teenage suicide and what can be done about them are explored. Kidsrights.

Teenage Suicide: Don't Try It. FS. This documentary establishes the extent of the problem and demonstrates what some communities are doing to prevent it. Alan Landsburg Productions.

Teenage Suicide: Is Anyone Listening? F. This film documents the problems of two young people who have attempted suicide. Barr Films.

Teenage Suicide: What to Do. V, 27 minutes. In this videotape, teens talk openly about their suicide attempts, and professionals clear up the myths and examine clues. What teenagers can say and do to help prevent their peers from attempting suicide is answered by teens and acted out to provide a model for viewers to use when they see someone who might be suidical. A companion workbook available. Ann Arbor Publishers.

Teens Who Choose Life: The Suicide Crisis. FS, V. Explores the special dynamics of teen suicide using the moving stories of three teenagers who attempted suicide and survived. Helps viewers understand the events and feelings that may precipitate a suicidal crisis. Emphasizes that there are other ways to cope with stress and depression and demonstrates that the first step is to "choose life." Three filmstrips. Sunburst Communications.

Too Sad to Live. F, 60 minutes. Four sensitive vignettes of troubled young people. Especially recommended for guidance counselors and mental health professionals. Massachusetts Committee for Children and Youth.

A Tribute to Time. F. Story of a teenage boy and how his friends attempt to help him. Suicide Prevention and Education Center.

Urgent Messages. F, 22 minutes. Patty Duke introduces the story of three suicidal teenagers. Two tell their own stories, and the classmates of a third tell what it feels like to lose their friend. Media Guild.

Young People in Crisis. F, V, 30 minutes. Through a series of moving dramatic sequences, this film introduces young people seeking relief from the pain of broken homes, broken romances, and unrealistic expectations. We learn what is troubling each one, how they misguidedly try to overcome their problems, and how the people who care about them try to help. Narrator Dr. Pamela Cantor's insights and observations emphasize the need for direct action and explain how effective intervention can mean the difference between life and death. EXAR Communications.

Youth Stress. F, 24 minutes. Introduces the active stress-inducing world of today's adolescents, with stresses that are unrelenting and can tear us apart. The film demonstrates that if we are to thrive, we must learn the essence of controlling our lives, so that every force that comes against us brings us one step closer to our desired goals. Before commanding such a powerful life-sustaining force as stress, we must first learn about it. Perennial Education, Inc.

Sources of Films and Videos

Alan Landsburg Productions
1554 Sepulveda Boulevard
Los Angeles, CA 90025
(213) 208-2111

American Educational Films
3807 Dickerson Road
Nashville, TN 37207
(800) 822-5678

American Personnel and Guidance Association
2 Skyline Place, Suite 400
5203 Leesburg Pike
Falls Church, VA 22041
(703) 823-9800

Ann Arbor Publishers
P.O. Box 7249
Naples, FL 33941

Audio Visual Narrative Arts
P.O. Box 9
Pleasantville, NY 10507
(914) 769-8545

Avna Media
Box 1040
Mount Kisco, NY 10549

BFA Educational Media
Broadcasting System, Inc.
Distributed by Phoenix/BFA
Films and Video, Inc.
470 Park Avenue South
New York, NY 10016

Barr Films
P.O. Box 5667
Pasadena, CA 91107
(213) 793-6153

Behavioral Sciences Media Laboratory
Neuropsychiatric Institute, UCLA
760 Westwood Plaza
Los Angeles, CA 90024
(213) 825-0448

Charles Press Publishing, Inc.
P.O. Box 830
Bowie, MD 20715

Coronet/MTI Teleprogram
108 Wilmot Road
Deerfield, IL 60015-9925
(800) 621-7870

Directions Unlimited Film Corporation
8271 Melrose Avenue
Los Angeles, CA 90046

EXAR Communications
267B McClean Avenue
Stanten Island, NY 10305

Filmmakers Library
113 East 58th Street, Suite 703A
New York, NY 10022

Films, Inc./PMI
5547 North Ravenswood
Chicago, IL 60640
(312) 878-2600

Films for the Humanities and Sciences, Inc.
P.O. Box 2053
Princeton, NJ 08543
(800) 257-5126

Hospital and Community Psychiatry Service
Film Library/Visual Aids Service
University of Illinois
Champaign, IL 61820

Kidsrights
120-A West Fifth Avenue
P.O. Box 851
Mount Dora, FL 32757

Lawren Productions, Inc.
P.O. Box 66
Mendocino, CA 95460
(707) 937-0536

McGraw-Hill Films
P.O. Box 641
Del Mar, CA 92014
(619) 453-5000 or (800) 421-0833

Mass Media Ministries
by FTY
and UAHC Television and Film Institute
838 Fifth Avenue
New York, NY 10021
(212) 249-0100

Massachusetts Committee for Children and Youth
14 Beacon Street, Suite 706
Boston, MA 02108

The Media Guild
11722 Sorrento Valley Road
Suite E
San Diego, CA 92121-1021

Michigan Media
University of Michigan
416 Fourth Street
Ann Arbor, MI 48109
(313) 764-5360

Neighborhood Service Organization
Suicide Prevention Center
220 Bagley, Suite 626
Detroit, MI 48226
(313) 963-7890

Paulist Productions
P.O. Box 1057
Pacific Palisades, CA 90272
(213) 454-0688

Perennial Education, Inc.
930 Pitner Avenue
Evanston, IL 60202
(313) 328-6700

SL Film Productions
P.O. Box 41108
Los Angeles, CA 90014
(213) 254-8528

Suicide Prevention and Education Center
982 Easter Parkway
Louisville, KY 40217
(502) 635-5924

Sunburst Communications
101 Castleton Street
Pleasantville, NY 10570-9971
(914) 769-5030 or (800) 431-1934

Vidcam, Inc.
6322 Kings Pointe Road
Grand Blanc, MI 48439
(313) 694-0996

Walt Disney Media Company
500 South Buena Vista Street
Burbank, CA 91521
(818) 956-3000

Wombat Productions, Inc.
P.O. Box 70
Ossining, NY 10562
(914) 762-0011

The Youth Suicide National Center
1825 I Street, N.W., Suite 400
Washington, DC 20006
(202) 429-2016

Resource B:
Resources for
Prevention Programs

Pamphlets

About Suicide Among Young People. Channing L. Bete Company, Inc., South Deerfield, MA 01373.

Grief After Suicide. Mental Health Association in Waukesha County, Inc., 414 West Moreland Boulevard, Room 101, Waukesha, WI 53186.

Responding to Adolescent Suicide. Phi Delta Kappa Task Force on Adolescent Suicide, Phi Delta Kappa Educational Foundation, P.O. Box 789, Bloomington, IN 47402-0789.

Suicide in Youth and What You Can Do About It: A Guide for Students. By C. P. Ross and A. R. Lee. Youth Suicide National Center, 1825 I Street, N.W., Suite 400, Washington, DC 20006.

Suicide: We Are All Victims and *Suicide: A Teenage Tragedy.* Publications Service, Family Service America, 11700 West Lake Park Drive, Milwaukee, WI 53224.

Suicide: Why? 85 Questions and Answers About Suicide. By Adina Wrobleski. Also companion audio cassettes.

Youth Suicide: Community Response to a National Problem.
Youth Suicide National Center, 1825 I Street, N.W., Suite 400,
Washington, DC 20006.

School District and State Suicide Manuals

California: *Suicide Prevention Program for California Public
Schools.* (ISBN 0-8011-0682-6). Available from California State Department of Education, Publication Sales, P.O. Box 271, Sacramento, CA 95802-0271. 1987. 260 pages.

Fairfax County, Virginia: *The Adolescent Suicide Prevention Program.* By Beatrice Cameron and Myra Herbert. Available from the
Fairfax County Public Schools, Department of Student Services and
Special Education, 10310 Layton Hall Drive, Fairfax, VA 22030.
1987.

Florida: *Youth Suicide Prevention: A Guide for Trainers of Adult
Programs.* Available from ERIC/CAPS Publications, 2108 School
of Education, University of Michigan, Ann Arbor, MI 48109-1259.
1989. 147 pages.

Parkway, Missouri: *Parkway School District Crisis Intervention
Manual.* By Stephen Colombo and David Oegema. Available from
Stephen Colombo, Ph.D., Coordinator for Special Education, Pupil
Personnel/Special Services Department, Parkway School District,
455 North Woods Mill Road, Chesterfield, MO 63017. 1986.

Toronto: *Suicide Prevention: A Resource for Student Services.* Bul-
letin no. 12. By Ester Cole and Michael Brotman. Available from
Psychological Services, Toronto Board of Education, Toronto,
Ontario.

Weld, Colorado: *Handbook: Suicide Prevention in the Schools.* By
Susy R. Ruof, Joann M. Harris, and Mary B. Robbie. Available
from Special Education, Weld BOCES, P.O. Box 578, La Salle, CO
80645-0578. 1987.

Youth Suicide: A Comprehensive Manual for Prevention and Intervention. By Barbara Barrett Hicks. National Educational Service, P.O. Box 8, Bloomington, IN 47402. 132 pp.

Preventing Teenage Suicide: The Living Alternative Handbook. By Polly Joan. Human Sciences Press, Inc. 1986. 147 pp.

National Organizations

American Association of Suicidology
2459 South Ash Street
Denver, CO 80222
(303) 692-0985

National Committee on Youth Suicide Prevention
666 Fifth Avenue 13th Floor
New York, NY 10103
(212) 247-6910

Suicide Information and Education Center
723 14th Street, #103
Calgary, Alberta T2N 2A4
(403) 283-3031

Youth Suicide National Center
1825 I Street, N.W., Suite 400
Washington, DC 10006

Resource C:
Readings on Suicide for
Children and Young Adults

Non-Fiction

Bernstein, J. E. *Loss and How to Cope With It.* Boston: Houghton Mifflin, 1981. How the death of a loved one affects the survivors. Grades 6+.

Bolton, I. *My Son, My Son.* Altanta, Ga.: Bolton Press, 1983. A mother's story of surviving the loss of her son to suicide. If the reader has sustained a loss, this book's message is one of realistic hope, reassurance, and practical emotional support and healing. In the absence of loss, the message is one of such heightened awareness of what is of value in life that it generates the resolve to nurture those things that in turn can only reduce many of the painful aspects of life that are conducive to loss.

Bradley, B. *Endings: A Book About Death.* Reading, Mass.: Addison-Wesley, 1979. The physical and emotional aspects of different ways of dying, including suicide. Grades 7+.

Gordon, S. *When Living Hurts.* New York: Yad Tikvah Foundation, 1985. A lively what-to-do book for anyone who feels discouraged, sad, lonely, hopeless, angry, frustrated, unhappy, bored, depressed, or suicidal.

Hyde, M., and Forsythe, E. F. *Suicide: The Hidden Epidemic*. New York: Franklin Watts, 1978. Explores and helps clarify complex aspects of suicide. Grades 9+.

Klagsbrun, F. *Too Young to Die: Youth and Suicide*. New York: Houghton Mifflin, 1976. Scientific research, literary illustrations, and case examples are mingled with suggestions for talking with a suicidal person, calming him or her through a crisis, and leading him or her to sources of help. Grades 7+.

Kubler-Ross, E. *Remember the Secret*. Millbrae, Calif.: Celestial Arts, 1981. Discusses important questions about life and death. There is sadness to the story, but also great happiness and victory. Grades 7+.

LeShan, E. *You and Your Feelings*. New York: Macmillan, 1975. Discusses problems that young people have with family, friends, and school. Grades 7+.

LeShan, E. *Learning to Say Good-Bye: When a Parent Dies*. New York: Macmillan, 1976. A nonfictional discussion of the death of a parent with many case histories. It focuses on the many feelings that children have and may not share. There is one case history involving a suicide. Grades 5+.

Mack, J. E., and Hickler, H. *Vivienne: The Life and Suicide of an Adolescent Girl*. Boston: Little, Brown, 1981. The writings and diary of fourteen-year-old Vivienne discovered after her suicide, combined with the insights of clinical psychiatrist Mack, tell the story of her secret life and her heartbreaking death. Grades 9+.

Madison, A. *Suicide and Young People*. New York: Houghton Mifflin, 1978. Grades 6+.

Myers, I., and Myers, A. *Why You Feel Down and What You Can Do About It*. New York: Scribner's, 1982. Topics include shifting relationships in the family, the influence of companions, danger signals, and sources of help. Grades 7+.

Segerberg, O. *Living with Death*. New York: Dutton, 1976. A non-fictional discussion of different views and different aspects of death. There is also a section on coping with death, including a brief section on suicide. Grades 6+.

Fiction

Agee, J. *A Death in the Family*. New York: Bantam Books, 1970. The story of a family shattered by the sudden death of the father in a car accident. Grades 9+.

Armstrong, W. H. *The Mills of God*. New York: Doubleday, 1973. The story of a boy who, having finally been able to buy the dog he has always dreamed of, is forced to give up that one thing that has given his life some meaning. He dreams of committing suicide and wakes up to a mystery and a suicide. Grades 6+.

Arrick, F. *Tunnel Vision*. Scarsdale, N.Y.: Bradbury Press, 1980. After a fifteen-year-old boy hangs himself, his family and friends must deal with feelings of guilt and bewilderment. Grades 6+.

Asinof, E. *Craig and Joan: Two Lives for Peace*. New York: Viking Penguin, 1971. Craig and Joan were two teenagers turning from their conservative upbringing to the antiwar movement of the Vietnam era. They were all-American kids who expressed their feelings about killing and their feelings of alienation somewhat ironically in a suicide pact. Grades 7+.

Beckman, G. *Admission to the Feast*. New York: Dell, 1973. The story of a girl confronting her own death, through stream-of-consciousness writing. Grades 7+.

Bridgers, S. E. *Notes for Another Life*. New York: Bantam Books, 1982. Two teenagers must cope with overwhelming crises in their family, and discover the durability of love. Grades 7+.

Calvert, P. *Hour of the Wolf.* New York: Scribner's, 1983. A young man comes to terms with his own life after the suicide of a friend. Grades 7+.

Cleaver, V., and Cleaver, B. *Grover.* New York: New American Library, 1975. This book tells of the confusion experienced by a child who must face the illness and suicide of a parent. Grades 5+.

Donovan, J. *Wild in the World.* New York: Harper & Row, 1971. The last survivor of a household riddled by death asks whether fate determines survival. Grades 5+.

Elfman, B. *A House for Jonnie O.* New York: Houghton Mifflin, 1977. A young man comes to terms with his own life after the suicide of a friend.

Ferris, J. *Amen, Moses Gardenia.* New York: Farrar, Straus & Giroux, 1983. Virtually ignored by her alcoholic and workaholic father, Farrel suffers bouts of depression, which worsen when she thinks that her new boyfriend is not serious. Grades 7+.

Gerson, C. *Passing Through.* New York: Dial, 1978. A high school girl must cope with her older brother's suicide. Grades 8+.

Green, H. *I Never Promised You a Rose Garden.* New York: Holt, Rinehart & Winston, 1964. A novel about a young schizophrenic who is desperately self-destructive but fiercely intelligent. Her struggle is given added poignancy by her youth, wit, and courage. Grades 9+.

Guest, J. *Ordinary People.* New York: Penguin, 1982. A young man makes an unsuccessful attempt at suicide after his brother drowns in an accident. The story depicts the pain of adolescent anxiety and fragile family relationships. Grades 7+.

Hale, J. C. *The Owl's Song.* New York: Doubleday, 1972. A story about a young Native American boy's struggle for self-worth as he deals with alcoholism and suicide. Grades 7+.

Horgan, P. *Whitewater*. New York: Farrar, Straus & Giroux, 1970. A trio of school friends growing up.

L'Engle, M. *Camilla*. New York: Dell, 1982. After her mother's suicide attempt, a daughter realizes that parents are fallible human beings. The story reveals an affirmation of the value of existence. Grades 7+.

Luger, H. *Lauren*. New York: Dell, 1981. Unable to solve the problems of an unwanted pregnancy, seventeen-year-old Lauren considers suicide. Grades 9+.

Madison, W. *Portrait of Myself*. New York: Random House, 1979. Fifteen-year-old Catherine yearns for beauty and self-assurance, but when the teacher she adores rejects her drawings and recommends her expulsion, she attempts suicide. Grades 7+.

Miklowitz, G. *Close to the Edge*. New York: Dell, 1984. Jenny Hartley takes the news of Cindy's suicide attempt seriously. When Cindy does kill herself, it's Jenny's association with a senior citizen group that helps her put the death in perspective. Grades 7+.

Oneal, Z. *The Language of Goldfish*. New York: Fawcett, 1981. Afraid of changing and growing up, thirteen-year-old Carrie suffers a nervous breakdown and retreats into her childhood world. Grades 6+.

Peck, R. *Remembering the Good Times*. New York: Dell, 1986. Buck and Kate know that their friend Tran is overwhelmed by the pressures in his life but never suspect that he might resort to suicide. Grades 7+.

Plath, S. *The Bell Jar*. New York: Bantam Books, 1975. A young woman suffers a breakdown and tries suicide. Although this is a novel, it is actually Plath's own story of attempted suicide and time spent in institutions. Grades 9+.

Radley, G. *The World Turned Inside Out*. New York: Crown, 1982. This story explores the efforts made by Jeremy and his family to cope with the stress and tragedy of a suicide.

Terris, S. *The Drowning Boy*. New York: Doubleday, 1972. A series of painful events bring Jason to the brink of suicide, but he realizes in time that he doesn't really want to die. Grades 6+.

Tolan, S. *Grandpa and Me*. New York: Scribner's, 1978. Kerry's grandfather begins acting strangely and eventually commits suicide. She can understand and remembers him with love. Grades 5+.

Walsh, J. P. *Goldengrove*. New York: Farrar, Straus & Giroux, 1972. Madge discovers that some things in life cannot be fixed, that some hurts are too deep. In her anger and depression, she makes a suicide attempt. Grades 5+.

Zalben, J. *Maybe It Will Rain Tomorrow*. New York: Farrar, Straus & Giroux, 1982. When Beth's mother committed suicide, she had to learn not only to accept her mother's death but also to live with her father, her stepmother, and a new baby. Grades 7+.

References

Abbey, K. J., Madsen, C. H., and Polland, R. "Short-Term Suicide Awareness Curriculum." *Suicide and Life Threatening Behavior*, 1989, *19*, 216–227.

Adams, P. L., and Fras, I. *Beginning Child Psychiatry*. New York: Brunner/Mazel, 1988.

Adelstein, A., and Mardon, C. *Suicides 1961–74*. Population Trends, no. 2. London: Her Majesty's Stationery Office, 1975.

Albert, N., and Beck, A. T. "Incidence of Depression in Early Adolescence: A Preliminary Study." *Journal of Youth and Adolescence*, 1975, *4*, 301–307.

American Educational Research Association, American Psychological Association, and National Council on Measurement in Education. *Standards for Educational and Psychological Testing*. Washington, D.C.: American Psychological Association, 1985.

American Psychiatric Association. *Diagnostic and Statistical Manual*. (3rd ed., rev.) Washington, D.C.: American Psychiatric Association, 1987.

American Psychological Association. *Standards for Educational and Psychological Testing*. Washington, D.C.: American Psychological Association, 1985.

American Psychological Association. "Ethical Principles of Psychologists." *American Psychologist*, 1990, *45*, 390–395.

Anderson, N. C. "Concepts, Diagnosis, and Classification." In E. Paykel (ed.), *Handbook of Affective Disorders*. New York: Guilford Press, 1982.

Appel, Y., and Matus, A. *Adolescent Suicide Training Manual*. Trenton: New Jersey State Department of Education, 1984.

Asarnow, J. R., Carlson, G. A., and Guthrie, D. "Coping Strategies, Self-Perceptions, and Hopelessness, and Perceived Family Environments in Depressed and Suicidal Children." *Journal of Consulting and Clinical Psychology*, 1987, *55*, 361–366.

Asberg, M., Traskman, L., and Thoran, P. "Biologic Factors in Suicide." In A. Roy (ed.), *Suicide*. Baltimore, Md.: Williams & Wilkins, 1986.

Beck, A. T. "Hopelessness as a Predictor of Eventual Suicide." *Annals of the New York Academy of Science*, 1986, *487*, 90–96.

Beck, A. T., and Greenberg, R. "The Nosology of Suicidal Phenomena: Past and Future Perspectives." *Bulletin of Suicidology*, Fall 1971, pp. 10–17.

Beck, A. T., Kovacs, M., and Weissman, A. "Hopeless and Suicidal Behavior: An Overview." *Journal of the American Medical Association*, 1975, *234*, 1146–1149.

Beck, A. T., Rush, A., Shaw, B., and Emery, G. *Cognitive Therapy of Depression*. New York: Guilford Press, 1979.

Beck, A. T., Schuyler, D., and Herman, I. "Development of Suicidal Intent Scales." In A. T. Beck, H.L.P. Resnik, and D. J. Lettieri (eds.), *The Prediction of Suicide*. Bowie, Md.: Charles Press, 1974.

Beck, A. T., Steer, R. A., Kovacs, M., and Garrison, B. "Hopelessness and Eventual Suicide: A 10-Year Prospective Study of Patients Hospitalized with Suicidal Ideation." *American Journal of Psychiatry*, 1985, *142*, 559–563.

Beck, A. T., Weissman, A., Lester, D., and Trexler, L. "The Measurement of Pessimism: The Hopelessness Scale." *Journal of Consulting and Clinical Psychology*, 1974, *42*, 861–865.

Bedrosian, R. C., and Epstein, N. "Cognitive Therapy of Depressed and Suicidal Adolescents." In H. S. Sudak, A. B. Ford, and N. B. Rushforth (eds.), *Suicide in the Young*. Littleton, Mass.: John Wright, 1984.

Beebe, J. E. "Evaluation of the Suicidal Patient." In C. P. Rosenbaum and J. E. Beebe (eds.), *Psychiatric Treatment: Crisis, Clinic and Consultation*. New York: McGraw-Hill, 1975.

Bell, A. P., and Weinberg, M. S. *Homosexualities: A Study of Diversity Among Men and Women*. New York: Simon & Schuster, 1978.

Benjamin, A. *The Helping Interview*. Boston: Houghton Mifflin, 1987.

Berger, M. "Temperament and Individual Differences." In M. Rutter and L. Hersov (eds.), *Child and Adolescent Psychiatry: Modern Approaches*. (2nd ed.) London: Blackwell Scientific, 1985.

Berlin, I. "Suicide Among American Indian Adolescents: An Overview." *Suicide and Life-Threatening Behavior*, 1987, *17*, 218–232.

Berman, A. L. "Playing the Suicide Game." *Readings: A Journal of Reviews and Commentary in Mental Health*, 1988, *3* (2), 20–23.

Bernard, M. L., and Bernard, J. L. "Institutional Responses to the Suicidal Student: Ethical and Legal Considerations." *Journal of College Student Personnel*, 1980, *21* (2), 109–113.

Bernstein, J. E. *Books to Help Children Cope with Separation and Loss*. New York: Bowker, 1977.

Blumenthal, S. J. "Suicide: A Guide to Risk Factors, Assessment, and Treatment of Suicidal Patients." *Medical Clinics of North America*, 1988, *72*, 937–971.

Blumenthal, S. J. and Kupfer, D. J. "Clinical Assessment and Treatment of Youth Suicidal Behavior." *Journal of Youth and Adolescence*, 1988, *17*, 1–23.

Botvin, G. *Life Skills Training*. New York: Smithfield Press, 1983.

Botvin, G. J., and Dusenbury, L. "Life Skills Training: A Psychoeducational Approach to Substance-Abuse Prevention." In G. A. Maher and J. E. Zins (eds.), *Psychoeducational Interventions in the Schools*. Elmsford, N.Y.: Pergamon Press, 1987.

Bradley, J., and Rotheram, M. J. *Suicide: Imminent Danger Assessment and Suicide Risk Among Adolescents: A Training Manual for Runaway Shelter Staff*. Manual produced with support from Office of Human Development Services, Administration of Children, Youth, and Families, Grant no. CDP 6638, n.d.

Bradley, J., and Rotheram-Borus, M. *Evaluating Suicidal Youth in Community Settings: A Training Manual*. Tulsa: University of Oklahoma Press, 1989.

Brent, D. A., and others. "Psychopathology and Its Relationship to Suicidal Ideation in Childhood and Adolescence." *Journal of the American Academy of Child Psychiatry*, 1986, *25* (5), 666–673.

Briere, J., and Runtz, M. "Suicidal Thoughts and Behaviours in

Former Sexual Abuse Victims." *Canadian Journal of Behavioural Science,* 1986, *18,* 413–423.

Briere, J., and Zaidi, L. Y. "Sexual Abuse Histories and Sequelae in Female Psychiatric Emergency Room Patients." *American Journal of Psychiatry,* forthcoming.

Brown, G. L., and Goodwin, F. K. "Cerebrospinal Fluid Correlates of Suicide Attempts and Aggression." *Annals of the New York Academy of Science,* 1986, *487,* 175–188.

Brown, S. L. "Adolescents and Family Systems." In M. L. Peck, N. L. Farberow, and R. E. Litman (eds.), *Youth Suicide.* New York: Springer, 1985.

Brown, T. R., and Sheran, T. J. "Suicide Prediction: A Review." *Life-Threatening Behavior,* 1972, *2,* 67–98.

Bryan, D. P., and Herjanc, B. "Depression and Suicide Among Adolescents and Young Adults with Selective Handicapping Conditions." *Exceptional Education Quarterly,* 1980, *12,* 57–65.

Bucy, J. "Runaway and Homeless Youth." In M. J. Rotheram, J. Bradley, and N. Obolensky (eds.), *Evaluating and Treating Suicidal Teens in Community Settings.* San Francisco: Jossey-Bass, forthcoming.

Cain, A. C. (ed.). *Survivors of Suicide.* Springfield, Ill.: Thomas, 1972.

California State Department of Education School Climate Unit. *Implementation Guide to the Youth Suicide School Prevention Program.* Sacramento: California State Department of Education, 1986.

California Suicide Intervention Training Program. Workshop material developed by the California State Department of Mental Health, 1988.

Canaday, D. C. "Children and Homosexuality." In A. Thomas and J. Grimes (eds.), *Children's Needs: Psychological Perspectives.* Washington, D.C.: National Association of School Psychologists, 1987.

Carlson, G. A., and Cantwell, D. P. "Suicidal Behavior and Depression in Children and Adolescents." *Journal of the American Academy of Child Psychiatry,* 1982, *21* (4), 361–368.

Carter, G., and Jancer, J. "Mortality in the Mentally Handicapped:

A 50 Year Survey at the Stoke Park Group of Hospitals." *Journal of Mental Deficiency,* 1983, *27,* 143–156.

Cavaiola, A. A., and Schiff, M. "Behavioral Sequelae of Physical and/or Sexual Abuse in Adolescents." *Child Abuse and Neglect,* 1988, *12,* 181–188.

Cheatham, A. *Annotated Bibliography for Teaching Conflict Resolution in Schools.* (2nd ed.) Amherst, Mass.: National Association for Mediation in Education, 1989.

Chess, S., and Thomas, A. *Origins and Evolution of Behavior Disorders: From Infancy to Early Adult Life.* New York: Brunner/Mazel, 1984.

Clarkin, J. F., and others. "Affective and Character Pathology of Suicidal Adolescents and Young Adult Inpatients." *Journal of Clinical Psychiatry,* 1984, *45,* 19–22.

Clopton, J. R., and Jones, W. C. "Use of the MMPI in the Prediction of Suicide." *Journal of Clinical Psychology,* 1975, *31,* 52–54.

Cohen, E., Motto, J., and Seiden, R. "An Instrument for Evaluating Suicidal Potential." *American Journal of Psychiatry,* 1966, *122,* 886–891.

Cohen-Sandler, R., Berman, A. L., and King, R. A. "Life Stress and Symptomology: Determinants of Suicidal Behavior in Children." *Journal of the American Academy of Child Psychiatry,* 1982, *21,* 178–186.

Cole, E., and Brotman, M. *Suicide Prevention: A Resource for Student Services.* Bulletin no. 12. Toronto: Toronto Board of Education Psychological Services, n.d.

Coleman, L. *Suicide Clusters.* Boston: Faber and Faber, 1987.

Colombo, S., and Oegema, D. *Parkway School District Crisis Intervention Manual.* Chesterfield, Mo.: Parkway School District, 1986.

Comstock, B. S., and McDermott, M. "Group Therapy for Patients Who Attempt Suicide." *International Journal of Group Psychotherapy,* 1975, *25,* 44–49.

Conti, A. P. "A Follow-Up of Families Referred to Outside Agencies." *Psychology in the Schools,* 1971, *8,* 338–342.

Conti, A. P. "A Follow-Up Investigation of Families Referred to Outside Agencies." *Journal of School Psychology,* 1973, *11,* 215–223.

Conti, A. P. "Variables Related to Contacting/Not Contacting Counseling Services Recommended by School Psychologists." *Journal of School Psychology,* 1975, *13,* 41-50.

Corder, B. F., and Haizlip, T. M. "Recognizing Suicidal Behavior in Children." *Medical Times,* Sept. 1982, pp. 26-30.

Corder, B. F., Page, P., and Corder, R. F. "Parental History, Family Communication, and Interaction Patterns in Adolescent Suicide." *Family Therapy,* 1974, *3,* 285-290.

Corder, B. F., Shorr, W., and Corder, R. F. "A Study of Social and Psychological Characteristics of Adolescent Suicide Attempts in an Urban Disadvantaged Area." *Adolescence,* 1974, *9,* 1-6.

County School Board of Fairfax County, Virginia. *The Adolescent Suicide Prevention Program, Revised Edition. 1987.* Fairfax: County School Board of Fairfax County, Virginia, 1987.

Cowen, E. "Person-Centered Approaches to Primary Prevention in Mental Health: Situation-Focused and Competence-Enhancement." *American Journal of Community Psychology,* 1985, *13,* 31-49.

Cronbach, L. J. "Coefficient Alpha and the Internal Structure of Tests." *Psychometrika,* 1951, *16,* 297-334.

Cull, J. G., and Gill, W. S. *Suicide Probability Scale.* Los Angeles: Western Psychological Services, 1982.

D'Andrea, V. J., and Salovey, P. *Peer Counseling: Skills and Perspectives.* Palo Alto, Calif.: Science and Behavior Books, 1983.

Dank, B. "Coming Out in the Gay World." *Psychiatry,* 1971, *34,* 180-197.

Davidson, L. E., and Gould, M. "Contagion as a Risk Factor for Youth Suicide." In Alcohol, Drug Abuse, and Mental Health Administration, *Report of the Secretary's Task Force on Youth Suicide.* Vol. 2. Washington, D.C.: U.S. Government Printing Office, 1989.

Davis, J. M., Bates, C., and Velasquez, R. "Faculty Suicide: Guidelines for Effective Coping with a Suicide in a Counselor-Training Program. *Counselor Education and Supervision,* 1990, *29,* 197-204.

Davis, J. M. and Sandoval, J. "Applied Ethics for School-Based Consultants." *Professional Psychology,* 1982, *13,* 543-551.

Davis, J. M., Sandoval, J., and Wilson, M. P. "Strategies for the

Primary Prevention of Adolescent Suicide." *School Psychology Review,* 1988, *17,* 559–569.

Delisle, J. R. "Death with Honors: Suicide Among Gifted Adolescents." *Journal of Counseling and Development,* 1986, *64,* 558–560.

DeMers, S. T., and Bersoff, D. "Legal Issues in School Psychological Practice." In J. R. Bergan (ed.), *School Psychology in Contemporary Society: An Introduction.* Westerville, Ohio: Merrill, 1985.

Dew, M. A., Bromet, E. J., Brent, D., and Greenhouse, J. B. "A Quantitative Literature Review of the Effectiveness of Suicide Prevention Centers." *Journal of Consulting and Clinical Psychology,* 1987, *55,* 239–244.

Diekstra, R.F.W., and Moritz, B.J.M. "Suicidal Behavior Among Adolescents: An Overview." In R.F.W. Diekstra and K. Hawton (eds.), *Suicide in Adolescence.* Dordrecht, the Netherlands: Martinus Nijhoff, 1987.

Diepold, J., Sr., and Young, R. D. "Empirical Studies of Adolescent Sexual Behavior: A Critical Review." *Adolescence,* 1979, *14,* 45–64.

Douglas, J. D. *The Social Meanings of Suicide.* Princeton, N.J.: Princeton University Press, 1967.

Drye, R. C., Goulding, R., and Goulding, M. "No-Suicide Decisions: Patient Monitoring of Suicidal Risk." *American Journal of Psychiatry,* 1973, *130,* 171–174.

Dunne, E. J., McIntosh, J. L., and Dunne-Maxim, K. (eds.). *Suicide and Its Aftermath: Understanding and Counseling Survivors.* New York: Norton, 1987.

Durkheim, E. *Suicide.* (J. A. Spaulding and G. Simpson, trans.) New York: Free Press, 1951.

Dyer, J.A.T., and Kreitman, N. "Hopelessness, Depression, and Suicidal Intent in Parasuicide." *British Journal of Psychiatry,* 1984, *144,* 127–133.

Eisenberg, L. "Does Bad News About Suicide Beget Bad News?" *New England Journal of Medicine,* 1986, *315,* 705–707.

Elias, M. J., and others. "Impact of a Preventive Social Problem Solving Intervention on Children's Coping with Middle-School

Stressors." *American Journal of Community Psychology*, 1986, *14*, 259–275.

Erikson, E. "Youth: Fidelity and Diversity." *Daedalus*, 1962, *29*, 5–27.

Evans, G., and Farberow, N. L. *The Encyclopedia of Suicide*. New York: Facts on File, 1988.

Everstine, D. S., and Everstine, L. *People in Crisis: Strategic Therapeutic Interventions*. New York: Brunner/Mazel, 1983.

Fairchild, T. N. "Suicide Intervention." In T. N. Fairchild (ed.), *Crisis Intervention Strategies for School-Based Helpers*. Springfield, Ill.: Thomas, 1988.

Farberow, N. L., and Devries, A. G. "An Item Differentiation Analysis of M.M.P.I.'s of Suicidal Neuropsychiatric Hospital Patients." *Psychological Reports*, 1967, *20*, 607–617.

Fassler, J. *Helping Children Cope*. New York: Free Press, 1978.

Felner, R. D., Jason, L. A., Moritsugu, B., and Farber, S. S. (eds.). *Preventive Psychology: Theory, Research, and Practice*. Elmsford, N.Y.: Pergamon Press, 1983.

Fine, M. J. "Issues in Adolescent Counseling." *School Psychology Review*, 1982, *11*, 391–398.

Fisher, P., and Shaffer, D. "Methods for Investigating Suicide in Children and Adolescents." In H. S. Sudak, A. B. Ford, and N. B. Rushforth (eds.), *Suicide in the Young*. Littleton, Mass.: Wright, 1984.

Fitts, W. H. *Tennessee Self-Concept Scale*. Los Angeles: Western Psychological Services, 1964.

Frederick, C. J. "Suicide in Young Minority Group Persons." In H. S. Sudak, A. B. Ford, and N. B. Rushforth (eds.), *Suicide in the Young*. Littleton, Mass.: Wright, 1984.

Freud, S. "Mourning and Melancholia." In J. Strachey (ed.), *The Complete Psychological Works of Sigmund Freud*. Vol. 14. London: Hogarth Press, 1957. (Originally published 1915.)

Friedman, J.M.H., Asnis, G. M., Boeck, M. B., and DiFiore, J. "Prevalence of Specific Suicidal Behaviors in a High School Sample." *American Journal of Psychiatry*, 1987, *144*, 1203–1206.

Friedman, R., and others. "Family History of Illness in the Seriously Suicidal Adolescent: A Life-Cycle Approach." *American Journal of Orthopsychiatry*, 1984, *54*, 390–397.

Fulmer, D. W. *Counseling: Group Theory and System.* (2nd ed.) Cranston, R.I.: Carroll Press, 1978.

Garfinkel, B. D., Froese, A., and Hood, J. "Suicide Attempts in Children and Adolescents." *American Journal of Psychiatry,* 1982, *139*, 1257–1261.

Garland, A., and Shaffer, D. "School-Based Adolescent Suicide Prevention Programs." Unpublished manuscript, College of Physicians and Surgeons of Columbia University, 1988.

Gesten, E. L., Weissberg, R. P., Amish, P. L., and Smith, J. K. "Social Problem-Solving Training: A Skills-Based Approach to Prevention and Treatment." In C. A. Maher and J. E. Zins (eds.), *Psychoeducational Interventions in the Schools.* Elmsford, N.Y.: Pergamon Press, 1987.

Gibbs, J. T. "Conceptual, Methodological, and Sociocultural Issues in Black Youth Suicide: Implications for Assessment and Early Intervention." *Suicide and Life-Threatening Behavior,* 1988, *18*, 73–89.

Gibson, P. "Gay Male and Lesbian Youth Suicide." In M. R. Feinleib (ed.), *Report of the Secretary's Task Force on Youth Suicide.* Vol. 3: *Prevention and Interventions in Youth Suicide.* DHHS Publication no. (ADM) 89-1623. Washington, D.C.: U.S. Government Printing Office, 1989.

Giddan, N. S., and Austin, M. J. (eds.). *Peer Counseling and Self-Help Groups on Campus.* Springfield, Ill.: Thomas, 1982.

Gispert, M., Wheeler, K., Marsh, L., and Davis, M. S. "Suicidal Adolescents: Factors in Evaluation." *Adolescence,* 1985, *20*, 753–762.

Goldney, R. D. "Attempted Suicide: Correlates of Lethality." Unpublished doctoral thesis, Department of Psychiatry, University of Adelaide, South Australia, 1979.

Golombek, H., and Garfinkel, B. D. *The Adolescent and Mood Disturbance.* New York: International University Press, 1983.

Gottfredson, G. D. *The Effective School Battery.* Odessa, Fla.: Psychological Assessment Resources, 1984.

Gould, M. S., and Shaffer, D. "The Impact of Suicide in Television Movies: Evidence of Imitation." *New England Journal of Medicine,* 1986, *315*, 690–694.

Gould, M. S., Wallenstein, S., and Davidson, L. "Suicide Clusters:

A Critical Review." *Suicide and Life-Threatening Behavior,* 1989, *19,* 17–29.

Gould. M. S., Wallenstein, S., and Kleinman, M. A. *A Study of Time-Space Clustering of Suicide: Final Report.* Atlanta, Ga.: Centers for Disease Control, 1987.

Green, A. H. "Self-Destructive Behavior in Battered Children." *American Journal of Psychiatry,* 1978, *135,* 579–582.

Grisso, T., and Vierling, L. "Minors' Consent to Treatment: A Developmental Perspective." *Professional Psychology,* 1978, *9,* 412–427.

Grob, M. C., Klein, A. A., and Eisen, S. V. "The Role of the High School Professional in Identifying and Managing Adolescent Suicidal Behavior." *Journal of Youth and Adolescence,* 1983, *12,* 163–173.

Gronlund, N. *Sociometry in the Classroom.* New York: Harper & Row, 1959.

Harkavy-Friedman, J., Asnis, G., Boeck, M., and DiFiore, J. "Prevalence of Specific Suicidal Behaviors in a High School Sample." *American Journal of Psychiatry,* 1987, *144,* 1203–1206.

Harlow, L. L., Newcomb, M. D., and Bentler, P. M. "Depression, Self-Derogation, Substance Use, and Suicide Ideation: Lack of Purpose in Life as a Mediational Factor." *Journal of Clinical Psychology,* 1986, *42,* 5–21.

Harry, J. *Gay Children Grown Up.* New York: Praeger, 1982.

Harry, J., and DeVall, W. *The Social Organization of Gay Males.* New York: Praeger, 1978.

Haugaard, J. J., and Reppucci, N. D. *The Sexual Abuse of Children: A Comprehensive Guide to Current Knowledge and Intervention Strategies.* San Francisco: Jossey-Bass, 1988.

Hauser, M. J. "Special Aspects of Grief After a Suicide." In E. J. Dunne, J. L. McIntosh, and K. Dunne-Maxim (eds.), *Suicide and Its Aftermath: Understanding and Counseling the Survivors.* New York: Norton, 1987.

Hawton, K. *Suicidal Behavior in Children and Adolescents.* Beverly Hills, Calif.: Sage, 1986.

Hawton, K., and Catalan, J. *Attempted Suicide: A Practical Guide to Its Nature and Management.* (2nd ed.) Oxford, England: Oxford University Press, 1987.

Hawton, K., Cole, D., O'Grady, J., and Osborn, M. "Motivational Aspects of Deliberate Self-Poisoning in Adolescents." *British Journal of Psychiatry*, 1982, *141*, 286-291.

Hayes, M. L., and Sloat, R. S. "Learning Disability and Suicide." *Academic Therapy*, 1988, *23*, 469-475.

Heiman, M., Lamb, F., Dunne-Maxim, K., and Sutton, C. *It's OK to Ask for Help: Manual for Curriculum.* Piscataway: Community Mental Health Center for the University of Medicine and Dentistry of New Jersey, 1986.

Henderson, A. S., and others. "A Typology of Parasuicide." *British Journal of Psychiatry*, 1977, *131*, 631-641.

Hendin, H. "Black Suicide." *Archives of General Psychiatry*, 1969, *21*, 407-422.

Herbert, D. A. "My Brother Tim and Me." In E. J. Dunne, J. L. McIntosh, and K. Dunne-Maxim (eds.), *Suicide and Its Aftermath: Understanding and Counseling Survivors.* New York: Norton, 1987.

Hildebrand, J. "School Sued in '84 Teen Suicide." *Sacramento Bee*, Mar. 16, 1987, p. A-11.

Hill, W. C. "Intervention and Postvention in Schools." In H. S. Sudak, A. B. Ford, and N. B. Rushforth, (eds.), *Suicide in the Young.* Littleton, Mass.: Wright, 1984.

Holding, T. A., and Barraclough, B. M. "Psychiatric Morbidity in a Sample of a London Coroner's Open Verdicts." *British Journal of Psychiatry*, 1975, *127*, 133-143.

Holinger, P. C. "Adolescent Suicide: An Epidemiological Study of Recent Trends." *American Journal of Psychiatry*, 1978, *135*, 754-756.

Hollon, S. D., and Beck, A. T. "Cognitive Therapy and Depression." In E. C. Kendall and S. D. Hollon (eds.), *Cognitive-Behavioral Interventions: Theory, Research, and Procedures.* Orlando, Fla.: Academic Press, 1979.

Hunter, J., and Schaecher, R. "Stresses on Lesbian and Gay Adolescents in Schools." *Social Work in Education*, 1987, *9* (3), 180-181.

Jan-Tausch, J. *Suicide of Children 1960-1963: New Jersey Public Schools.* Trenton: Division of Curriculum and Instruction, Of-

fice of Special Education Services, New Jersey Department of
Education, 1964.

Janus, M. D., McCormack, A., Burgess, A. W., and Hartman, C.
Adolescent Runaways: Causes and Consequences. Lexington,
Mass.: Heath, 1987.

Jones, R. M. *Fantasy and Feeling in Education.* New York: New
York University Press, 1968.

Kaminer, Y., Feinstein, C., and Barrett, R. P. "Suicidal Behavior in
Mentally Retarded Adolescents: An Overlooked Problem." *Child
Psychiatry and Human Development*, 1987, *18*, 90–94.

Kane, J. S., and Lawler, E. E., III. "Methods of Peer Assessment."
Psychological Bulletin, 1978, *85*, 555–586.

Kaslow, N., and others. "Problem-Solving Deficits and Depressive
Symptoms Among Children." *Journal of Abnormal Child Psychology*, 1983, *11*, 497–502.

Kaufman, G. G., and Johnson, J. C. "Scaling Peer Ratings: An
Examination of the Differential Validities of Positive and Negative Nominations." *Journal of Applied Psychology*, 1974, *59*,
445–451.

Kazdin, A. E., Rodgers, A., and Colbus, D. "The Hopelessness Scale
for Children: Psychometric Characteristics and Concurrent Validity." *Journal of Consulting and Clinical Psychology*, 1986, *54*,
241–245.

Kazdin, A. E., and others. "Hopelessness, Depression, and Suicidal
Intent Among Psychiatrically Disturbed Inpatient Children."
Journal of Consulting and Clinical Psychology, 1983, *51*, 504–
510.

Kempe, C. H., and Heyfer, R. E. *The Battered Child.* Chicago:
University of Chicago Press, 1980.

Kempe, R. S., and Kempe, C. H. *The Common Secret: Sexual Abuse
of Children and Adolescents.* New York: Freeman, 1984.

Kenny, T. J., and others. "Visual-Motor Problems of Adolescents
Who Attempt Suicide." *Perceptual and Motor Skills*, 1979, *48*,
599–602.

Khan, A. U. "Heterogeneity of Suicidal Adolescents." In S. Chess,
A. Thomas, and M. E. Hertzig, (eds.), *Annual Progress in Child
Psychiatry and Child Development: 1988.* New York: Brunner/
Mazel, 1989.

Kinsey, A. C., Pomeroy, W. B., and Martin, C. E. *Sexual Behavior in the Human Male.* Philadelphia: Saunders, 1948.

Kinsey, A. C., Pomeroy, W. B., Martin, C. E., and Gebhard, P. H. *Sexual Behavior in the Human Female.* Philadelphia: Saunders, 1953.

Klagsbrun, F. *Too Young to Die: Youth and Suicide.* Boston: Houghton Mifflin, 1976.

Klingman, A., and Eli, Z. B. "A School Community in Disaster: Primary and Secondary Prevention in Situational Crisis." *Professional Psychology,* 1981, *12,* 523–533.

Klosterman-Fields, S. J. "Bulimia, Binge Eating, and Suicidal Ideation Among College Women." Unpublished doctoral dissertation, University of Wisconsin, Madison, 1985.

Kneisel, P. J., and Richards, G. P. "Crisis Intervention After the Suicide of a Teacher." *Professional Psychology,* 1988, *19,* 165–169.

Knesper, D. J. "A Study of Referral Failures for Potentially Suicidal Patients: A Method of Medical Care Evaluation." *Hospital and Community Psychiatry,* 1982, *33,* 49–52.

Kogan, L. S. "The Short-Term Case in a Family Agency. Parts I–III." *Social Casework,* 1957, *38,* 231–238, 296–302, 366–374.

Kosky, R. "Childhood Suicidal Behavior in Battered Children." *American Journal of Psychiatry,* 1983, *24,* 457–468.

Kreitman, N., Philip, A. E., Greer, S., and Bagley, C. R. "Parasuicide." *British Journal of Psychiatry,* 1969, *115,* 746–747.

Kremer, E., Zimpfer, D., and Wiggers, T. "Homosexuality, Counseling and the Adolescent Male." *Personnel and Guidance Journal,* 1975, *54,* 94–101.

Lam, J. A. *The Impact of Conflict Resolution Programs on Schools: A Review and Synthesis of the Evidence.* Amherst, Mass.: National Association for Mediation in Education, 1988.

Lamb, F., and Dunne-Maxim, K. "Postvention in Schools: Policy and Process." In E. J. Dunne, J. L. McIntosh, and K. Dunne-Maxim (eds.), *Suicide and Its Aftermath: Understanding and Counseling the Survivors.* New York: Norton, 1987.

Lambert, N. M., and Bower, E. M. *A Process for In-School Screening of Emotionally Handicapped Children.* Atlanta, Ga.: Educational Testing Service, 1974.

Lanktree, C., Briere, J., and Zaidi, L. "Differential Identification of Sexually Abused Children in Psychiatric Outpatient Charts." Paper presented at the annual convention of the American Psychological Association, New Orleans, La., Aug. 1989.

Lefkowitz, M. M., and Tesiny, E., "Assessment of Childhood Depression." *Journal of Consulting and Clinical Psychology*, 1980, *48*, 43–51.

Lefkowitz, M. M., and Tesiny, E., "Depression in Children: Prevalence and Correlates." *Journal of Consulting and Clinical Psychology*, 1985, *53*, 647–656.

Leroux, J. A. "Suicidal Behavior and Gifted Adolescents." *Roeper Review*, 1986, *9*, 77–79.

Lester, D. "Demographic Versus Clinical Prediction of Suicidal Behaviors: A Look at Some Issues." In A. T. Beck, H.L.P. Resnik, and D. J. Lettieri (eds.), *The Prediction of Suicide*. Bowie, Md.: Charles Press, 1974.

Lester, D., and Beck, A. T. "What the Suicide's Choice of Method Signifies." *Omega: Journal of Death and Dying*, 1980, *11*, 146–155.

Lettieri, D. J. "Suicidal Death Prediction Scales." In A. T. Beck, H.L.P. Resnick, and D. J. Lettieri (eds.), *The Prediction of Suicide*. Bowie, Md.: Charles Press, 1974.

Levenson, M., and Neuringer, C. "Problem-Solving Behavior in Suicidal Adolescents." *Journal of Consulting and Clinical Psychology*, 1971, *37*, 433–436.

Linden, L. L., and Breed, W. "The Demographic Epidemiology of Suicide." In E. S. Schneidman (ed.), *Suicidology: Contemporary Developments*. Orlando, Fla.: Grune & Stratton, 1976.

Linehan, M. M., Goodstein, J. L., Nielsen, S. L., and Chiles, J. A. "Reasons for Staying Alive When You Are Thinking of Killing Yourself: The Reasons for Living Inventory." *Journal of Consulting and Clinical Psychology*, 1983, *51*, 276–286.

Linehan, M. M., and Nielsen, S. "Assessment of Suicide Ideation and Parasuicide: Hopelessness and Social Desirability." *Journal of Consulting and Clinical Psychology*, 1983, *49*, 773–775.

Linehan, M. M., and others. "Interpersonal Problem Solving and Parasuicide." *Cognitive Therapy and Research*, 1987, *11*, 1–12.

Litman, R. E., Wold, C. I., Farberow, N. L., and Brown, T. R.

"Prediction Models of Suicidal Behaviors." In A. T. Beck, H.L.P. Resnick, and D. J. Lettieri (eds.), *The Prediction of Suicide*. Bowie, Md.: Charles Press, 1974.

Litt, I. F., Cuskey, W. R., and Rudd, S. "Emergency Room Evaluation of the Adolescent Who Attempts Suicide: Compliance with Follow-Up." *Society for Adolescent Medicine*, 1983, *4*, 106–108.

Luscomb, R., Clum, G., and Patsiokas, A. "Mediating Factors in the Relationship Between Life Stress and Suicide Attempting." *Journal of Nervous and Mental Diseases*, 1980, *168*, 644–699.

Maag, J. W., Rutherford, R. B., and Parks, B. T. "Secondary School Professionals' Ability to Identify Depression in Adolescents." *Adolescence*, 1988, *23*, 73–82.

McCarthy, P. D., and Walsh, D. "Suicide in Dublin: I. The Underreporting of Suicide and the Consequences for Material Statistics." *British Journal of Psychiatry*, 1975, *126*, 301–308.

McDermott, P. "Law, Liability, and the School Psychologist: Malpractice and Liability." *Journal of School Psychology*, 1972, *10*, 397–407.

Mack, J. E., and Hickler, H. *Vivienne: The Life and Suicide of an Adolescent Girl*. Boston: Little, Brown, 1981.

McKenry, P. C., Tishler, C. L., and Kelly, C. "The Role of Drugs in Adolescent Suicide Attempts." *Suicide and Life-Threatening Behavior*, 1983, *13*, 166–175.

McWhirter, R. J., and McWhirter, J. J. "Legal Issues of Adolescent Suicide." *Journal of Educational Equity and Leadership*, 1987, *7*, 332–337.

Matson, J. L., and Ollendick, T. H. *Enhancing Children's Social Skills*. Elmsford, N.Y.: Pergamon Press, 1988.

Mayfield, D., and Montgomery, D. "Alcoholism, Alcohol Intoxication, and Suicide Attempts." *Archives of General Psychiatry*, 1972, *27*, 349–353.

Meichenbaum, D. *Stress Inoculation Training*. Elmsford, N.Y.: Pergamon Press., 1985.

Melton, G. B., Koocher, G. P., and Saks, M. J. (eds.). *Children's Competence to Consent*. New York: Plenum Press, 1983.

Menninger, K. A. *Man Against Himself*. San Diego, Calif.: Harcourt Brace Jovanovich, 1938.

Moody, M., and Limper, H. *Bibliotherapy: Methods and Materials.* Chicago: American Library Association, 1971.

Moos, R. H., and Trickett, E. J. *Classroom Environment Scale.* (2nd ed.) Palo Alto, Calif.: Consulting Psychologists Press, 1987.

Moreno, J. L. *Who Shall Survive?* Washington, D.C.: Nervous and Mental Disease Publishing, 1934.

Motto, J. A. "Suicide in Male Adolescents." In H. S. Sudak, A. B. Ford, and N. B. Rushforth, (eds.), *Suicide in the Young.* Littleton, Mass.: Wright, 1984.

Motto, J. A. "Treatment Concerns in Preventing Youth Suicide." In M. L. Peck, N. L. Farberow, and R. E. Litman (eds.), *Youth Suicide.* New York: Springer, 1985.

Murphy, G. E., and others. "Suicide and Alcoholism." *Archives of General Psychiatry,* 1979, *36,* 65–69.

Myers, K. M., Burke, P., and McCauley, E. "Suicidal Behavior by Hospitalized Preadolescent Children on a Psychiatric Unit." *Journal of the American Academy of Child Psychiatry,* 1985, *24,* 474–480.

National Center for Health Statistics. "Annual Summary of Births, Marriages, Divorces, and Deaths. United States, 1987 (Provisional Data)." *Monthly Vital Statistics Report,* 1988, *36* (13), 1–23.

National Gay Task Force. *Anti-Gay/Lesbian Victimization.* New York: National Gay Task Force, 1984.

Neimeyer, R. A., and MacInnes, W. D. "Assessing Paraprofessional Competence with the Suicide Intervention Response Inventory." *Journal of Counseling Psychology,* 1981, *28,* 176–179.

Nelson, F. L. *State of California Youth Suicide Prevention School Evaluation of Classroom Instruction.* Program Evaluation Report 1985–86. Los Angeles: Institute for Students of Destructive Behaviors and Suicide Prevention Center, 1986.

Nelson, F. L. "Evaluation of a Youth Suicide Prevention Program." *Adolescence,* 1987, *38,* 813–825.

Nelson, F. L., Farberow, N. L., and Litman, R. E. "Youth Suicide in California: A Comparative Study of Perceived Causes and Interventions." *Community Mental Health Journal,* 1988, *24,* 31–42.

Neuringer, C. "Suicide and the Rorschach: A Rueful Postscript." *Journal of Personality Assessment,* 1974, *38,* 535-539.

O'Carroll, P. W. "A Consideration of the Validity and Reliability of Suicide Mortality Data." *Suicide and Life-Threatening Behavior,* 1989, *19,* 1-16.

O'Carroll, P. W., Mercy, J. A., and Steward, J. A. "CDC Recommendations for a Community Plan for the Prevention and Containment of Suicide Clusters." *Centers for Disease Control Morbidity and Mortality Weekly Report,* 1988, *37,* (S-6).

Ojanlatva, A., Hammer, A. M., and Mohr, M. G. "The Ultimate Rejection: Helping the Survivors of Teen Suicide Victims." *Journal of School Health,* 1987, *57,* 181-182.

Orbach, I. "Attraction and Repulsion by Life and Death in Suicidal and Normal Children." *Journal of Consulting and Clinical Psychology,* 1983, *51,* 661-670.

Orbach, I. "The 'Insolvable Problem' as a Determinant in the Dynamics of Suicidal Behavior in Children." *American Journal of Psychotherapy,* 1986, *40,* 511-520.

Orbach, I. *Children Who Don't Want to Live: Understanding and Treating the Suicidal Child.* San Francisco: Jossey-Bass, 1988.

Otto, U. "Suicidal Acts by Children and Adolescents." *Acta Psychiatrica Scandinavia,* 1972, Supplement 233, 7-123.

Pallis, D. J., and others. "Estimating Suicide Risk Among Attempted Suicides." *British Journal of Psychiatry,* 1982, *141,* 37-44.

Patrick, J. H., and Overall, J. E. "Multivariate Analysis of Clinical Rating Profiles of Suicidal and Nonsuicidal Psychiatric Patients." *Journal of Projective Techniques,* 1969, *33,* 138-145.

Patsiokas, A., Clum, G., and Luscomb, R. "Cognitive Characteristics of Suicide Attempters." *Journal of Consulting and Clinical Psychology,* 1979, *47,* 478-484.

Paykel, E. S., Myers, J. K., Lindenthal, J. J., and Tanner, J. "Suicidal Feelings in the General Population: A Prevalence Study." *British Journal of Psychiatry,* 1974, *124,* 1099-1102.

Paykel, E. S., and Rassaby, E. "Classification of Suicide Attempters by Cluster Analysis." *British Journal of Psychiatry,* 1978, *133,* 45-52.

Paykel, E. S., and others. "Treatment of Suicide Attempters: A Descriptive Study." *Archives of General Psychiatry,* 1974, *31,* 487–491.

Peck, D. L. "Lethality of Method of Choice Among a Youthful Sample of Committers: An Examination of the Intent Hypothesis." *Psychological Reports,* 1984, *55,* 861–862.

Peck, D. L. "Social-Psychological Correlates of Adolescent and Youthful Suicide." *Adolescence,* 1987, *22,* 863–878.

Peck, M. L. "Crisis Intervention Treatment with Chronically and Acutely Suicidal Adolescents." In M. L. Peck, N. L. Farberow, and R. E. Litman (eds.), *Youth Suicide.* New York: Springer, 1985.

Perry, J. D., and others. "Suicide: School Psychology Assessments and Interventions." Paper presented at the National Association of School Psychologists Convention, Chicago, Apr. 1988.

Pfeffer, C. R. "Clinical Assessment of Suicidal Behavior in Children." In H. S. Sudak, A. B. Ford, and N. B. Rushforth (eds.), *Suicide in the Young.* Littleton, Mass.: Wright, 1984a.

Pfeffer, C. R. "Modalities of Treatment for Suicidal Children: An Overview of the Literature on Current Practice." *American Journal of Psychotherapy,* 1984b, *38,* 364–372.

Pfeffer, C. R. *The Suicidal Child.* New York: Guilford Press, 1986.

Pfeffer, C. R. "The Family System of Suicidal Children." In S. Lesse (ed.), *What We Know About Suicidal Behavior and How to Treat It.* Northvale, N.J.: Jason Aronson, 1988.

Pfeffer, C. R., Conte, H. R., Plutchik, R., and Jerrett, I. "Suicidal Behavior in Latency-Age Children: An Empirical Study: An Outpatient Population." *Journal of American Academy of Child Psychiatry,* 1980, *19,* 703–710.

Phillips, D. P., and Carstensen, L. L. "Clustering of Teenage Suicides After Television News Stories About Suicide." *New England Journal of Medicine,* 1986, *315,* 685–689.

Piaget, J. *The Child and Reality: Problems of Genetic Psychology.* (A. Rosin, trans.) New York: Grossman, 1973.

Platt, J. J., Spivack, G., and Bloom, M. *Means End Problem Solving Procedure (MEPS): Manual and Tentative Norms.* Philadelphia: Department of Health Sciences, Hahnemann Medical College and Hospital, 1971.

Poland, S. *Suicide Prevention Overview (Cypress Fairbanks Public Schools)*. Houston, Tex.: S. Poland, 1986.

Pryzwansky, W., and Bersoff, D. "Parental Consent for Psychological Evaluations: Legal, Ethical and Practical Considerations." *Journal of School Psychology*, 1978, *16*, 274-281.

Puig-Antich, J., Perel, J. M., and Lupatkin, W. "Imipramine Effectiveness in Pre-Pubertal Major Depressive Disorders: 1. Relationship of Plasma Levels to Clinical Response of the Depressive Syndrome." *Archives of General Psychiatry*, 1985, *42*, 237-242.

Puig-Antich, J., and others. "Psychosocial Functioning in Prepubertal Major Depressive Disorders: I. Interpersonal Relationships During the Depressive Episode." *Archives of General Psychiatry*, 1985a, *42*, 500-507.

Puig-Antich, J., and others. "Psychosocial Functioning in Prepubertal Major Depressive Disorders: II. Interpersonal Relationships After Sustained Recovery from Affective Episode." *Archives of General Psychiatry*, 1985b, *42*, 511-517.

Reynolds, C. R., Gutkin, T. B., Elliott, S. N., and Witt, J. C. *School Psychology: Essentials of Theory and Practice*. New York: Wiley, 1984.

Reynolds, C. R., and Kaiser, S. M. "Bias in Assessment of Aptitude." In C. R. Reynolds and R. W. Kamphaus (eds.), *Handbook of Psychological and Educational Assessment of Children: Intelligence and Achievement*. New York: Guilford Press, 1990.

Reynolds, W. M. "A Model for the Screening and Identification of Depressed Children and Adolescents in School Settings." *Professional School Psychology*, 1986, *1*, 117-129.

Reynolds, W. M. *About My Life: S.I.Q. Form H.S.* Odessa, Fla: Psychological Assessment Resources, 1987a.

Reynolds, W. M. *Suicidal Ideation Questionnaire: Preliminary Model*. Odessa, Fla.: Psychological Assessment Resources, 1987b.

Reynolds, W. M. *Suicidal Ideation Questionnaire: Professional Manual*. Odessa, Fla.: Psychological Assessment Resources, 1988.

Reynolds, W. M., and Graves, A. "Depression and Suicidal Ideation in Behavior Disordered Youngsters." Unpublished manuscript, 1987.

Rich, C. L., Fowler, R. C., Young, D., and Blenkush, M. "San

Diego Suicide Study: Comparison of Gay to Straight Males."
Suicide and Life-Threatening Behavior, 1986, *14,* 448-457.

Richman, J. "Family Therapy of Attempted Suicide." *Family Process,* 1979, *18,* 131-142.

Richman, J. "The Family Therapy of Suicidal Adolescents: Promises and Pitfalls." In H. S. Sudak, A. B. Ford, and N. B. Rushforth (eds.), *Suicide in the Young.* Littleton, Mass.: Wright, 1984.

Richman, J. *Family Therapy for Suicidal People.* New York: Springer, 1986.

Robins, E. "The Final Months: A Study of the Lives of 134 Persons Who Committed Suicide." *New England Journal of Medicine,* 1982, *306,* 1117.

Robins, L. N. "Suicide Attempts in Teen-Aged Medical Patients." In Alcohol, Drug Abuse, and Mental Health Administration, *Report of the Secretary's Task Force on Youth Suicide.* Vol. 4: *Strategies for the Prevention of Youth Suicide.* DHHS Publication no. (ADM) 89-1624. Washington, D.C.: U.S. Government Printing Office, 1989.

Rofes, E. *I Thought People Like That Killed Themselves: Lesbians, Gay Men, and Suicide.* San Francisco: Grey Fox, 1983.

Rogawski, A. B., and Edmundson, B. "Factors Affecting the Outcome of Psychiatry Interagency Referral." *American Journal of Psychiatry,* 1971, *127,* 925-934.

Rosenbaum, M., and Richman, J. "Suicide: The Role of Hostility and Death Wishes from the Family and Significant Others." *American Journal of Psychiatry,* 1970, *126,* 1652-1655.

Rosenberg, P. H., and Latimer, R. "Suicide Attempts by Children." *Mental Hygiene,* 1966, *50,* 354-359.

Rosenfield, L., and Prupas, M. *Left Alive: After a Suicide Death in the Family.* Springfield, Ill.: Thomas, 1984.

Ross, C. P. "Mobilizing Schools for Suicide Prevention." *Suicide and Life-Threatening Behavior,* 1980, *10,* 239-243.

Ross, C. P. "Teaching Children the Facts of Life and Death: Suicide Prevention in the Schools." In M. L. Peck, N. L. Farberow, and R. E. Litman (eds.), *Youth Suicide.* New York: Springer, 1985.

Ross, C. P., and Lee, A. R. *Suicide in Youth and What You Can Do About It: A Guide for School Personnel.* Burlingame, Calif.: Suicide Prevention and Crisis Center of San Mateo County, n.d.

Ross, C. P., and Motto, J. A. "Group Counseling for Suicidal Adolescents." In H. S. Sudak, A. B. Ford, and N. B. Rushforth (eds.), *Suicide in the Young.* Littleton, Mass.: Wright, 1984.

Ross-Reynolds, G. "Intervention with the Homosexual Adolescent." In J. Sandoval (ed.), *Crisis Counseling, Interventions, and Prevention in the Schools.* Hillsdale, N.J.: Erlbaum, 1987.

Rotheram, M. J. "Evaluation of Imminent Danger for Suicide Among Youth." *American Journal of Orthopsychiatry,* 1987, *57,* 102–110.

Rotheram-Borus, M. J. "Assertiveness Training with Children." In R. H. Price, E. L. Cowen, R. P. Lorion, and J. Ramos-McKay (eds.), *Fourteen Ounces of Prevention: A Casebook for Practitioners.* Washington, D. C.: American Psychological Association, 1988.

Rotheram-Borus, M. J., and Trautman, P. D. "Hopelessness, Depression, and Suicidal Intent Among Adolescent Suicide Attempters." *Journal of the American Academy of Child and Adolescent Psychiatry,* 1988, *27,* 700–704.

Rourke, B. P. "Socio-Emotional Disturbances of Learning-Disabled Children." *Journal of Consulting and Clinical Psychology,* 1988, *56,* 801–810.

Rourke, B. P., Young, G. C., and Lenaars, A. A. "A Childhood Learning Disability That Predisposes Those Afflicted to Adolescent and Adult Depression and Suicide Risk." *Journal of Learning Disabilities,* 1989, *22,* 169–175.

Rourke, B. P., Young, G. C., Strang, J. D., and Russell, D. L. "Adult Outcomes of Central Processing Deficiencies in Childhood." In I. Grant and K. M. Adams (eds.), *Neuropsychological Assessment in Neuropsychiatric Disorders: Clinical Methods and Empirical Findings.* New York: Oxford University Press, 1986.

Roy, A. "Suicide in Chronic Schizophrenia." *British Journal of Psychiatry,* 1982, *141,* 171–177.

Roy, A. "Family History of Suicide." *Archives of General Psychiatry,* 1983, *40,* 971–974.

Roy, A. "Genetics of Suicide." *Annals of the New York Academy of Science,* 1986a, *487,* 97–105.

Roy, A. "Suicide in Schizophrenia." In A. Roy (ed.), *Suicide.* Baltimore, Md.: Williams & Wilkins, 1986b.

Rubenstein, J. L., and others. "Suicidal Behavior in 'Normal' Adolescents: Risk and Protective Factors." *American Journal of Orthopsychiatry*, 1989, *59*, 59-71.

Ruof, S. R., Harris, J. M., and Robbie, M. B. *Handbook: Suicide Prevention in the Schools.* Lasalle, Colo.: Special Education, Weld Board of Cooperative Educational Services, 1987.

Ryerson, D. M. " 'ASAP'—an Adolescent Suicide Awareness Programme." In R.F.W. Diekstra and K. Hawton (eds.), *Suicide in Adolescence.* Dordrecht, the Netherlands: Martinus Nijhoff, 1987.

Sabbath, J. C. "The Suicidal Adolescent—the Expendable Child." *Journal of the American Academy of Child Psychiatry*, 1982, *8*, 272-289.

Sacks, M., and Eth, S. "Pathological Identification as a Cause of Suicide on an Inpatient Unit." *Hospital and Community Psychiatry*, 1981, *32*, 36-40.

Saffer, J. B. "Group Therapy with Friends of an Adolescent Suicide." *Adolescence*, 1986, *21*, 743-745.

Saghir, M. T., and Robins, E. *Male and Female Homosexuality: A Comprehensive Investigation.* Baltimore, Md.: Williams & Wilkins, 1973.

Saltzman, L. E., Levenson, A., and Smith, J. C. "Suicides Among Persons 15-24 Years of Age, 1970-1984." *Morbidity and Mortality Weekly Report*, 1988, *37*, 61-68.

Sandoval, J. *Crisis Counseling, Intervention, and Prevention in the Schools.* Hillsdale, N.J.: Erlbaum, 1988.

Sandoval, J., and Irvin, M. G. "Legal and Ethical Issues in the Assessment of Children." In C. R. Reynolds and R. W. Kamphaus (eds.), *Handbook of Psychological and Educational Assessment of Children: Intelligence and Achievement.* New York: Guilford Press, 1990.

Schotte, D., and Clum, G. "Suicide Ideation in a College Population: A Test of a Model." *Journal of Consulting and Clinical Psychology*, 1982, *50*, 690-696.

Schotte, D. E., and Clum, G. A. "Problem-Solving Skills in Suicidal Psychiatric Patients." *Journal of Consulting and Clinical Psychology*, 1987, *55*, 49-54.

Schuckit, M. A. *Drug and Alcohol Abuse: A Clinical Guide to Diagnosis and Treatment*. (2nd ed.) New York: Plenum, 1984.

Schulsinger, R., Ketz, S., Rosenthal, D., and Wender, P. "A Family History of Suicide." In M. Schon and E. Strongren (eds.), *Origins, Prevention, and Treatment of Affective Disorders*. Orlando, Fla.: Academic Press, 1979.

Segal, B. E., and Humphrey, J. "A Comparison of Suicide Victims and Suicide Attempters in New Hampshire." *Diseases of the Nervous System*, 1970, *31*, 830–838.

Shaffer, D. "Suicide in Childhood and Early Adolescence." *Journal of Child Psychology and Psychiatry*, 1974, *15*, 275–291.

Shaffer, D. "Depression, Mania, and Suicidal Acts." In M. Rutter and L. Hersov (eds.), *Child and Adolescent Psychiatry: Modern Approaches*. (2nd ed.) London: Blackwell Scientific, 1985.

Shaffer, D., and Bacon, K. "A Critical Review of Preventive Intervention Efforts in Suicide, with Particular Reference to Youth Suicide." In Alcohol, Drug Abuse, and Mental Health Administration, *Report of the Secretary's Task Force on Youth Suicide*. Volume 3: *Prevention and Interventions in Youth Suicide*. DHHS Publication no. (ADM) 89-1623. Washington, D.C.: U.S. Government Printing Office, 1989.

Shaffer, D., and Caton, C. "Runaway and Homeless Youth in New York City: A Report to the Ittleson Foundation." Unpublished manuscript, College of Physicians and Surgeons of Columbia University, New York State Psychiatric Institute, 1984.

Shaffer, D., and Fisher, P. "Suicide in Children and Young Adolescents." In C. F. Wells and I. R. Stuart (eds.), *Self-Destructive Behavior in Children and Adolescents*. New York: Van Nostrand Reinhold, 1981.

Shaffer, D., and Garland, A. "An Evaluation of New Jersey Youth Suicide Prevention Programs: Draft Report Preliminary Findings." Unpublished manuscript, College of Physicians and Surgeons of Columbia University, 1987.

Shaffer, D., Garland, A., and Bacon, K. *Prevention Issues in Youth Suicide*. Report prepared for Project Prevention, American Academy of Child and Adolescent Psychiatry. New York: Adolescent Study Unit, College of Physicians and Surgeons of Columbia University, 1987.

Shafti, M., Carrigan, S., Whittinghill, J. R., and Derrick, A. "Psychological Autopsy of Completed Suicide in Children and Adolescents." *American Journal of Psychiatry*, 1985, *142*, 1061-1064.

Shapiro, R. J., and Budman, S. H. "Defection, Termination and Continuation in Family and Individual Therapy." *Family Process*, 1973, *12*, 55-67.

Shepherd, D. M., and Barraclough, B. M. "The Aftermath of Parental Suicide for Children." *British Journal of Psychiatry*, 1976, *129*, 267-276.

Shneidman, E. S. "Preventing Suicide." *American Journal of Nursing*, 1965, *65*, 111-116.

Shneidman, E. S. "Classification of Suicidal Phenomena." *Bulletin of Suicidology*, July 1968, pp. 1-9.

Shneidman, E. S. *Deaths of Man*. New York: Quandrangle Books, 1973.

Shneidman, E., and Farberow, N. "Statistical Comparisons Between Attempted and Committed Suicides." In N. Farberow and E. Shneidman (eds.), *The Cry for Help*. New York: McGraw-Hill, 1965.

Siegel, L., and Griffin, N. "Correlates of Depressive Symptoms in Adolescence." *Journal of Youth and Adolescence*, 1984, *13*, 475-487.

Simons, R. L., and Murphy, P. I. "Sex Differences in the Causes of Adolescent Suicide Ideation." *Journal of Youth and Adolescence*, 1985, *14*, 423-434.

Singer, M. T. "Teenage Suicide: A Growing Problem." *Forecast for Home Economics*, 1980, *25*, 34-36.

Slaikeu, K. A. *Crisis Intervention. A Handbook for Practice and Research*. Boston: Allyn & Bacon, 1984.

Slaikeu, K. A., Tulkin, S. R., and Speer, D. C. "Process and Outcome in the Evaluation of Telephone Counseling Referrals." *Journal of Consulting and Clincial Psychology*, 1975, *43*, 700-707.

Slenkovich, J. "No Duty to Refer Potential Suicide to Licensed Psychiatrist/Psychologist." *The School's Advocate*, 1986, *1*, 270-271.

Smith, G. M. "Usefulness of Peer Ratings of Personality in Educational Research." *Educational and Psychological Measurement*, 1967, *27*, 967–984.

Smith, K., Conroy, R. W., and Ehler, B. D. "Lethality of Suicide Attempt Rating Scale." *Suicide and Life-Threatening Behavior*, 1984, *14* (4), 215–242.

Smith, K., and Crawford, S. "Suicidal Behavior Among 'Normal' High School Students." *Suicide and Life-Threatening Behavior*, 1986, *16*, 313–325.

Smith, K., Eyman, J., Dyck, R., and Ryerson, D. "Draft Report of School-Related Suicide Programs." Draft 2, 12-4-87. Unpublished report, School Programs Committee, American Association of Suicidology, 1987.

Spirito, A., Overholser, J., and Stark, L. J. "Common Problems and Coping Strategies II: Findings with Adolescent Suicide Attempters." *Journal of Abnormal Child Psychology*, 1989, *17*, 213–221.

Spirito, A., Stark, L. J., and Williams, C. "Development of a Brief Checklist to Assess Coping in Pediatric Populations." *Journal of Pediatric Psychology*, 1988, *13*, 555–574.

Spivack, G., and Shure, M. B. *Social Adjustment of Young Children: A Cognitive Approach to Solving Real-Life Problems*. San Francisco: Jossey-Bass, 1974.

Stack, S. "Divorce and Suicide: A Time Series Analysis, 1933–1970." *Journal of Family Issues*, 1981, *2* (1), 77–90.

Stanley, M., and Stanley, B. "Biochemical Studies in Suicide Victims: Current Findings and Future Implications." *Suicide and Life-Threatening Behavior*, 1989, *19*, 30–42.

Szasz, T. "The Case Against Suicide Prevention." *American Psychologist*, 1986, *41*, 806–812.

Taylor, E. A., and Stansfield, S. A. "Children Who Poison Themselves: I. Clinical Comparison with Psychiatric Controls, and II. Predictions of Attendance for Treatment." *British Journal of Psychiatry*, 1984, *145*, 127–135.

Teri, L. "The Use of the Beck Depression Inventory with Adolescents." *Journal of Abnormal Child Psychology*, 1982, *10*, 277–284.

Thomas, A., and Chess, S. *Temperament and Development*. New York: Brunner/Mazel, 1977.

Tishler, C., McKenry, P., and Morgan, K. "Adolescent Suicide Attempts: Some Significant Factors." *Suicide and Life-Threatening Behavior*, 1981, *11*, 86–92.

Toolan, J. M. "Depression in Children and Adolescents." *American Journal of Orthopsychiatry*, 1962, *32*, 404.

Toolan, J. M. "Psychotherapeutic Treatment of Suicidal Children and Adolescents." In H. S. Sudak, A. B. Ford, and N. B. Rushforth (eds.), *Suicide in the Young*. Littleton, Mass.: Wright, 1984.

Toolan, J. M. "Depression and Suicide in Children." In S. Lesse (ed.), *What We Know About Suicidal Behavior and How to Treat It*. Northvale, N.J.: Jason Aronson, 1988.

Trautman, P. D. "Specific Treatment Modalities for Adolescent Suicide Attempters." In Alcohol, Drug Abuse, and Mental Health Administration, *Report of the Secretary's Task Force on Youth Suicide. Volume 3: Prevention and Interventions in Youth Suicide*. DHHS Publication no. (ADM) 89-1623. Washington, D.C.: U.S. Government Printing Office, 1989.

Trautman, P. D., and Shaffer, D. "Treatment of Child and Adolescent Suicide Attempters." In H. S. Sudak, A. B. Ford, and N. B. Rushforth (eds.), *Suicide in the Young*. Littleton, Mass.: Wright, 1984.

Tsuang, M. T. "Genetic Factors in Suicide." *Disorders of the Nervous System*, 1977, *38*, 49.

Tsuang, M. T. "Risk of Suicide in the Relatives of Schizophrenics, Manics, Depressives, and Controls." *Journal of Clinical Psychiatry*, 1983, *44*, 396–400.

United Press International. "A Stubborn Suicide Rate." *San Francisco Chronicle*, Mar. 11, 1988, p. A4.

U.S. Department of Health and Human Services. *Trends and Current Status in Childhood Mortality: United States, 1900–85*. DHHS Publication no. (PHS) 89-1410. Washington, D.C.: U.S. Government Printing Office, 1989.

Varenhorst, B. B. "Peer Counseling: A Guidance Program and a Behavioral Intervention." In J. D. Krumboltz and C. E. Thoresen (eds.), *Counseling Methods.* New York: Holt, Rinehart & Winston, 1976.

Walberg, H. J., and Thomas, S. C. "Defining Open Education." *Journal of Research and Development in Education,* 1974, *8,* 4–13.

Warshauer, M. E., and Monk, M. "Problems in Suicide Statistics for Whites and Blacks." *American Journal of Public Health,* 1978, *68,* 383–388.

Watzlawick, P., Weakland, J. H., and Fisch, R. *Change: Principles of Problem Formation and Problem Resolution.* New York: Norton, 1974.

Weiner, I. B. *Child and Adolescent Psychopathology.* New York: Wiley, 1982.

Welu, T. C. "A Follow-Up Program for Suicide Attempters: Evaluation for Effectiveness." *Suicide and Life-Threatening Behavior,* 1977, *7,* 17–30.

Werner, E. E., and Smith, R. S. *Vulnerable but Invincible: A Longitudinal Study of Resilient Children and Youth.* New York: McGraw-Hill, 1986.

Westat, Inc. *Independent Living, Services for Youth in Substitute Care.* Rockville, Md.: Westat, Inc., 1986.

Wilson, M. P. *Peer Counseling in California Public Schools: Summary of a Survey of Status and Scope.* Sacramento: School Climate Unit, California State Department of Education, 1986.

Withers, L. E., and Kaplan, D. W. "Adolescents Who Attempt Suicide: A Retrospective Clinical Chart Review of Hospitalized Patients." *Professional Psychology: Research and Practice,* 1987, *18,* 391–393.

Wolfe, D. A. *Child Abuse: Implications for Child Development and Psychopathology.* Beverly Hills, Calif.: Sage, 1987.

Woodruff, R. A., Clayton, P. J., and Guze, S. B. "Suicide Attempts and Psychiatric Diagnosis." *Disorders of the Nervous System,* 1972, *33,* 617–621.

Woolfolk, R. L., and Richardson, F. C. *Stress, Sanity and Survival.* New York: Signet, 1987.

Wright, L. S. "Suicidal Thoughts and Their Relationship to Family Stress and Personal Problems Among High School Seniors and College Undergraduates." *Adolescence,* 1985, *20,* 575–580.

Zins, J. E., and Hopkins, R. A. "Referral Out: Increasing the Number of Kept Appointments." *School Psychology Review,* 1981, *10,* 107–111.

Zung, W.W.K. "A Rating Scale for Suicide Prevention." In A. T. Beck, H.L.P. Resnik, and D. J. Lettieri (eds.), *The Prediction of Suicide.* Bowie, Md.: Charles Press, 1974.

Name Index

Subject Index